The Immigration
Handbook

The Immigration Handbook

A Practical Guide to
United States Visas, Permanent
Residency and Citizenship

IVAN VASIC

McFarland & Company, Inc., Publishers
Jefferson, North Carolina, and London

LIBRARY OF CONGRESS CATALOGUING-IN-PUBLICATION DATA

Vasic, Ivan.
The immigration handbook : a practical guide to United States visas,
permanent residency and citizenship / Ivan Vasic.
p.   cm.
Includes bibliographical references and index.

ISBN 978-0-7864-4009-2
softcover : 50# alkaline paper ∞

1. United States—Emigration and immigration—Handbooks, manuals,
etc.   2. Immigrants—United States—Handbooks, manuals, etc.
I. Title.
JV6543.V37   2009   323.6'230973—dc22   2008039821

British Library cataloguing data are available

Cover photograph ©2008 Shutterstock

Manufactured in the United States of America

McFarland & Company, Inc., Publishers
Box 611, Jefferson, North Carolina 28640
www.mcfarlandpub.com

Table of Contents

Part IV. Inadmissibility and Deportability

Preface

As an attorney who has been practicing immigration law for more than ten years, it has been my desire for the past couple of years to come up with a simple, easy-to-read reference book on immigration. A guide that is helpful to a regular person trying to obtain an immigration benefit. A guide that will lead a person through an immigration process from start to finish.

I have read and examined numerous publications on immigration, including books and Web sites. Some are better than the others. However, I have found that unless you are somewhat versed in immigration law and procedure, you will have trouble navigating through all the rules, laws, forms and explanations. You may very well find the process frustrating and end up getting an attorney after all.

This book will attempt to give essential knowledge about immigration, and empower a person who has little, if any, experience with immigration law to tackle a variety of immigration issues. There is no reason why immigration law must remain a mystery to the majority of people. In this book, I have tried to simplify immigration rules and procedures, break them down, and explain them in simple language.

This reference book is primarily aimed at people seeking immigration benefits for themselves or their relatives, and for businesses seeking immigration benefits for their employees. Nevertheless, it may be used by anyone who wishes to decipher and understand immigration-law rules and procedures, including students, lawyers new to immigration, and interested citizens.

This book does not attempt to cover every aspect of immigration proceedings. For certain immigration procedures, which I will discuss later, it would be wise to have the help of an immigration attorney. But for a multitude of people seeking everyday immigration benefits, this book will serve as a step-by-step guide to getting a successful result, an approval, without needing additional help and incurring extra legal fees. If you decide to retain an attorney for your particular case, this book will still give you a basic understanding of the rules and processes involved so that you can meaningfully participate in your case without appearing totally helpless.

This book will explain laws, rules and procedures, but do not hesitate to ask for help. Immigration law is not easy to understand. If you have a question or are unsure about something, contact a lawyer who can clarify things or help you with a certain issue you do not understand.

If you do not speak the English language well, find a lawyer who speaks your language. Often, immigrants sitting in front of an American lawyer pretend that they understand everything so that they do not appear stupid or ignorant. As you can imagine, this can cause misunderstandings and frustration, and a person is left in the dark as to what is going on with his or her case. If you cannot find an immigration lawyer who speaks your language, hire a translator to go with you, or ask a relative or friend who is fluent in English to accompany you.

Finally, I am not just an attorney, I am an immigrant myself. I came to the United States more than eighteen years ago and I know what you are going through. I have gone through the same process myself. I came to the United States as a permanent resident; my wife, who is a United States citizen, was my sponsor. At the time of my arrival in the United States, I was already a law school graduate from a university in Europe. You would think that it should not have been too difficult for me to understand the process I was going through. Nevertheless, I remember clearly that I was absolutely at a loss as to what needed to be done, which forms needed filling out and why, where to send them, whom to call, and so on. I remember a feeling of helplessness, and that my destiny was in someone else's hands. That is why I have decided to write this book. I want you to understand the immigration process you are going through, so that you can meaningfully participate in this process which is of utmost importance to you and your family.

Introduction

Before we get into discussions on specific immigration issues, you have to become familiar with some of the most essential immigration terms. First are some of the labels the U.S. Citizenship and Immigration Service — USCIS from now on — uses in dealing with the public. Unless you are a U.S. citizen, the USCIS will refer to you, if you are obtaining a benefit for yourself, or to the person for whom you are trying to obtain an immigration benefit, as an "alien."

When they say "alien," we all think of a being from outer space. I am sure that for some of us coming to the United States for the first time felt like arriving on another planet. In the immigration discussions following, I generally do not use this term. To be perfectly frank, I do not like the term "alien," as it feels impersonal, cold, and somehow not human enough. Therefore, when I refer to a person who is not a U.S. citizen, and who is seeking immigration benefits, I will try, as much as I am able, to refer to him or her as a "person," "petitioner," or "applicant."

A person who desires to enter the United States for a temporary visit needs a "nonimmigrant visa," and is called a "nonimmigrant." A person attempting to permanently live in the United States is seeking an "immigrant visa." If a person obtains an immigrant visa, he or she is called a "permanent resident alien" or "immigrant."

Next, for each immigration benefit sought, a person must file a form which is usually called either a "petition" or an "application." A person filing a form in order to obtain a benefit for another person is called a "sponsor" or "petitioner." A person who is receiving an immigration benefit is called a "beneficiary." If a person is seeking benefits for himself or herself, the person may also be called an "applicant." Sometimes, the sponsor and beneficiary are two different persons. Sometimes, the sponsor and the beneficiary may be the same person, if a person is allowed to seek immigration benefits without a sponsor.

For each immigration issue discussed in this book, you will get (1) an overview; (2) a detailed explanation of the process for each type of benefit; (3) an explanation as to who can apply for the benefit; (4) an explanation of who can qualify for an immigration benefit; (5) information about the forms and fees needed to initiate the proceeding; (6) instructions on completing the forms; (7) a list of the documents that need to be sent along with the forms; (8) information about where to get forms; and (9) valuable Web sites and addresses.

This book is divided into four parts, and each part has several chapters. The first part is dedicated to the concept of permanent residency. The first chapter contains an overview of the most important immigration concepts in connection with all processes for permanent residency, such as adjustment of status and backlog, among others. Chapter 2 covers issues arising in family immigration, such as someone filing a petition for an immigrant visa for a relative. Chapter 3 covers other family categories, like orphans, adoptees, and widows and widowers, among others. Chapter 4 discusses all aspects of employment immigration, when an employer attempts to obtain an immigrant visa for a foreign worker. Immigration lottery is discussed in chapter 5. Chapter 6 covers issues in relation to asylum and refugee procedure and status. The final chapter in Part I, chapter 7, discusses certain useful forms and tips for permanent residents, nonimmigrants and employers of immigrants.

The second part of the book is dedicated to issues related to U.S. citizenship. There are three chapters in this part. The first chapter analyzes citizenship by birth. Chapter 2 talks about citizenship by naturalization. The third chapter discusses ways of losing U.S. citizenship.

The third part of the book covers various nonimmigrant visas and ways and methods of obtaining them. I have included material on the most frequently sought after nonimmigrant visas in this part, nonimmigrant visas which are needed by travelers, students, and various temporary employees.

The final part, Part IV, is dedicated to issues relating to deportation of immigrants from the United States. Chapter 1 discusses inadmissibility of persons in the United States. Chapter 2 discusses deportability and removal of persons from the United States.

Appendix A lists form packages for the family immigration categories. Appendix B contains sample immigration forms. Appendix C lists Web sites and gives instructions on obtaining all forms either through the mail or via the Internet, lists applicable fees and gives mailing addresses. I have deliberately included applicable Web sites throughout the text in this book, as I believe that the reader will be able to best use these while reading about a particular issue.

PART I

—∞—

Permanent Resident Status

CHAPTER 1

Overview

A. Permanent Resident Status

Permanent resident status allows a person to live and work in the United States "permanently." There is no requirement that a permanent resident must eventually become a United States citizen. Sometimes, a permanent resident decides to remain a citizen of the country where he or she was born. The person can freely travel abroad with his or her own passport and will be allowed to return to the United States. However, under certain circumstances, permanent resident status can be revoked. For example, lying to the USCIS in order to obtain permanent resident status and being convicted of a felony are grounds for revocation.

There are several ways a person can obtain permanent resident status in the United States. Most commonly, permanent resident status is obtained through a family sponsor, an employer sponsor, or immigration lottery, or gaining asylum or refugee status.

The immigration process that leads to the permanent resident status is twofold. Sometimes, as you will see later, each part of the process is separate. Sometimes both parts are done at the same time.

The first part of the process always starts with a filing of a petition. It could be a family or employment petition. Let us imagine that you have a family member in the United States who is willing to sponsor you for permanent resident status. Your sponsor must file a family petition. The purpose of the family petition is for the USCIS to determine if the sponsor is indeed eligible to apply for you, and whether you and your sponsor have a family relationship which may lead to your permanent residency.

If the first part is successful and the petition is approved, the second part of the process kicks in. The second part is called either "adjustment of status," or "visa processing," and is commenced by either filing an application for adjustment of status in the United States, or applying at the U.S. consulate in the country where the alien resides. The term "adjustment of status" refers to the process of changing a person's immigration status from nonimmigrant to that of permanent resident. Visa processing refers to the process of getting an immigrant visa at a U.S. consulate.

The purpose of the second part of the process is to determine whether you are eligible to become a permanent resident, because not everyone can become a permanent resident of the United States, even if the original family, employment, or other petition is approved. For example, you will be most likely precluded from adjusting status if you are a convicted felon or you entered the United States illegally. Also, during this process, it will be determined whether you belong to an immigration category allowing you to obtain permanent resident status immediately, or whether you will have to wait to obtain permanent residency.

You will be allowed to apply for adjustment of status or visa processing immediately if, for example, your family member is your spouse and he or she is a U.S. citizen. If your spouse in the preceding example is not a U.S. citizen, but is only a permanent resident of the United States, you will have to wait before you can adjust your status or go through visa processing.

Before we continue, it will be helpful to explain some very important terminology and concepts in connection with the process of getting a permanent resident status.

B. Backlog

"Backlog" is a waiting period before one can get permanent resident status. For example, a family member files a petition to bring a relative into the United States. When the petition is approved, two things can occur, depending on the sponsor's immigration status and the alien's relationship to the sponsor: the alien is either eligible to receive permanent resident status immediately, or not. For a spouse, unmarried child under twenty-one, or a parent of a U.S. citizen there are no backlogs, which means that they are automatically eligible for permanent resident status in most circumstances. For others there is a waiting period. Waiting periods exist because the U.S. government has decided to allow a certain number of immigrant visas per year for various family categories. For example, a brother or sister of a U.S. citizen must wait more than twelve years before getting a green card. Also, nationals of Mexico, the Philippines, China and India have longer waiting times than the rest of the world. The U.S. Department of State issues a Visa Bulletin every month which shows current dates for various family or employment categories. You can check the dates in your category every month by visiting *www.travel.state.gov.* Click on "frequently requested visa information," then click on Visa Bulletin. When a petition (family or employment) is approved, you will receive an approval in writing from the USCIS. The approval will contain a "priority date," which is essentially the date when the petition was filed.

Whether you may apply for permanent residency immediately depends on whether your priority date is "current." Your priority date is current if it is prior to the date in the Visa Bulletin for a specific category. For example, if the Visa Bulletin shows that in your category the date is January 1, 2001, that means that the people whose petitions were filed before that date have a ready immigration number and may apply for per-

manent residency. If your priority date is December 31, 2000, you are "current," which means that an immigration number is immediately available to you. Visa Bulletin might be confusing to understand. To make it easier to find out which category you may fit in, please note the following designations for each category.

1. Family-sponsored preferences

(1) Unmarried sons and daughters of U.S. citizens (23,400 visas per year — F1)

(2) Spouses and children and unmarried sons and daughters of permanent residents (226,000 per year): Spouses and children —(F2A); Unmarried sons and daughters—(F2B)

(3) Married sons and daughters of U.S. citizens (23,400 per year)—(F3)

(4) Brothers and sisters of adult U.S. citizens (65,000 per year)—(F4)

2. Employment-sponsored preferences

(1) Priority workers—(E1)

(2) Members of the professions holding advanced degrees or persons of exceptional ability—(E2)

(3) Skilled workers, professionals and other workers—(E3)

(4) Certain special immigrants (religious workers)—(E4)

(5) Investors—(E5)

C. Immediate Relatives

An "immediate relative" is a parent, spouse or minor child (under twenty-one years of age) of a U.S. citizen. Immediate relatives are not subject to backlog, and in most circumstances may apply for permanent residency immediately after the family petition is approved.

D. Derivative Beneficiaries

A person who obtains permanent residency through a family petition (or employment or lottery) is called a "principal alien." That person's spouse and children are called "derivative beneficiaries" because they derive their benefit through the principal alien; in other words, they are eligible to become permanent residents without having to get approved through a separate family or employment petition, like the principal alien. However, they have to either adjust their status if they are in the United States or go through visa processing if they live abroad (see explanation for adjustment of status and visa processing below in Sections F and K). For example, if a person becomes a permanent resident through lottery, that person's spouse and unmarried children under twenty-one will get permanent resident status as well.

An important detail: a spouse will be considered a derivative beneficiary if the marriage took place before the principal alien adjusted his or her status or went through visa processing. A child will be considered a derivative beneficiary if he or she was born from a marriage that took place before the principal alien adjusted status or went through visa processing.

E. Aging Out—The Child Status Protection Act

In August 2002, the Child Status Protection Act (CSPA) became law in the United States. The act allows an immigrant who has reached twenty-one years of age to be still considered a "child" for immigration benefits under certain circumstances. First, let me explain what could have happened before the act. A sponsor who was a permanent resident of the United States might file a family petition for a spouse and minor child, but before the petition was approved, or before the visa number became available, the child turned twenty-one. The child would have been automatically transferred to a lower category with a longer wait time.

What are the consequences of the act?

(1) If a sponsor is a U.S. citizen filing for a child who was under twenty-one when the family petition was filed, the date of filing will "freeze" the child's age. In other words, even if the child is over twenty-one when the petition is approved or when the child adjusts his or her status, he or she will still be considered a

child for immigration purposes. However, the child must file for adjustment of status or visa processing within one year after the petition is approved.

(2) If a sponsor is a permanent resident of the United States, the child's age will be "frozen" when the "priority date" becomes current, or when a visa becomes available. At that time, the number of days the family petition was pending will be subtracted from the child's age. If the child's age is under twenty-one by using this formula, the child will be able to file for adjustment of status. For example, let's say a child was fifteen when a family petition was filed, and she turned twenty when the petition was approved. A visa number became available four years later when the child was twenty-four. The child will still be considered under twenty-one for immigration purposes because the petition was pending for five years, and this time is subtracted from the child's actual age. Keep in mind, however, that the child must file for adjustment status or visa processing within one year after the priority date.

(3) The same applies for derivative children of employment petitions.

(4) For children of asylum seekers and refugees, the date when the age is locked is the date when the asylum or refugee petition is filed, or when asylum seekers or refugees file a petition for a child to join them.

(5) Under the act, if a permanent resident files a family petition for a child under the second preference (F2A — unmarried sons and daughters under twenty-one of permanent residents) and the permanent resident becomes a naturalized U.S. citizen after the child turns twenty-one, the family petition will be automatically converted to family-based first-preference-category F1— unmarried sons and daughters over twenty-one of a U.S. citizen. This sometimes could result in a beneficiary having to wait longer then if he or she was left in the previous category. Therefore, the beneficiary (child) may "opt out" of this automatic conversion and request that he or she remain in the F2A category.

F. Adjustment of Status

When a sponsor's petition for an immigrant visa (through family, employment, lottery or otherwise) is approved by USCIS and the beneficiary trying to obtain permanent resident status is in the United States, the beneficiary may be able to "adjust status" to that of permanent resident without having to leave the United States. This is accomplished by filing an Application to Adjust Status, Form I-485.

However, adjustment of status is not always available. It may depend on whether the sponsor is a U.S. citizen or not. It also depends on the beneficiary's current immigration status in the United States.

After the application for adjustment of status is filed, the applicant will receive a request to have fingerprints and photographs taken (so-called "biometrics"). Fingerprints do not have to be taken if the person is under fourteen or over seventy-four years of age. About a couple of months later, the applicant will receive a request to appear at an interview at a local immigration office. If the interview goes well, the application will be approved and the applicant will receive a green card in the mail within a couple of months of the interview.

1. Who is eligible to apply for adjustment of status?

You are eligible to apply for adjustment of status when:

(1) an immigrant visa number is immediately available to you based on an approved immigrant petition (if there is no backlog). Under most circumstances, an immigrant petition is based on family, employment, or a lottery.

(2) you are a derivative beneficiary (a spouse or a child of a person who is adjusting his or her status). If the spouse and child are in the United States, they should file their adjustment of status applications at the same time when the principal applicant is filing his or her application, to speed up the process. If the spouse or child is outside the United States, the person adjusting status should concurrently file I-824 Form, Application for Action on an Approved Application or Petition, at the same time when the adjustment of status application is filed. The filing of this form will reduce a possible delay in processing for this person's spouse and child living abroad. The notice of adjustment of status approval will be immediately sent to

the U.S. consulate where the spouse and child (or children) are located. Note that this form cannot be used for the spouse or children of a person who is adjusting status as an "immediate relative" of the petitioner. In such a case separate family petitions must be prepared for the spouse and/or children of the beneficiary. For example, a person whose child is residing outside the United States marries a U.S. citizen. The U.S. citizen would file a family petition, and at the same time the beneficiary would file application for adjustment of status. The United States citizen would have to file a separate family petition for the child, and cannot use Form I-824.

(3) you have been admitted as the fiancé or fiancée of a U.S. citizen and you marry such person within ninety days after being admitted in the United States. Also, any child of the fiancé or fiancée can adjust his or her status based on the parent's application to adjust and it should be filed at the same time.

(4) you have been granted asylum in the United States and you have been living in the United States more than one year after being granted asylum.

(5) you have been admitted to the United States as a refugee and have been living in the United States more than one year after being admitted.

(6) you are a citizen of Cuba, arrived in the United States after January 1, 1959, and have been living in the United States for more than one year after your arrival.

(7) you have been continuously living in the United States since January 1, 1972.

2. Who is not eligible to apply for adjustment of status?

You cannot adjust your status if:

(1) you entered the United States without a visa;

(2) you entered as a nonimmigrant crewmember;

(3) you were not allowed in the United States after being inspected at the border by an immigration officer;

(4) your visa expired while still in the United States;

(5) you worked in the United States without a proper work permit;

(6) you failed to maintain your legal nonimmigrant status even though it was not your fault or because of a technical reason, unless you fall under one of these categories:

(a) you are an immediate relative of a U.S. citizen.

(b) you are the fiancé or fiancée (under K-1 visa) or the fiancé's or fiancées child (under K-2 visa), and if you married the U.S. citizen within ninety days after arriving in the United States; see Part III.

(c) your nonimmigrant visa is based on your status as a foreign medical graduate (H visa) (see Part III), or international organization employee or derivative family members (G visa).

(7) you had a fiancé or fiancée (K1 visa) but did not marry your fiancé or fiancée within ninety days of entering the United States.

(8) you entered as an exchange student under a visa (J1 or J2) and you are subject to a two-year foreign residency requirement (see explanation on J1/Js visas, Part III, Chapter 4).

(9) you were admitted into the United States as a visitor under the Visa Waiver Program; see Part III, Chapter 2.

A) Immediate relative exception

If your nonimmigrant visa expired, or you worked without a proper work permit, you may be able to adjust your status and get a green card if you entered the United States with a valid nonimmigrant visa, such as a visitor visa B2, and if your family sponsor is your immediate relative and a U.S. citizen. However, this will not be the case if your nonimmigrant visa is exchange student J1/J2, with a two-year foreign residence requirement, or a visitor visa under the Visa Waiver Program. The above immediate relative exception also does not apply if your family sponsor is only a permanent resident of the United States.

Also note that if you are married to a U.S. citizen, and you are a citizen of a country participating in the Visa Waiver Program, you will not be able to adjust status in the United States. Lucky citizens of certain countries do not have to apply for a visa at the U.S. Embassy. (See discussion of the Visa Waiver Program Part III, Chapter 2.) Instead, they receive a green I-94 card at the U.S. border, giving them ninety days in the United States. The downside is that they cannot adjustment their status or extend their visas in the United States, but will have to go back to their European country and go through visa processing there.

B) LIFE Act exception

If you are unable to adjust your status under any of the conditions outlined above, you may be able to do it under the LIFE Act. The so-called LIFE Act was enacted on December 21, 2000, and although it did not represent an outright amnesty to persons who were at that time living illegally in the United States, it gave a large number of people an opportunity to adjust their status in the United States by paying a $1,000 penalty. If you are subject to the LIFE Act, you must file Supplement A to Form I-485 Adjustment of Status.

Who is eligible under LIFE Act?

To apply for adjustment of status under the LIFE Act, you must have been present in the United States on December 21, 2000, and:

(1) you are physically present in the United States when you apply for the adjustment of status; and

(2) an immigrant visa is immediately available to you (your family or employment petition is approved); and

(3) you are otherwise admissible into the United States for permanent residence (you are not a felon); and

(4) you are a beneficiary of an approved family petition or labor certification filed before April 30, 2001; and

(5) you pay a $1,000 penalty.

In addition, you must also fall under one of the following categories:

(1) Alien crewmember;

(2) Alien working without work authorization;

(3) Alien in an unlawful immigrant status (entered the United States illegally, for example);

(4) Alien who fails to maintain a lawful status after arriving in the United States (your nonimmigrant visa expired after you legally entered the United States);

(5) Alien who was admitted in transit without a visa;

(6) Alien admitted as a nonimmigrant under the Visa Waiver Program;

(7) Alien seeking employment-based adjustment of status who does not have lawful immigration status (nonimmigrant visa expired or entered illegally, for example).

What does this mean in simple language? If you were lucky enough to have someone file a family or employment petition for you on or before April 30, 2001, and the petition was approved, you may apply for adjustment of status in the United States if you fall under one of the above-mentioned categories. You do not have to leave the United States to get a green card. And, most importantly, it does not matter if you came to the United States with a nonimmigrant visa or sneaked over the border. It does not matter if you worked in the United States without a work permit. So, though not called "amnesty," on some level, this could be considered amnesty.

c) Other exceptions

Even if you fall under one or more categories listed in the LIFE Act, you may not have to use the LIFE Act to adjust your status. Do not file the Supplement A and do not send the fee if:

(1) you are the spouse or a minor child of a U.S. citizen or the parent of a U.S. citizen twenty-one years or older, and you entered the United States with a valid nonimmigrant visa; or

(2) you were granted asylum in the United States; or

(3) you have continuously resided in the United States since January 1, 1972; or

(4) you entered the United States as a K-1 fiancé or fiancée of a U.S. citizen; or

(5) you have an approved I-360 petition under one of the following categories: Amerasian, widow or widower, battered or abused spouse or child, or special immigrant (you are applying for adjustment of status as a juvenile court dependent or have served in the U.S. armed forces).

G. Travel During Adjustment of Status

Travel during the process for adjustment of status is possible; however, several conditions must be satisfied. Note that if a person, while adjustment of status is proceeding, leaves the United States without a travel permit, he or she may not be able to reenter the United States, and may be subject to a 3–10-year ban on entry. If a person who left the United States was found to have stayed illegally in the United States for more than 180 days but less than one year, he or she may be barred from entering the United States for three years after the departure from the United States. If a person has been found to have stayed illegally in the United States for more than one year, he or she may be barred from reentering the United States for ten years. It does not matter whether the person is in the adjustment of status process or not. If a person was illegally in the United States at the time of filing for adjustment of status, he or she may be barred from reentry into the United States for up to ten years.

Worse yet, even if you receive a travel document from USCIS and manage to reenter the United States, if it is determined that you had been illegally in the United States before your departure from the country, you may be barred from adjustment of status. In that case you may have to apply for a waiver of inadmissibility before the adjustment of status application is approved (see discussion on inadmissibility in Part IV).

The bottom line is that you can apply for a travel document if you were legally in the United States when you applied for adjustment of status. When I refer to the travel document, I mean the "advance parole" document issued by the USCIS. "Advance parole" means exactly that, a person gets an advance permit to reenter the United States after travel abroad. The form which must be used is Form I-131 Application for Travel Document. You must state the reasons for travel while your adjustment of status application is pending. Emergent personal or business reasons are acceptable. Documents needed:

- copy of the USCIS receipt showing that a person has applied for adjustment of status;
- letter/statement explaining the reasons for travel;
- two passport photographs.

Processing time is about thirty business days. Therefore it is the best to include the I-131 Form along with the adjustment of status application.

H. Work During Adjustment of Status

A person who is applying for adjustment of status is eligible to work while the application is pending. However, any employment must first be authorized by USCIS. The form needed is Form I-765, Application for Employment Authorization. This form should be filed at the same time that the application for adjustment of status is filed. It takes up to ninety days to get a work permit or Employment Authorization Document (EAD). If it passes more than ninety days after the application is filed, the alien should make an appointment with the local USCIS office to get a temporary EAD card (see discussion on INFOPASS in chapter 7). Documents needed:

- copy of the receipt for adjustment of status application;
- copy of I-94 document (attached to your passport when you entered the United States);
- copy of the old EAD card, if applicable;
- two passport-style photographs.

I. Denial of Application for Adjustment of Status

If the USCIS makes a finding that the application for adjustment of status should be denied, it will first send a Notice of Intent to Deny. The alien will be granted thirty days to rebut the findings by the USCIS. If an adjustment of status application is denied, there is no appeal available. The alien may file a motion to reopen or a motion to reconsider within thirty days of the denial. Motion to reopen must state new facts warranting the approval. Motion to reconsider must state the reasons for reconsideration and why the decision was inappropriate. Both motions are done on Form I-290B, Notice of Appeal or Motion. Also, since the USCIS will commence a deportation proceeding against the alien if the application is denied, the alien will have an opportunity to reapply for adjustment of status during the deportation proceeding (see Part IV for discussion on deportation).

J. Rescission of Adjustment of Status

Note that if the adjustment of status was granted, and within five years of the approval the USCIS determines that the person was not entitled to the adjustment of status, the approval may be rescinded. The rescission will place the person in an immigration status he or she would have been in if the adjustment of status was not granted in the first place (usually that means no status). Please also note that all persons who received permanent resident status as derivative beneficiaries will lose their status as well, unless they independently moved for the removal of conditions on residence. That may apply even in cases when they became U.S. citizens.

K. Visa Processing

Visa processing refers to situations where the original family or employment petition — or the immigration lottery application — is approved and the beneficiary is not in the United States, or for some reason is not allowed to adjust his or her status in the United States. The final part of the immigration process is done at the U.S. embassy/consulate in the country where the beneficiary lives. After a family or employment petition is approved, the USCIS closes its case and sends the entire immigration package to the National Visa Center located in New Hampshire. In a couple of months or so, the National Visa Center sends a letter to the sponsor in the United States, explaining the next step in the process, requesting additional documents and additional forms to be filled out and signed. After the sponsor collects all the requested documentation, he or she must mail the package back to the National Visa Center. If everything is in order, the National Visa Center will send the documents to the U.S. embassy/consulate where the beneficiary lives. The beneficiary is contacted by the consulate, must attend a couple of interviews, and if everything checks out fine, he or she will receive a sealed envelope containing the beneficiary's file. The beneficiary will have to enter the United States within a certain period of time or the approval lapses. After timely entering of the

United States, he or she will receive a stamp in the passport at the border, I-551, indicating that the person has permanent resident status and authorization to work. The actual green card will arrive in the mail shortly thereafter.

L. Required Documents

The first letter the National Visa Center sends will ask for certain fees to be paid. Once the fees are sent to the National Visa Center, the second package will arrive. In the second package, the sponsor will be asked to prepare an Affidavit of Support, I-864, and attach his or her three most current federal income tax returns, along with his or her W-2s and 1099s, whichever is applicable (W2 is given to regular employees, 1099 is given to an independent contractor). In addition, the package will contain "Instructions for Immigrant Visa Applicants." You will have to send to the National Visa Center the following original documents:

(1) Application for Immigrant Visa and Alien Registration Form DS-230 Part I and Part II. This application must be filled out and signed by the beneficiary; therefore, it must be mailed to the beneficiary and returned to the sponsor;

(2) a photocopy of the passport biographical page. This is the page containing passport photograph, address, date of birth, passport expiration date, etc.;

(3) birth certificates for the beneficiary, his or her spouse and children under twenty-one;

(4) any court and prison records;

(5) any military records;

(6) a marriage certificate, if married;

(7) any divorce judgments and/or death certificates for previous marriages.

After all the documents and forms are collected, they must be sent to the National Visa Center. Note that you have one year to prepare a response after the date of the first letter from the National Visa Center. If a response is not made to the National Visa Center within one year, the entire process, starting with the original family or employment petition, will have to be done all over again.

If the responses to the second package are satisfactory and timely, the National Visa Center will send a final letter stating that visa processing is completed, and will send the entire package to the U.S. consulate designated in the letter. This is the same U.S. consulate where the beneficiary is residing. The letter will also state the date and time for the first interview with the consular officer. Your beneficiary will have to do one more thing, however. The beneficiary will have to get a satisfactory medical exam, as requested and instructed by the consular officer. If that checks out, the consular officer will issue the final approval.

CHAPTER 2

Obtaining Permanent Resident Status Through Family Relations

Family immigration is the essence of immigration in this country, and the process is generally straightforward. If you follow these steps carefully, you should be able to get legal immigration status for your relative without a problem. In most cases, the process starts with filing a Petition for Alien Relative, Form I-130. The purpose of this form is to prove to the USCIS that you have a qualifying relationship with the relative you are trying to sponsor and that you are eligible to sponsor a relative.

A. Relatives You Can Sponsor

If you are a United States citizen, you may file for:

(1) your husband or wife;

(2) your unmarried child under twenty-one years of age; "child" includes your natural child, stepchild or adopted child;

(3) your unmarried son or daughter, age twenty-one or older;

(4) your married son or daughter of any age;

(5) your brother or sister if you are over twenty-one years of age;

(6) your mother or father if you are over twenty-one years of age.

If you are a permanent resident of the United States, you may file for:

(1) your husband or wife;

(2) your unmarried child under twenty-one years of age;

(3) your unmarried son or daughter age twenty-one or older.

B. Relatives You Cannot Sponsor

You may not file for:

(1) your adopted child unless you adopted the child before the child's sixteenth birthday, or if the child was not in your legal custody and has not lived with you for at least two years before the adoption decree became final;

(2) your natural parent if you are a U.S. citizen but gained permanent resident status through adoption;

(3) your stepparent or stepchild if the marriage that created the relationship took place after the child's eighteenth birthday;

(4) your husband or wife if you and your spouse were not physically present at the marriage ceremony (marriage by proxy);

(5) your subsequent husband or wife if you became a permanent resident alien by marrying a U.S. citizen or a permanent resident, unless five years have passed since you received a green card, or you can prove to USCIS that your previous marriage was a

valid, "real" marriage and not a sham, or that your previous spouse died;

(6) your husband or wife if the marriage took place after your spouse was placed in a deportation or removal proceeding, unless your spouse has resided outside the United States for more than two years after the date of marriage;

(7) your husband or wife if it was legally determined that your spouse has attempted or conspired to enter into the marriage in order to evade immigration laws;

(8) a grandparent, grandchild, nephew, niece, uncle, aunt, cousin or in-law.

Filling out the form itself is, of course, not enough to prove that you are eligible to sponsor your relative and that you have a qualifying relationship with the relative. You must prove those points with documentary evidence.

C. Evidence of United States Citizenship

In order to show that you are a U.S. citizen, you may produce the following:

(1) If you were born in the United States you may provide your birth certificate issued by the civil registrar, vital statistics office or other appropriate civil authority. If such a document is not available for some reason, you will need to provide substitute documents, which include a statement from the appropriate civil authority certifying that a birth certificate is not available and as many of the following as you are able to get:

(a) Church record; a copy of a document with a church seal showing a baptism or comparable church rite performed within two months of your birth, stating the date and place of your birth, date of the church ceremony and the names of your parents;

(b) School record; a letter from a school authority stating the date of admission to the school, your birth date and age at the time of admission, place of birth and your parents' names;

(c) Census record; state or federal census

record showing your name, place of birth, date of birth or age; or

(d) Affidavits; written statements by at least two persons who were living at the time of your birth and have personal knowledge of your birth. Good examples are your godfather or godmother and their spouses.

(2) if you were not born in the United States but are a naturalized U.S. citizen, a copy of your Naturalization Certificate;

(3) if one of your parents was a U.S. citizen at the time of your birth, and you were born abroad, a copy of your Report of Birth Abroad of a Citizen of the United States, Form FS-240, issued by an American Embassy or consulate;

(4) a copy of your unexpired U.S. passport; or

(5) an original statement from a United States consular officer verifying that you are a U.S. citizen with a valid U.S. passport.

D. Evidence of Permanent Residence Status

In order to prove that you are a permanent resident of the United States, you need to provide:

(1) a copy of your permanent resident card, front and back;

(2) or, if you have not yet received a card in the mail, then evidence that you were admitted as a permanent resident, such as the "Welcome Letter" from the USCIS, or a copy of your passport page with the I-551 stamp you received at the border.

E. Evidence of Family Relationship

In order to sponsor a relative, you must prove that you have a qualifying relationship with the relative. Below is a list of documents you must provide in order to prove that the relationship exists.

(1) Husband and wife

(a) U.S. marriage certificate, or, if you were married abroad, a marriage certificate in the original language and a translation into English;

(b) for each of you, copies of all judgments for divorce and/or death certificates for any former spouses, in the original language and translated into English, if applicable;

(c) one passport size photograph for each of you.

Note that you will have to provide other documents to prove that your marital relationship is a real one and not fraudulent. Below is a list of some of the documents which you can use. You should bear in mind that every document bearing both of your names should be saved, as it is important in proving your relationship to USCIS.

• checking, savings or investment account statements in both of your names;
• mortgages in both names; title to real estate or personal property in both names;
• rental leases in both names;
• your children's birth certificates;
• affidavits of persons who know you and your spouse, and have personal knowledge of your marriage and life together;
• utility statements, insurance cards in both names.

(2) Child (sponsor is the mother)

(a) child's birth certificate showing your child's name and your name.

(3) Child (sponsor is the father)

(a) child's birth certificate showing both parents' names; and
(b) parents' marriage certificate.

(4) Child born out of wedlock (parents were not married at the time of birth) and sponsor is the father

(a) If the child was not legitimized by the father before the child reached the age of eighteen, the father must provide evidence that the father and child had a real father-child relationship before the child reached the age of twenty-one. Evidence could be support payments or a life together.

(5) Brother or sister

(a) copy of your birth certificate;
(b) copy of your brother's or sister's birth certificate showing that you have at least one common parent.

(6) Mother

(a) copy of your birth certificate.

(7) Father

(a) copy of your birth certificate showing the names of both parents;
(b) parents' marriage certificate;
(c) copies of any divorce judgments or death certificates showing that any prior marriages of your mother and father were legally terminated.

(8) Stepparent/stepchild

(a) copy of the marriage certificate of the stepparent to the alien's natural parent showing that the marriage took place before the child's eighteenth birthday;
(b) copies of any divorce decrees and death certificates showing that any prior marriages were legally terminated.

(9) Adoptive parent or child

(a) copy of the adoption decree showing that the adoption took place before the child's sixteenth birthday.
(b) if you have adopted the sibling of a child who you already adopted, copy of the adoption decree showing that the adoption took place before the sibling's eighteenth birthday.
(c) evidence that each child was in your legal custody and lived with you at least two years before the adoption was finalized.

F. Special Rules Regarding Marriage

This is the category which every immigrant is familiar with, because almost every person who is currently illegally in the United States believes that this is the best ticket to a permanent resident status. Why? Because if the sponsoring spouse is a United States citizen, it allows the illegal alien to adjust his or her status in the United States without having to leave the

United States. In many circumstances that may be true. But, because this avenue is so popular with illegal aliens, the USCIS will be highly suspicious of your "love."

The USCIS acknowledges that a person living in the United States will probably eventually meet a future spouse who is a U.S. citizen, and that most marriages are true marriages born out of love and affection. Nevertheless, it is also true that a lot of people try to use this avenue to get to permanent resident status though their marriage is a total sham. Note that if one tries to defraud the USCIS, penalties are stiff, and not only for the sponsor, but also for the beneficiary, and may include jail time and substantial fines. Of course, for many aliens currently in the United States, this is the only remaining ticket to "freedom," and they will risk a lot.

Frequently, if you hire an attorney to do your papers based on a marriage to a U.S. citizen, the attorney will ask you to sign a paper stating that you were advised of the fact that an attempt to defraud the United States may be punishable by jail and fines, and that you both positively state that your relationship is a valid and true one. This letter protects the attorney in case it turns out that you were lying to the USCIS.

This book only deals with true and valid marriages. Nothing contained in this publication will advise you on how to circumvent the law or process. This discussion proceeds on the assumption that the marriage is true and valid. It is crucial that you do not forget that the fact that you married a U.S. citizen and filed immigration forms is not the end of your road to the permanent resident status. You will need a lot more evidence in order to get approved and get your status adjusted to permanent resident status.

Some persuasive evidence includes photographs of both of you together; photo albums are convenient. The immigration officer will want to see photographs of your wedding, a wedding album and a wedding video, if you have one. If you go on a honeymoon, include those photographs as well. Even after the wedding, any photographs memorializing your relationship are helpful, like outings with friends, vacations, dinners, and celebrations. Second, make the effort to establish a checking and savings account in both names. I know that this is sometimes difficult

because an alien cannot get a social security card without a valid work permit. However, even an alien without legal status in the United States may apply for a tax number; use this opportunity. The immigration officer will ask to see that you have filed federal and state income taxes together. Try to put both names on the utility bills, car and medical insurance cards. If you lease an apartment, include both of your names on the lease. Make sure that after marriage both of you update driver's licenses and state identification cards with your new address. And memorize your spouse's cell phone number. I know that it is easy just to store it in the phone, but do yourself a favor and store it in your memory, as well. It simply does not look good if the spouses do not know each other's cell phone numbers.

The USCIS generally does not have enough officers to go to everyone's home in order to ascertain whether two people are really living together. You may be selected for a visit, though, and you will not be notified in advance. Sometimes, there are circumstances when spouses make a decision to maintain two residences because of work or for other reasons. However, I strongly discourage it. No matter how sincere your reasons are, it will not look good in the eyes of USCIS officials.

At the time of the interview, bring all those documents mentioned above. You must bring a translator if you do not understand the English language. The immigration officer will ask you certain questions and examine the forms and documents you've submitted. If he or she is satisfied with the documentation you have submitted, you are going to be approved. If the immigration officer cannot make a decision at that time because some of the required documents are missing, you will be asked to mail the required documents. Finally, if the immigration officer does not believe that your marriage is valid, you and your spouse may be separated into different rooms and asked a series of very personal questions. You do not want to go through that experience; it is not fun. In those situations, a decision on your case may take months.

1. Conditional permanent resident status

When an alien marries a U.S. citizen, and the marriage is less than two years old, such a person will get a conditional resident status if the adjustment of status is approved. Children of the alien will also get a conditional resident status. This conditional resident status is valid for two years. It gives the alien the same rights as the permanent resident status. The alien can stay in the United States, work, and travel abroad. In order to remove conditions on residence and obtain the final permanent resident status, both parties— the U.S. citizen and the alien spouse — must petition the USCIS within ninety days before the expiration of the conditional resident status to get the conditional status removed. This also applies to children of the alien who also have to file for the removal of conditional resident status. This is accomplished by filing I-751 Form, Petition to Remove Conditions on Residence. If the form is not filed, the alien will lose the conditional resident status as of the date of the second anniversary of your conditional residence. What does that mean? The alien will be left in the immigration status he or she would have been in if the adjustment of status was not granted. Ultimately, the USCIS may remove the alien from the United States.

This form must generally be filed and signed by both spouses, and supported by documentation. However, there may be situations when that is not possible. The conditional resident alone may file the form alone, but only in limited situations, if

(1) you entered the marriage in good faith, but your spouse subsequently died;

(2) you entered the marriage in good faith but your marriage was subsequently terminated due to divorce or annulment;

(3) you entered the marriage in good faith, you remain married, but have been battered or subjected to extreme cruelty by your spouse;

(4) the termination of your conditional status would result in extreme hardship.

A) REQUIRED DOCUMENTS IF YOU ARE BOTH FILING

If you thought that you were done with pictures and documents after your adjustment of status interview (when you obtained your conditional status), you are wrong. You must provide the following along with your Petition to Remove Conditions on Residence:

(1) copy of your conditional resident card, both sides;

(2) birth certificates for any children born to both of you during marriage;

(3) apartment leases, real estate mortgages, real estate titles to your marital residence;

(4) financial documents showing joint ownership of checking, savings, investment accounts;

(5) car and medical insurance documents showing coverage for the family;

(6) at least two affidavits from family members or friends who have personal knowledge of your marriage and relationship. The affidavits must be notarized.

In addition, if you have a criminal history, you must send additional documents. If you were ever arrested or detained by a law enforcement official and no charges were filed, you must send:

(1) an original official statement by the arresting agency or court that no charges were filed.

If you were arrested or detained and charges were filed, or charges were filed against you without an arrest, you must submit:

(1) an original or court-certified copy of the complete arrest record for each arrest and the disposition for each incident (conviction, dismissal, acquittal).

If you were ever convicted or placed in an alternative sentencing program or rehabilitative program (community service), you must submit:

(1) an original or certified copy of the probation or parole record, or

(2) evidence that you completed the alternative sentencing program or rehabilitative program, and

(3) evidence that your record was set aside, sealed and expunged or otherwise removed from your record, such as:

(a) an original or court-certified order vacating, setting aside, sealing, expunging or otherwise removing your arrest and conviction, or

(b) original statement from the court that no record exists of your arrest or conviction.

B) REQUIRED DOCUMENTS WHEN FILING ALONE

If you are filing without your spouse, you must prove that you fall under one of the permitted categories listed above. It is generally harder to have conditions on residence removed if you are filing alone, and you can almost certainly expect to have an interview with an immigration officer. Documents needed are the following:

(1) a copy of the death certificate for your spouse;

(2) a copy of your divorce decree, or annulment;

(3) court documents, such as court orders of protection, police reports, records from social services or churches, photographs of injuries, showing that you were battered or abused by your spouse or subjected to extreme cruelty by your spouse;

(4) if you are basing your petition on extreme hardship, evidence that your removal from the United States would result in a hardship significantly greater than the hardship encountered by other aliens removed from the United States.

Whether the form is filed by husband and wife together or when a person files alone, once the required documentation is submitted, the petitioner will receive a receipt from the USCIS automatically extending his or her conditional status for one year. The USCIS will send a request for fingerprints. They may ask for another interview. If the petition is approved, the petitioner's conditional status will be removed, and he or she will become a permanent resident of the United States.

G. Affidavit of Support

In all family-based categories listed in this chapter, a family sponsor, a U.S. citizen or a permanent resident must get over one more hurdle in order to receive a full approval for his or her relative. He or she must prove that the relative being sponsored will have sufficient means of financial support once in the United States, and that he or she will not become so-called "public charge."

To prove that the intending immigrant will not become a burden on the local, state or federal government, the sponsor must file an Affidavit of Support, Form I-864 or I-864 EZ, along with the Form I-130, Petition for Alien Relative. The sponsor must show that he or she has enough income or assets to support the intending immigrant in case the intending immigrant cannot support himself or herself in the United States. Both forms are identical, and you may use either of them. However, a sponsor may use Form I-864EZ if he or she is sponsoring only one relative and his or her income is entirely based on his or her salary or pension. If you are sponsoring more than one relative, you should use Form I-864, and you must have one form for each relative.

The Affidavit of Support is essentially a contract between the sponsor and the U.S. government. If the immigrant, after coming to the United States, receives local, state or federal public aid (food stamps, insurance, etc.) because of his or her poor financial situation, the actual agency giving such aid may request that the sponsor repay the cost of the benefits. Importantly, if the sponsor fails to repay the cost of the benefit, the agency has the right to sue in court for damages. The obligations created by the Affidavit of Support end once the immigrant becomes a U.S. citizen, or if he or she can be credited with forty qualifying quarters of work in the United States.

1. Proof of income

The sponsor must be at least eighteen years of age with a residence in the United States. To determine whether the sponsor has sufficient income, he or she must compare his or her income to the required minimum income levels listed in the Poverty Guidelines, Form I-864P. The sponsor's income must be at least 125 percent of the current federal poverty guideline for the sponsor's household size. Let me explain. If a sponsor is married and has two children, his or her household size should be four; however, to this number he or she must add the number of immigrants he or she is sponsoring. For example, a sponsor is sponsoring his or her father and mother. The total household size would be six. In the current Poverty Guidelines, minimum income required for a household of six is $35,500. Therefore, the sponsor's income must be at least that much to be eligible to sponsor his or her parents.

How can a sponsor prove that he or she has

enough income? Along with the Affidavit of Support, he or she must send a copy of his or her latest federal income tax return, and copies of W-2 forms if the sponsor is a salaried employee, or 1099 forms if the sponsor is an independent contractor. Also required is a letter from the sponsor's employer stating that the sponsor indeed works there, for how long the sponsor has been employed, and the amount of wages paid. Finally, a copy of the latest pay check stub is helpful.

2. Use of assets

What happens if the sponsor does not have enough income? There are a couple of options. First, if the sponsor does not have enough income, but has other assets, he or she may use them to show that he or she is financially able to sponsor an immigrant. Example of other assets could be savings, stocks and bonds, cash, equity in a real estate (equity is the difference between the fair market value of your property minus the mortgage balance), and other personal property owned by you (cars, boats, etc.) If a sponsor uses equity in real estate, he or she should send a copy of the latest mortgage statement and a copy of a recent appraisal of the property.

3. Income from household members

Income from other persons from the sponsor's household may be used to reach the required income threshold. That person must be living in the sponsor's residence and be related to the sponsor as his or her spouse, parent, sibling or adult child. To use income from other household members, both sponsor and the household member must fill out and sign Form I-864A, Contract between Sponsor and Household Member. Note that in these cases, the household member must send the same documents required of the sponsor (the most recent federal income tax re-turn, W2 or 1099 forms, letter from employer and the most recent pay stub.) Also note that even the intended immigrant may be considered a household member for purposes of getting to the required income level. Two requirements must be satisfied: the intended immigrant must have the same residence as the sponsor, and he or she will continue receive income from the same source after becoming a permanent resident (trust fund, annuity, etc.).

4. Joint sponsor

If a sponsor does not have enough income or assets, and there are no household members living with the sponsor or the household members are unable or unwilling to help, a sponsor may find a joint sponsor. A joint sponsor is usually a friend or a distant relative willing to act as a joint sponsor with the original sponsor. He or she must be a U.S. citizen or a permanent resident, eighteen years of age or older, and have a residence in the United States. A joint sponsor must also prepare a separate Form I-864, and satisfy the same documentary requirements as the principal sponsor.

5. Substitute sponsor

A person willing to be substituted for the original sponsor — if the original sponsor has died after the relative petition was approved, but before the beneficiary obtained permanent resident status — is called a substitute sponsor. A substitute sponsor must be a U.S. citizen or a permanent resident, eighteen years of age or older, and be related to the intending immigrant as his or her spouse, parent, mother- or father-in-law, sibling, child over eighteen, brother- or sister-in-law, grandparent, grandchild, or legal guardian. A substitute sponsor must satisfy the same documentary requirements as the original sponsor.

CHAPTER 3

Other Family Categories

There are several family classifications that require a separate discussion. They are generally based on a family relationship, but because of their specific circumstances require a different treatment. They are not used as frequently as the main family classifications listed in chapter 2. They require separate forms and for the most part must satisfy different document requirements.

For the first three classifications discussed here, Form I-360, Petition for Amerasian, Widow(er) or Special Immigrant must be used. For the orphan classification, there are two forms which may be used depending on circumstances, Form I-600A, Application for Advance Processing of Orphan Petition, or Form I-600, Petition to Classify Orphan as an Immediate Relative. In addition, starting April 1, 2008, the Hague Convention on Adoption became effective in the United States. Two new additional forms have been created, I-800A, Application for Determination of Suitability to Adopt a Child from a Convention Country, and I-800, Petition to Classify Convention Adoptee as an Immediate Relative.

A. Amerasians

For purposes of this classification, an Amerasian is a person born between December 31, 1950, and October 22, 1982, in Korea, Vietnam, Laos, Kampuchea, or Thailand, and whose father is a U.S. citizen. Petition for an Amerasian may be filed by any person eighteen years or older, including the Amerasian, or a U.S. corporation.

Petition must be filed with:

(1) evidence that the Amerasian was indeed born in one of the listed countries between December 31, 1950, and October 22, 1982. If the person was born in Vietnam, he or she must also provide a copy of the Vietnamese ID card or an affidavit stating why the card is not available.

(2) evidence that the U.S. citizen was his or her father. Evidence may include birth records, church baptismal records, local civil records, an affidavit from the father, evidence of financial support from the father, photographs of the father, especially with the child, or if those documents are not available, affidavits of persons with facts and knowledge of the father-child relationship, including a statement as to how they acquired those facts and knowledge.

(3) a photograph of the Amerasian.

(4) a copy of the marriage certificate if the Amerasian is married, or a copy of the divorce decree or a spouse's death certificate if the Amerasian is no longer married.

In addition to Form I-360 and copies of the above documents, the petitioner for an Amerasian must also file Form I-361, Affidavit of Financial Support and Intent to Petition for Legal Custody of Amerasian. Sponsor must be a U.S. citizen or permanent resident, twenty-one years of age or older, and of good moral character. The sponsor must agree to provide financial support for the Amerasian five years from the date the Amerasian becomes a permanent resident of the United States or until the Amerasian reaches the age of twenty-one, whichever is longer. Sponsor's household income must be at least equal to 125 percent of the poverty line for the sponsor's household size (see discussion on Form I-864, Affidavit of Support, chapter 2).

Evidence of adequate income, in duplicate, may include:

(1) a statement from a bank officer on the bank's letterhead showing the date the account was opened, the present balance, and the total deposited in the last year;

(2) a statement from the employer on the employer's letterhead showing the date when employment started, whether the employment is temporary or permanent, and the wages or salary;

(3) a copy of the last federal income tax return along with all W2 and 1099 forms;

(4) a list of stocks and bonds with serial numbers and denominations, and the name of the owner;

(5) statements from the holder of a trust or annuity on the financial institution's letterhead showing the name of the trust fund or annuity, name of the beneficiary, and the amount distributed each year.

If the petition for Amerasian classification is approved, one must wait for a visa number. Because the youngest Amerasian is now at least twenty-five years of age, the waiting time will depend on whether the Amerasian is married or not.

B. Widows and Widowers

A widow or widower of a deceased U.S. citizen may petition for a permanent resident status by filing Form I-360. There are certain requirements which must be satisfied.

(1) The widow or widower must have been married for at least two years to someone who was a U.S. citizen at the time of his or her death.

(2) The deceased spouse must have died less than two years before Form I-360 was filed.

(3) The widow or widower and the spouse must not have been legally separated at the time of the spouse's death. Legally separated does not mean just living separately at the time of death. It means that

the widow or widower or the spouse filed a petition for legal separation in a state court before that spouse's death, and that a state court entered a judgment of legal separation.

(4) The widow or widower must not have remarried.

This petition must be filed with certain documentary evidence. The widow or widower must provide the following evidence:

(1) a copy of the marriage certificate and copies of any divorce judgments or death certificates for any of widow's, widower's, or the deceased spouse's prior spouses;

(2) evidence that the deceased spouse was a U.S. citizen (a copy of the spouse's birth certificate if born in the United States, Certificate of Naturalization if a naturalized U.S. citizen, Certificate of Citizenship, or Form FS-240 report of Birth Abroad of a Citizen of the United States, or a copy of the spouse's U.S. passport, which was valid at the time of the spouse's death;

(3) a copy of the death certificate.

The widow or widower is exempt from filing an Affidavit of Support Form I-864. Instead, she or he must file Form I-864W, Intending Immigrant's Affidavit of Support Exemption. Finally, the petition may be filed concurrently with the Adjustment of Status Application, Form I-485.

C. Battered or Abused Spouses or Children of U.S. Citizens or Permanent Residents

A battered spouse or child may petition for permanent residence by filing Form I-360 if the following is true:

(1) petitioner is now the spouse or a child of an abusive U.S. citizen or a permanent resident. Note that if the petitioner divorces from the U.S. citizen or permanent resident after the petition is filed this will not automatically invalidate the petition. However, if the petitioner remarries before becoming a permanent resident of the United States, the petition will not be granted or it will be revoked if it was approved;

(2) he or she is residing in the United States now and has resided with the abusive U.S. citizen or a permanent resident in the past;

(3) he or she has been battered or abused by a U.S. citizen or a permanent resident spouse during the marriage; or he or she is a parent of a child who has been battered or abused by a U.S. spouse or a permanent resident spouse; or he or she is a child battered or abused by a U.S. citizen or a permanent resident parent;

(4) he or she is a person of good moral character;

(5) removal or deportation of him or her would result in extreme hardship to himself or herself, or to his or her child or children; and

(6) he or she entered into the marriage with the U.S. citizen or permanent resident abuser in good faith. This means that the marriage was not fraudulent, entered into only in order to obtain permanent resident status, but a real, valid marriage.

Petitioner must also provide documentary evidence in support of the petition. The evidence may be some or all of the following:

(1) evidence of the abuser's U.S. citizenship or permanent resident status, such as birth certificate if born in the United States, Certificate of Naturalization if a naturalized U.S. citizen, or a Certificate of Citizenship, Form 240, Report of Birth Abroad by a United States Citizen; copy of U.S. passport; copy of the permanent resident card if a permanent resident;

(2) marriage certificate to the abuser spouse, or birth certificate for a child;

(3) evidence that the petitioner resided with the abusive U.S. citizen or permanent resident. Evidence may be employment records, utility receipts, school records, hospital records, children's birth certificates, mortgages, leases, insurance policies, or affidavits from persons with personal knowledge of the marriage and relationship with the abuser spouse;

(4) documents showing that the petitioner is residing in the United States now (see previous paragraph);

(5) evidence of abuse, such as police reports, orders of protection, court records, church records, medical records, social services records, photographs of injuries;

(6) if the petitioner is over fourteen years of age, evidence that he or she is of good moral character, such as state-issued police background check, or local police clearance from each locality in the United States or abroad where the petitioner lived for more than six months at the time in the three years prior to the date of filing the petition;

(7) affidavits, medical records, children's birth certificates showing that removal of the petitioner from the United States would result in extreme hardship;

(8) evidence that the marriage was entered into in good faith (copies of leases, mortgages, federal income tax returns, bank account information, utility bills, wedding photographs, children's birth certificates, affidavits of family and friends).

A petitioner under this category does not have to file an Affidavit of Support, Form I-864 with the petition. The petitioner should file form I-864W, Intending Immigrant's Affidavit of Support Exemption. The petition may be filed with the Application to Adjust Status, Form I-485, if the petitioner is a spouse or a child of a U.S. citizen.

D. Orphans

Adoption of foreign-born orphans by U.S. citizens has been steadily increasing over the years in spite of inherent difficulties. The process itself is costly, long, and very emotional, and the result is uncertain as well. There are numerous stories of families adopting foreign-born children who simply could not adapt to the new family and the new environment. Sometimes innocent children are saddled with the inevitable results of their natural mother's excessive consumption of alcohol and drugs while pregnant. The process of adopting a foreign child in a foreign country is by itself extremely difficult. There are different laws, cultures and procedures to wrestle with. Some countries do not allow adoptions by foreigners, or they have stopped all adoptions by foreigners for the time being.

If you are determined to adopt a foreign child, this section will help you navigate the immigration part of the process. This segment is divided into two parts. The first part will examine procedures involved in adoptions from countries who are not signatories to the Hague Adoption Convention. The second part will discuss adoptions from countries which are signatories to the Hague Convention. In the first part, I will discuss what comes next after you have decided to adopt a foreign child, but have not identified a child you wish to adopt, or when the child you wish to adopt is known and you are traveling to his or her country to meet with him or her. The first part will cover what to do next when you have already adopted a child or will adopt a particular child.

1. Advance processing

If you have decided to adopt a child from a foreign country, but have not identified a child you wish to adopt, you may use Form I-600A, Application for Advance Processing of Orphan Petition. The purpose of this form is to determine in advance whether you satisfy the requirements for a foreign adoption. The first question you must answer is whether the child is considered an orphan for immigration purposes. A child is considered an orphan if:

(1) the child has no parents because of their death or disappearance, or because the child was abandoned or deserted by his or her parents, or separation or loss from both parents; or

(2) the child has only one parent who is not capable of taking care of the child and who has irrevocably, in writing, released the child for adoption and emigration to the United States. Mind you, this could be tricky. There may be instances when a parent was swindled or pressured into signing such a document by unscrupulous go-between, not really knowing that he or she was relinquishing his or her parental rights to the child.

Who can adopt a foreign child? A married couple can if at least one spouse is a U.S. citizen, and the other spouse is at least a permanent resident of the United States. An unmarried U.S. citizen twenty-five years of age or older can also adopt a foreign child. In order to prove that an adopting person is a U.S. citizen, you can use any evidence listed in chapter 2. In addition, for a married couple, you must provide a copy of the marriage certificate and proof of termina-

tion of all of your previous marriages (divorce judgment, annulment, death certificate). Finally, you must provide a home study by a person or agency authorized to provide a home study, and this must have been completed not more than six months before being submitted with Form I-600A. There are numerous agencies providing home studies and you should easily find one that is located in your city and state. The home study must contain a discussion of the following elements:

- personal interview with you and your spouse, if applicable, and home visits;
- assessment of your capabilities to be a proper parent or parents to the orphan, including the assessment of you and your spouse's physical, mental and emotional capabilities, your finances, history of abuse or violence, history of previous rejections for adoption or prior unfavorable home study, and any criminal history. You must include evidence of all criminal history, even if your arrest or conviction has been sealed, pardoned, or expunged. Failure to disclose all information regarding criminal history may result in denial of the application I-600A;
- assessment of your living accommodations;
- your capabilities to take care of a handicapped or special-needs orphan;
- summary of the counseling given to you and plans for any post-adoption counseling;
- specific approval of you and your spouse for adoption, if applicable;
- the home-study preparer's certification and statement of authority to conduct home studies;
- if required, review of the home study by an appropriate state agency if you live in the United States, or an appropriate private or public adoption agency licensed in the United States if you live abroad and will adopt the child abroad.

2. Classification of child as immediate relative

Petition I-600 is used when you have already adopted a child or intend to adopt him or her shortly. Initially, the petition must prove that the child is an orphan and that the petitioner is a U.S. citizen.

If the orphan was already adopted abroad, you must establish that both you, the petitioner, and your spouse, personally saw and observed the child before and during the adoption proceedings. The foreign adoption decree must show that the child was adopted by both spouses jointly, if the petitioner is married, or that the petitioner was at least twenty-five years of age at the time of adoption if the petitioner is single.

If you and your spouse have not seen and observed the child before the child was adopted by you (adoption by proxy), both you and your spouse must submit a sworn statement that you will readopt the child once the child enters the United States. You must provide evidence that the readoption is possible in your home state, such as a statement by a state official. You also have to provide evidence that you have satisfied your state's pre-adoption requirements.

In addition to documentary requirements for Form I-600A, you also must provide the following:

(1) orphan's birth certificate;
(2) death certificates for the orphan's parents, if applicable;
(3) certified copy of the adoption decree;
(4) statement in writing from the only surviving parent that he or she is incapable of taking care of the child and that he or she irrevocably releases the child for emigration and adoption;
(5) evidence that the child has been unconditionally abandoned to an orphanage.

If the petition is approved, the child will be considered an immediate relative of the U.S. citizen, will be admitted into the United States as a permanent resident, and will simultaneously become a U.S. citizen.

E. Hague Adoption Convention

The United States is a signatory to the Hague Adoption Convention, in full force as of April 1, 2008. Procedures and forms are different if a child to be adopted is from a convention country.

As of February 26, 2008, 75 countries had become parties to the Hague Adoption Convention. See *www.hcch.net* or *www.travel.state.gov*, for the current list of countries. The purpose of the Convention is to establish internationally agreed-upon rules and procedures for adoptions from the countries which are signatories to the Convention. Note that if a child to be adopted was born in a country which is a signatory to the Convention, the procedure must be in compliance with the rules and procedures outlined by the Convention. Otherwise, refer to the previous discussion of adoptions.

If you have decided to adopt a child from a country which is a signatory to the Convention, the first thing is to determine if the particular placement agency you are using is accredited by the Department of State. Refer to *www.travel.state.gov*, and click on "Children & Family."

According to the rules of the Convention, every country will establish a so-called "central authority" for dealing with this type of adoptions. In the United States, the central authority is the Department of State, Office of Children's Issues, Bureau of Consular Affairs.

The procedure under Convention differs from the procedure discussed in the previous section on orphans. Under the Convention rules, before prospective parents are allowed to adopt a child, the USCIS must first determine whether the U.S. citizens are suitable to be adoptive parents. Second, the country in which the child was born will determine if the adoption would be in the child's best interest, and whether all necessary consents to adoption have been given freely (consent from legal guardian). Finally, the USCIS must determine whether the proposed adoption will be in agreement with the Convention rules and U.S. immigration law. If everything checks out, only then may a child be adopted.

1. Determination of suitability to adopt

The adoption process under the Convention begins with filing of Form I-800A, Application for Determination of Suitability to Adopt a Child from a Convention Country. Supplement 1 must be filled out for every additional adult living in the same household.

First, a person must demonstrate that he or she is eligible to adopt. A person is eligible to adopt if he or she is a U.S. citizen and is habitually residing in the United States. Habitual residence means:

- person is domiciled in the United States;
- person is domiciled in the United States but is temporarily living abroad;
- person is not currently domiciled in the United States but will establish a domicile in the United States on or before the child's admission to the United States for permanent residence;
- person is domiciled abroad, but intends to bring the child who was adopted abroad to the United States before the child's eighteenth birthday so that the child may obtain U.S. citizenship.

In addition, a U.S. citizen, if unmarried, must be at least 25 years of age, or, if married, both spouses will adopt the child and both are U.S. citizens, or the other spouse has a lawful status in the United States. Documents needed to prove U.S. citizenship are:

- birth certificate;
- Certificate of Naturalization;
- Certificate of Citizenship;
- unexpired U.S. passport issued for ten years;
- Report of Birth Abroad, Form FS-240;
- statement from a consular officer that you are a U.S. citizen.

Documents needed to prove lawful status in the United States could be a green card, I-94 card, stamp in the passport, or any other evidence showing lawful status in the United States.

For married couples, please provide a copy of the marriage certificate and evidence that all prior marriages have been terminated through divorce, annulment or death. For all applicants, if a child is not going to be adopted abroad, please provide evidence that all pre-adoption requirements in a particular state have been met. Finally, please provide a home study from a qualified, accredited agency. Please see discussion on home studies in the section above on orphans. In addition, the home study must:

- be tailored to the applicant's particular situation and the particular country of adoption;
- identify all adults in the household, their dates of birth and immigration alien numbers, if any;
- include an interview with the applicant and other adults in the household;
- state the number of visits and interviews, dates, locations and participants;

- summarize the pre-placement preparation and training provided;
- provide results of any checks done and referrals made;
- evaluate adoption in light of any history of past abuse, violence or substance abuse;
- provide answers to questions regarding abuse;
- provide description of overall physical, mental and emotional health of the applicant and other adults in the home;
- describe any problem areas.

Once a home study is completed, it may have to be updated or amended in the following situations:

- change in marital status (adoptive parent marriage or divorce) requires a new I-800A and an updated home study;
- change of residence, including change of state (evidence that any pre-adoption requirements of the new state have been met);
- any arrest, child abuse, substance abuse, or domestic violence by either prospective adoptive parent;
- change to a different Convention country (requires an updated home study);
- addition of other children to a home, or other adults (requires an updated home study);
- seeking a disabled or special needs child, if the home study did not address the special need;
- change in the number of children or their characteristics (age and gender).

If the original I-800A application was approved, send an updated home study with Form I-800A, Supplement 3. Supplement 3 may also be used if a person is requesting an extension of the I-800A approval. The request for extension should be filed within ninety days of its expiration.

2. Classification of child as immediate relative

Once the I-800A has been approved and the central authority of the child's country has proposed placing a child for adoption, the prospective adoptive parents must file Form I-800, Petition to Classify Convention Adoptee as an Immediate Relative. If the central authority of the child's country placed the child for adoption more than six months after the child's fifteenth birthday, the I-800 must be filed before the child's sixteenth birthday. If the evidence of placement by central authority is not yet available, the adoption service provider must submit a statement confirming that the central authority has indeed made the adoption placement on a particular date.

The I-800 petition may be filed if the I-800A application has been approved, the central authority has proposed an adoption placement, no significant changes have occurred in the adoptive parents' circumstances since the I-800A approval, and the adoptive parent, if unmarried, is at least twenty-five years of age.

The I-800 petition must be filed with the I-800A approval, a statement from the primary provider that all pre-placement preparation and training has been completed, and a report containing the following information:

- that the child is eligible for adoption;
- that the adoption is in the child's best interest;
- that the child's legal custodian has consented to the adoption in writing irrevocably, after first being counseled regarding the effects of adoption;
- that no consideration was paid to obtain necessary approvals;

The report must be sent along with the child's birth certificate; a copy of the legal guardian's irrevocable consent to adoption; a statement by the primary provider that the report is true, correct and complete; and a summary given to the prospective adoptive parents regarding the child's medical and social history. In addition, the prospective adoptive parents must file either Form I-864, Affidavit of Support, or Form I-864W, Intending Immigrant's I-864 Exemption. Form I-601, Application for Waiver of Grounds of Inadmissibility may be required, usually for medical grounds of inadmissibility. Please refer to discussion on waivers of inadmissibility in part IV.

If a petition is approved, the child may be adopted either abroad or in the United States. In case the child will reside in the United States, the applicant should seek an immigrant visa for the child. In case the child will reside abroad, the applicant should ask for a nonimmigrant visa for the child so that the child may enter the United States for purposes of getting U.S. citizenship.

CHAPTER 4

Obtaining Permanent Resident Status Through Employment

This chapter will discuss employment immigration. Employment immigration refers to the procedure of getting permanent resident status in the United States through employment. A person may be able to obtain a permanent resident status through employment if the person's future U.S. employer can prove to the U.S. Department of Labor (DOL) and USCIS, that for a particular occupation which the employer is trying to fill by hiring a foreign worker, there are not enough available U.S. workers with the desired skills, experience and education. The employer must offer to the foreign worker at least the amount of the prevailing wages for this particular position. A prevailing wage is defined as the amount of wages being earned by a U.S. worker with the same or similar skills, education and experience in that occupation in the United States locality where the foreign worker would be employed.

Similarly to family immigration, a person trying to obtain permanent resident status in the United States in most circumstances needs a sponsor who will petition for him or her. Here a sponsor is an employer who needs workers with certain skills and who cannot find available U.S. workers with the same or similar skills. There are exceptions, however; a person can petition for himself or herself without an employer in certain circumstances, and I will discuss this in detail. For the majority of employment petitions, though, an employer sponsor is necessary.

Employment immigration is divided into several "preference" categories, meaning that to each employment category USCIS has assigned a certain level of importance — which corresponds to the speed of getting an immigrant visa. The higher the preference level the shorter time to get an immigrant visa.

Each employment category carries a higher or lower preference in the eyes of the USCIS. Preference is based on the alien's qualifications, experience, and education, lack of U.S. workers for the same position, and the benefit of having aliens with a certain level of education, skills, and work experience contributing their efforts to an employer in the United States and therefore benefiting the United States in general.

The first preference includes "priority workers." Priority workers are either "outstanding professors or researchers," "extraordinary ability aliens," or multinational executives or managers. The second preference includes "advanced degree professionals" and "exceptional ability aliens." The third category includes "skilled workers," "professional workers" and "unskilled workers." The fourth category includes such "special immigrants," as "religious workers." The fifth category is reserved for foreign investors.

In the context of employment immigration, note that the employer is the "petitioner," and that the employee is the "beneficiary." The employer may be an individual, a partnership, corporation, or a limited liability company. A job offered must be a permanent or a full-time position. For all categories, except for the first category — "priority workers" — and certain workers in the second category, the process is twofold. First, the employer must obtain a Labor Certification for the Permanent Employment of Aliens in the United States (PERM) from the U.S. Department of Labor for the particular position the employer is seeking to fill, if required for a particular position. The certification may be granted by DOL where the employer can demonstrate that there are insufficient U.S. workers qualified, available and willing to work in this particular position, at the prevailing wages for this type of work in the geographic area of employment. If the DOL issues a labor certificate for a particular position, then and only then may an Immigrant Petition for Alien Worker, I-140, be filed on behalf of an immigrant.

Please note that if there are enough available immigrant visas in a particular category when I-140 Petition For Alien Worker is filed, the petition may be filed concurrently with Form I-485, Adjustment of Status, if the alien is in the United States and is otherwise eligible for adjustment of status. In addition, for most categories, except multinational executives and managers, Premium Processing Service (PPS) is allowed. The request for PPS is filed on Form I-907, and the fee is $1,000. You will get an answer within fifteen days.

A. Priority Workers

The most important feature of this category is that Labor Certification is not required. Therefore, the employer must only file Form I-140 with the relevant documentation.

1. Outstanding professors or researchers

This category includes professors or researchers with at least three years of experience in teaching or research in the academic area, and who are internationally recognized as being outstanding. They may be employed

- in a tenure or tenure-track teaching position at a university or similar institution of higher education;
- in a comparable research position at a university or similar institution of higher education; or

- in a comparable research position for a private employer. The employer must employ at least three persons in the full-time research activities, and must have documented achievements in an academic field.

Please note that the term "outstanding" should mean that the person, because of his or her academic achievements, belongs to the very top of the academic field, or has achieved national and international acclaim. The employer does not need to go through a labor certification process; however, there are a number of documents which must be sent to the USCIS, along with the I-140 Form. Documents should include:

(1) evidence that the professor or researcher is internationally recognized as being outstanding in an academic field. Evidence may include:

- receipt of major prizes or awards for outstanding achievements in the academic field (provide copies of certificates, awards, letters, etc.);
- proof of membership in associations in the academic field, which require outstanding academic achievement as a condition for membership (provide letters from the associations outlining the eligibility requirements for the membership and stating that the person has satisfied the necessary requirements for the membership);
- articles, books, and other published work written by others about the person's work in the academic field (provide copies of the articles and other writings);
- original scientific or scholarly research contributions to the academic field (copies of relevant writings by others recognizing the research as original scientific work);
- participation by the professor or researcher as a judge on a panel evaluating work by others in the academic field (copies of brochures or other writings evidencing both an invitation to participate and the actual participation as a judge in competitions, exams or other panels;
- evidence of published works, books, articles, essays in scientific, scholarly, or other journals or magazines in the academic field with international circulation (copies of the relevant writings);

(2) evidence that the professor or researcher has at least three years of experience in teaching or research in the academic field (provide letters from the current and previous employers, including specific points on the nature of positions, dates of employment, places of employment, and whether the positions were tenured or tenure-track positions;

(3) if the employer is a university or other institution of higher education, evidence that the position is either a tenure or tenure-track position for a professor, or a permanent research position in an academic field (a letter from the university will suffice, outlining particular terms of employment);

(4) if the employer is a private entity, evidence that it employs at least three full-time researchers, that it has documented accomplishment in scientific or academic fields, and that it intends to employ the researcher on a full-time basis (a letter from the employer outlining the particular terms of employment, along with written material regarding the scientific accomplishments, and a list of full-time employees, and the terms of their employment — starting dates, full-time status, names of the positions).

2. Aliens with extraordinary ability in sciences, arts, education, business or athletics

Similarly to the previous category, outstanding professors and researchers, the term "extraordinary" refers to persons who have reached the very top of their fields, and have received national and international acclaim. Importantly, in this category, the petitioner can vouch for himself or herself; in other words, an employer is not necessary. Again, labor certification is not required. The documentation needed is the following:

(1) evidence of a one-time achievement, such as a major internationally recognized award (Nobel Prize, for example); or at least three of the following (preferably more than three)

(2) receipt of lesser national or international prizes or awards for excellence in a particular field (copies of the certificates, awards, letters, etc.);

(3) membership in associations and organizations which require outstanding achievements in the particular field, as judged by recognized national and international experts in the field (copies of letters from the associations and organizations, including the list of requirements for the membership, and a statement that the person has satisfied the membership requirements);

(4) published material about the person in journals, magazines, books, major media reports (copies of the publications, videos and pictures);

(5) participation as a judge on a panel evaluating the work of others in a particular field (copies of the invitations to participate in exams, competitions, etc.);

(6) original work in a particular field (copies of writings or other evidence of the original contribution);

(7) publication of scholarly writings in professional or major trade publications or other media (TV, radio, etc.);

(8) display of the person's work in exhibitions, showcases (pictures, news articles, videos, etc.);

(9) evidence that the person has performed a leading or critical role for organizations or associations with distinguished reputations (letters from the organizations or establishments outlining the role played by the person, dates of employment or involvement, and the results achieved);

(10) evidence that the person is receiving a high salary for services (copies of letters from the current and previous employers);

(11) evidence of commercial success in the performing arts (such as copies of box-office receipts, attendance lists, and sales of books, videos, or records);

(12) evidence that the person will continue working in the United States in the same field (a letter from an employer, copies of employment contracts, or statement from the petitioner explaining his or her plans once in the United States).

3. Multinational managers or executives

This category applies to executives or managers living abroad, who have worked abroad for a company which also has a presence in the United States. The company abroad is the parent, branch, affiliate or subsidiary of a company in the United States. The executive or manager must have been employed in that capacity by the company located abroad for at least one year in the last three years in an executive or managerial position. The actual employer — the sponsor — is the company in the United States. A simple example of when this category might apply: after a large car company from Japan opens a plant in the United States.

Evidence should include a statement from the employer:

(1) that the executive or manager has been employed for at least one year in the last three years by the company located abroad;

(2) that the U.S. company where the foreign worker is going to work is the same employer, or a subsidiary, branch or affiliate of the company where the alien was employed abroad (provide documentary evidence of the connection between the company in the United States and abroad, such as articles of incorporation and other corporate documents, accounting and legal documents);

(3) that the U.S. employer has been doing business in the United States for at least one year (copies of corporate documents, leases, contracts, etc.);

(4) that the foreign worker is going to be employed in the United States in an executive or managerial position (description of the duties, salary, etc.).

B. Advanced Degree Professionals and Aliens with Exceptional Ability in Sciences, Arts, or Business

This employment category is considered the second preference category. Generally, an alien in this category needs an employer sponsor who will have to go through the labor certification process with the DOL. However, an alien may be able to apply alone for himself or herself, and circumvent the labor certification process, if he or she seeks an exception to the requirement of a job offer from an employer in the national interest of the United States.

"Advanced degree" means a degree beyond a four-year college degree or bachelor's degree. In addition, a person may be eligible if he or she has the equivalent of an advanced degree because of work ex-

perience, however, such a person must have the minimum of a four-year college degree. Generally, an advance degree is considered a master's degree, or a doctoral degree, but keep in mind that if a profession requires a doctoral degree, master's degree will not be enough. Alternatively, a bachelor's degree, plus at least five years of work experience, may be sufficient to satisfy the second preference requirement.

I've already discussed persons with "extraordinary" abilities. What then are persons with "exceptional" ability? There is fine line here. Obviously the standard is somewhat lower, but there are no clear answers as to what constitutes one or the other. Importantly, if a person is classified as a person with "extraordinary" ability, he or she will not have to obtain a labor certificate from the DOL.

1. Professionals with advanced degrees

The I-140 employment petition must include a labor certification from the DOL, or a request for a waiver on the grounds that the employment is deemed to be in the national interest of the United States. In addition, the following must be sent: an official academic (university) record (diploma, certificate, etc.) demonstrating that the worker holds a U.S. advanced degree in a particular profession, or a foreign equivalent, or evidence that the worker has at least a bachelor's degree and five years of work experience in the profession.

It is essential to have the foreign diploma or certificate evaluated by one of the foreign degree evaluator companies (there are a number of them in the United States, and they can be easily found on the internet by putting "foreign degree evaluator companies" in the search engine). After reviewing the diploma, certificate or other type of evidence of a degree, the evaluators issue a report stating that in their opinion a person does or does not have a certain degree equivalent to that in the United States. In addition, to prove that the worker has five years of experience in the profession, send letters from previous employers showing the dates of employment, salary or wages paid, and the specific duties performed.

2. Aliens with exceptional ability in sciences, arts, or business

For workers with exceptional ability in the sciences, arts or business, a labor certificate is required, unless an exception is applicable (see below, Exception to Labor Certification), or a request for a waiver of labor certification based on the U.S. national interest, and at least three of the following (the more the better):

(1) an official academic record showing that the worker has the degree, diploma, certificate or similar document from an academic institution relating to the worker's exceptional ability (a foreign document should be evaluated as discussed above);

(2) letters from current and former employers demonstrating that the worker has at least ten years of experience in a field and has exceptional ability (include dates of employment, salary or wages paid, specific duties performed);

(3) a copy of the license to practice a particular profession or specialty (note that if the state where the worker would be employed requires a state license in order to be engaged in a particular profession or specialty, be prepared to provide that as well);

(4) evidence that the foreign worker has been receiving a high salary for his or her work which demonstrates exceptional ability (letters from employers would suffice);

(5) evidence of membership in professional organizations, associations, and clubs;

(6) evidence of awards and recognition for work and contributions to the profession or specialty, by peers, governmental entities, professional or business organizations (good reference letters from people from the industry are very important).

C. Skilled Workers, Professionals and Unskilled Workers

In this employment category, labor certification is required, but there are exceptions (see below discussion on exceptions to labor certification). This employment group consists of professionals holding a bachelor's degree, skilled workers with at least two years of work experience, and unskilled workers.

1. Skilled workers

Skilled workers are considered workers with at least two years of relevant work experience, and where the position an employer is seeking to fill requires at least two years of relevant experience. In addition to the labor certification, the following documents are needed:

(1) evidence that the foreign worker has the required training, education and work experience needed for the job (for example, a high school diploma, specialty diploma, trade school diploma, specialty school diploma, certificates, and other documents awarded for the successful completion of a work program);

(2) letters from current and previous employers showing that the foreign worker has the required two years of experience in the occupation, including the dates of employment, salary and wages paid, specific job duties, etc.

2. Professionals

Professionals are considered aliens with a bachelor's degree, where the position an employer is seeking to fill requires a bachelor's degree. The required documents, in addition to the labor certification, are:

(1) official academic record from a college, university, or other appropriate school showing that the foreign worker has received a degree, diploma, certificate or other document for successful completion of a four-year college program;

(2) evidence that the position the employer is seeking to fill requires a bachelor's degree.

3. Unskilled workers

This is the last category, a category which one can use when all other hope is lost (in other words, when an employer cannot fit a worker into any of the previous employment categories). Frequently, a person will try this category when he or she has no other avenue available to get a permanent resident status. Documents required, in addition to the labor certification, are:

(1) evidence that the worker meets the qualifications required for the job, including work experience and education; letters from former employers showing dates of employment, salary and wages paid, specific job duties, and official school records, such as high school diploma or the equivalent.

D. Special Immigrants

There are several categories under the heading "Special Immigrants." Keep in mind that these categories do not require a labor certification and the form that must be used is not Form I-140, Petition for Alien Worker, but Form I-360, Petition for Amerasian, Widow(er), Battered Spouse or Child or Special Immigrant. I will discuss two categories, Special Immigrant Juvenile, and Special Immigrant Religious Worker. I will mention the other categories without discussion, as the other categories generally do not come up very often.

1. Special immigrant juvenile

An unmarried juvenile under twenty-one, or a person on his or her behalf, may file a I-360 Petition to obtain permanent resident status. This immigration benefit is allowed only if:

(1) the juvenile has been declared a juvenile court dependent in the United States, or

(2) the juvenile court has placed such juvenile in the custody of a state agency and the juvenile is found to be eligible for long-term foster care; and

(3) the juvenile has been subject to an administrative or judicial court proceeding where it was determined that it would not be in the juvenile's best interest if the juvenile was returned to his or her home country.

The petition may be filed concurrently with the Form I-485, Application to Adjust Status. Petitioner should send copies of the juvenile's birth certificate and court and/or administrative agency's records.

2. Special immigrant religious worker

A religious worker may petition for himself or herself, or a person may petition for a religious worker to obtain permanent resident status in the United States if:

(1) such religious worker has been a member of a religious denomination having nonprofit status in the United States;

(2) such religious worker has been a minister of that nomination continuously for the past two years, and

(3) the religious worker seeks to enter the United States as a minister of that denomination.

The I-360 petition must be filed with:

(1) a letter from the authorized official of the religious organization stating that the religious worker qualifies for the work as minister of that denomination, attesting to the religious worker's membership in the religious denomination, and explaining in detail the religious worker's work as a minister in the past two years;

(2) evidence showing that the religious denomination is a legal nonprofit religious organization in the United States and that it is exempt from taxation.

A petition may not be filed at the same time as the Form I-485 Application for Adjustment of Status. If the religious worker is in the United States, adjustment of status may be commenced after the I-360 petition is approved. If the religious worker is outside the United States, he or she will have to resort to regular visa processing and may be subject to a backlog (there are only 5,000 available visas per year).

3. Other special immigrants

Other immigrants which fall under the category of "Special Immigrants" and are required to use Form I-360 are:

- Panama Canal employees— persons who were at the time the Panama Canal Treaty of 1977 became effective either a Panama Canal Company employee, a Canal Zone government employee, or an employee of the United States government in the Canal Zone;
- Physicians— graduates from a foreign medical school or physicians qualified to practice medicine in a foreign country, who entered the United

States in H or J visa status before January 9, 1978, who was licensed to practice medicine in a state of the United States on January 9, 1978, and was practicing medicine in such state on that date, and has been continuously residing in the United States and has been practicing medicine in the United States since his or her entry in the United States;

• International organization employees and family members—nonimmigrant employees in G or N visa status of a qualifying international organization and certain relatives of such employees;

• Armed forces members—a person who served honorably in active duty as a member of armed forces after October 15, 1978, who enlisted outside the United States under a treaty or agreement in effect on October 1, 1991, for a period aggregating twelve years, who is a national of a country having such treaty or agreement with the United States, and the executive department under which he or she served has recommended the special immigrant status;

• Afghanistan or Iraq national translators—a national of Afghanistan or Iraq working with the United States armed forces as a translator for at least twelve months, and who has obtained a favorable written recommendation from a general or flag officer in the chain of command in the unit that the translator supported, and whose background check has been cleared.

E. Investors

Each year, 10,000 immigrant visas are allocated to so-called "alien entrepreneurs," their spouses and children. In order to qualify as an alien entrepreneur, and obtain permanent resident status in the United States, a person must invest in a new enterprise in the United States (at least $1,000,000, or less if the enterprise is in a federally designated target area), create at least ten more jobs for U.S. workers, and be actively involved in the business of the new enterprise.

If a person invests in a "targeted area," which includes rural areas and areas with high unemployment, the minimum investment is $500,000. A rural area is defined as any area outside of metropolitan areas, or

an area outside of city or town having a population of at least 20,000. A high-unemployment area is defined as an area (county, city, town) having an unemployed rate of at least 150 percent of the national unemployment rate. In simple terms that means that if the national unemployment rate is 5 percent, the required percentage of unemployment for a targeted area would be 7.5 percent. Go to the United States Census Bureau (*www.census.gov*) and the United States Bureau of Labor Statistics (*www.bls.gov*) to research specific areas.

To apply for permanent resident status, an investor must use Form I-526, Immigrant Petition for Alien Entrepreneur. If the petition is approved, the investor will either be eligible for adjustment of status or visa processing. Note that the investor will initially receive conditional resident status for two years. Ninety days before the expiration of the initial two-year period, the investor must petition to remove conditions on residence by filing Form I-829, Petition by Entrepreneur to Remove Conditions.

To satisfy the first requirement, the investor must establish a totally new company, purchase an established business, or expand an existing business. If the investor is expanding an existing business, the investor must demonstrate that his or her investment has either increased the number of employees by 40 percent or the net worth of the business. Note that purchasing a home in the United States will not qualify you for an immigrant visa.

The amount of the investment capital must be either $500,000 (if a new commercial establishment is located in a targeted area), or $1,000,000 (if the new commercial establishment is located in other areas). Investment is defined as a contribution of capital. Capital includes cash, equipment, inventory, and indebtedness secured by the alien's personal assets. The entire amount of the investment capital must be directed to the new enterprise. Attorney fees, commissions, finders' fees, and other administrative expenses are not counted toward the required amount of capital. It goes without saying that the capital must have been obtained by the investor by lawful means. Therefore, be prepared to show the trail of money, through balance sheets, bank accounts, accounting reports, etc.

Regardless of the amount of capital invested, and whether or not the new commercial enterprise is in a targeted area, the alien entrepreneur must create at least ten new jobs for U.S. workers. Copies of tax records for employees will be needed. If the employees have not been hired yet, the investor must produce a comprehensive business plan showing the need for ten additional workers. If the employer has purchased a troubled business (a business which has been in existence for at least two years and has a net loss for accounting purposes of at least 20 percent of the business's net worth), the investor must demonstrate that he or she will maintain the pre-investment number of employees for at least two years.

The fact that a new commercial enterprise has been established, that the amount of the required capital is satisfactory, and that at last ten new U.S. workers have been hired will not be enough to get the visa approved, unless the investor is ready to step in and be intimately involved with the business. That means exercising managerial control of the day-to-day operations or business policy formulation.

To prove that the four requirements have been met, an investor seeking permanent resident status must send documentary evidence for each of the requirements.

Evidence may include:

- articles of incorporation, articles of organization, certificate of merger or consolidation, partnership agreement, certificate of limited partnership, asset purchase agreement, stock purchase agreement, investment agreement, joint venture agreement, certified financial records, payroll records, and certificate evidencing authority to conduct business in a state or municipality (business license);
- evidence that the new business has been established in a targeted area; statistical records for a particular area;
- evidence of required investment (copies of bank statements, bills of sale for equipment and inventory, deeds for real property, evidence of money transfers, promissory notes, security agreements);
- evidence that capital was lawfully obtained (foreign tax returns for the last five years, foreign business and registration records, evidence of any pending civil and criminal actions against the alien — or judgments — in the last fifteen years, or a statement that there are none);

- evidence of job creation (copies of payroll records, tax forms, or a comprehensive business plan);
- evidence of personal involvement in business (statement showing the investor's job title, description of job duties, whether an officer of the business, board member, managing partner, etc.).

If the immigrant visa is approved and the investor has successfully either adjusted his or her status or finished visa processing, he or she will receive conditional resident status for two years. Ninety days before the expiration of the two-year period, the investor must file Form I-829, Petition by Entrepreneur to Remove Conditions. This form is filed by the investor, and his or her spouse and children as well. Once the petition is filed, conditional status is extended for six months. Travel with the old green card and receipt for the filed petition is enough for travel while the petition is pending.

Documentary evidence required for the investor:

- copy of the permanent resident card;
- evidence of establishment of a new commercial enterprise; past federal tax returns for the business; also see discussion above on the initial documentary evidence;
- evidence that investor has invested the required capital (send audited financial statement);
- evidence that the business has been sustained and operating in the past two years (invoices, receipts, contracts, bank statements, business licenses, federal and state tax returns, quarterly tax statements);
- evidence of the number of employees at the beginning of the investment and now; copies of payroll records, tax documents;

Evidence required for those filing as spouse or child of principal investor:

- copy of the permanent resident card;
- copy of the alien entrepreneur's spouse's resident card; if the investor is deceased, his or her death certificate;
- copy of evidence required for the investor to remove conditions on residence.

If the investor, spouse or child has ever been arrested or detained by any law enforcement official and no charged were filed, send an original official statement by the arresting agency or court order confirming that no charges were filed. If a person was arrested and charges were filed, or charges were filed without an arrest, send an original or court-certified copy of the entire arrest record, and court disposition for each incident (dismissed, convicted, acquitted, etc.).

If a person was convicted or placed in an alternative sentencing program or rehabilitative program (for example, community service or a drug program), send original court-certified copy of the sentencing record and evidence that the sentence was completed (certified copy of the parole record or evidence of the completion of the alternative sentencing program or rehabilitative program).

If a person's arrest or conviction was vacated, set aside, or expunged, send a court-certified copy of the order vacating, setting aside, or expunging the record, or an original court statement that no record of the arrest or conviction exists.

Do not submit documentation for regular traffic incidents where the fine was less than $500, unless it was alcohol- or drug-related.

F. Labor Certification

As an employer, you must approach the labor certification process seriously. The process is not easy, especially for an employer who has never done it before, and the task could appear daunting. Like any other immigration procedure, the devil is in the details. Let me suggest how you should approach the problem.

The essence of the labor certification process is to protect U.S. workers. In other words, if there is a job opening, and there are qualified U.S. workers willing and able to perform the job, then the job should be given to them. The purpose of the labor certification process is to determine whether there are any U.S. workers available for the job, and whether the employer tried diligently enough to find them.

1. General information

The formal process for a labor certification commences by filing an Application for Permanent Employment Certification (ETA Form 9089 or PERM). The Form 9089 must be filled out and signed by the employer and submitted either through e-mail or regular mail. If the application is submitted via e-mail, the authorized person must thereafter print out and sign the application and keep it in the employer's records. I suggest the use of e-mail; it is easier and quicker. Go to *www.plc.doleta.gov/eta* to file electronically.

Before doing anything further, the first step is to create a job description for a particular position, based on the job requirements and duties. To make it easier, the employer should go to *www.onetcenter.org*. This Web site contains more than 900 job descriptions, with specific work duties and requirements. The employer should find the closest occupation to the one the employer is trying to fill. Second, the employer must determine if the salary or wages the employer intends to pay to the alien worker are indeed at the prevailing wage level.

A) Prevailing wages

Once an employer decides to hire a foreign worker for a particular position, the employer must determine what should be the salary or wages paid to the worker. The amount of wages to be paid to a foreign worker have to be at least at the 100 percent level of the prevailing wages paid to U.S. workers employed in the same or similar occupation, who also have the same or similar education, skills and experience possessed by the foreign worker, in the U.S. locality where the work is to be done.

The essence of this requirement again entails protection of U.S. workers. The employer cannot pay the foreign worker less than that paid to a U.S. worker with same or similar qualifications. If the employers were allowed to pay foreign workers less, wages for U.S. workers would become depressed, and more foreign workers would apply, further depressing wages in the United States and effecting U.S. workers.

There are two things to keep in mind. First, the state workforce agency (SWA) will give an employer its determination of the prevailing wage in writing, upon request. Each request is made on a form which requires the employer to provide essential information about the position the employer is seeking to fill. A sample form from the Illinois Department of Employment Security can be found in Appendix B. For other states, go to *www.doleta.gov*, and click on "Regions and States." The employer must provide the following information:

- job title (for example, architect, cook, medical doctor, fashion designer, etc.);
- job description and duties;
- location of work, hours per week worked, and salary or wages paid;
- education and training level required (the minimum education level required for this position);
- field of study required (for example, civil engineering, medicine, architecture, cooking, etc.);
- length of education and training required if a bachelor's degree is required for a position, state eight years of elementary school, four years of high school and four years of college);
- work experience and field of experience (state minimum years of experience needed);
- special skills required (for example, proficiency in a language other than English, particular license or certification, live-in requirement, etc.);
- information about whether the position requires supervision of other workers; state the number of workers to be supervised in this position.

I suggest that before an employer submits a form for a wage determination, the employer should find out what to expect once the form is submitted. How do you do that? The Internet, of course. Go to Foreign Labor Certification Data Center OnLine Wage Library, *www.flcdatacenter.com*. Click on "FLC Wage Search Wizard." Choose the state where the work will be performed. Select the appropriate area (county) in the state. Click on "DOT crosswalk" and choose the appropriate occupation from the list. Click on "Search" and you will get the prevailing wage in your locality in four different levels.

Level I (entry level) wage rates are for entry-level workers with only a basic understanding of the occupation. Level II (qualified) wage rates are for workers who have attained, through education and/or experience, a good understanding of the occupation. Level III (experienced) wage rates are for workers who have attained through education and/or experience special skills and knowledge and a sound knowledge of the occupation. Level IV (fully competent) wage rates are for workers with advanced skills and diversified

knowledge, fully competent, with sufficient understanding of the occupation to plan and conduct work, requiring judgment and independent evaluation, selection and application of standard procedures and techniques, such as managers and supervisors.

B) EMPLOYMENT CATEGORIES REQUIRING LABOR CERTIFICATION

The next step is to determine if the particular position you are seeking to fill requires a labor certification. The first preference category, Priority Workers, does not need labor certification. The second preference category, Advance-degree Professionals and Exceptional-ability Aliens, generally requires a labor certification, unless the alien is seeking a waiver based on the U.S. national interest. Labor certification is also required for the third category, Skilled Workers, Professionals and Other (Unskilled) Workers. Labor certification is not required for the fourth category, Special Immigrants, or the fifth category, Investors.

C) NATIONAL INTEREST WAIVER

Petition for a National Interest Waiver is allowed only in the second preference category, Professionals with Advanced Degrees and Aliens with Exceptional Ability in Sciences and Arts. Note that getting this waiver is no simple matter. I suggest that if you decide to petition for this waiver you get the help of a specialist.

A person is never automatically eligible for a waiver. Eligibility is decided on a case-by-case basis, depending on the specifics of a particular situation. However, in order to petition for a waiver, the employer must satisfy certain basic requirements.

First, it must be demonstrated that the foreign worker will be employed in an occupation of great importance and value. An occupation which would satisfy this requirement would be one which would improve the United States economy; improve wages and working conditions; improve education and training for U.S. children and underqualified workers; improve health care; provide more affordable housing for young, poor and older U.S. residents; improve the U.S. environment and use of natural resources; or involves a request from a U.S. agency.

Second, the benefit from the foreign worker's employment would be national in scope.

Third, the employer and the worker must show

that his or her work would benefit the national interest to a higher degree than the work of an available U.S. citizen in the same occupation.

One occupation that is subject to a National Interest Waiver is that of medical doctor. Foreign physicians are subject to the second employment preference. A foreign physician may be able to obtain a National Interest Waiver if he or she agrees to work full time as a physician in an area or areas designated by the U.S. Secretary of Health as lacking in health care professionals, or at a health care facility under the authority of the U.S. Department of Veterans Affairs. Go to *www.hpsafind.hrsa.gov* or *www.va.gov*. In addition, either a federal agency or a state's department of public health must issue an attestation that the alien physician's work would be in the national interest.

The foreign physician files a Petition for Immigrant Worker, I-140, along with a request for National Interest Waiver, and the Adjustment of Status Application, Form I-485. However, the status will not be adjusted and the foreign physician will not be able to get permanent resident status unless he or she proves that he or she has worked for five years in an underserved area or a Veterans Affairs health facility.

D) EXCEPTIONS TO LABOR CERTIFICATION

The DOL has determined that there are insufficient U.S. workers for certain occupations. Most of them are grouped in so-called Schedule A occupations ("Schedule A" refers to Federal Register, Section 20 CFR 656.5). If an occupation is a Schedule A occupation, labor certification is not necessary. The other occupation where a labor certification is not necessary is sheepherder. However, in all situations, the employer still must fill out and sign the 9089 Application and send it to USCIS along with the I-140 petition. In addition, the employer needs to send evidence that he or she provided a notice of filing of Form 9089 to either the bargaining representative for the employer's workers or the employer's employees directly (see discussion on notice below in Section D). Schedule A occupations are the following:

- physical therapists;
- professional nurses;
- aliens with exceptional ability in sciences and arts

(except performing artists), including college and university teachers of exceptional ability;
- aliens with exceptional ability in performing arts.

To demonstrate that a foreign worker belongs to one of the Schedule A occupations, required documentation needs to be sent along with the Form 9089 and I-140, depending on a particular occupation:

(1) Physical Therapists—a letter or statement signed by an authorized physical therapy licensing official from the state where the worker will be employed, stating that the worker is qualified to take the state's written licensing examination for a physical therapist.

(2) Professional Nurses—documentation that the worker has received a certificate from the Commission on Graduates of Foreign Nursing Schools (*www.cgfns.org*), attesting that the worker holds full and permanent license to practice nursing in the state where the worker will be employed. Alternatively, evidence can be submitted that the worker has passed the National Council Licensure Examination for registered nurses (*www.ncsbn.org*).

(3) Aliens with Exceptional Ability in the Sciences and Arts (except performing artists):

- documentation evidencing international recognition of the person's work (articles, books, journals, videos, etc., discussing the person's work);
- evidence that the worker has been engaged in this type of work for at least the past twelve months (letters from current and previous employers with dates of employment, job description, description of specific job duties);
- evidence that the worker will be engaged in this type of work requiring exceptional ability in the United States (employment contract, letters from employers); *and*
- at least two of the following (the more the better):
  — evidence of national and international awards, certifications, commendations received by the worker for the exceptional work done in his or her field (send copies);
  — documentation evidencing worker's membership in national and international associations, organizations, clubs, which accept membership based on person's exceptional achieve-

ments in the particular field (send copies of the membership card, acceptance letters, letters from the entities showing the requirements for the membership);

— published articles in national and international journals and magazines, also books (send copies of all of those) in a particular field;

— evidence that the worker participated as a judge on a panel of experts judging works of others in the field (send copies of invitation letters, printed brochures about a competition, exam, certification, etc.);

— evidence that the person's work has been a major contribution to a particular field of study nationally and internationally;

— evidence that the person's work has been exhibited nationally and internationally (copies of the exhibition invitations, brochures, videos, etc.).

(4) Aliens with Exceptional Ability in Performing Arts:

• evidence that in the past twelve months, the person's work experience required exceptional ability, and that his or her work in the United States will require exceptional ability;

• evidence of national and international awards, prizes, certifications showing international and national acclaim and recognition (send copies);

• articles about the worker published in national and international journals, magazines, newspapers, etc. (send copies of the articles);

• evidence of the worker's salary and earnings, showing worker's exceptional ability (letters from current and prior employers showing the dates of employment, job descriptions, specific duties, salary or wages paid, or copies of contracts as an independent contractor, if applicable);

• evidence showing the outstanding reputation of the theaters, clubs, concert halls and other establishments where the worker has performed (copies of the brochures, news articles, etc.);

• evidence showing the outstanding reputation of the theater companies, ballet troupes, orchestras, etc., in which the worker has performed in the last twelve years (copies of the news articles, brochures, etc.);

• playbills and star bills (printed for a particular show, showing names of cast members, cast biographies, cast photographs, description of scenes, venues, etc.).

(5) College and University Teachers—evidence that the worker was selected for the job "in a competitive recruitment and selection process is needed." However, note that the Application 9089 must still be filed within eighteen months after the worker was selected. To prove that the recruitment process was competitive, send evidence of the following:

• statement from an official of the school with authority to hire workers, written on the school's letterhead, describing the recruitment process, including the total number of applicants who applied for the position and specific reasons why it is the opinion of the hiring committee that the foreign worker is more qualified for the job than the U.S. applicants;

• final report by the school body making a recommendation to hire the worker;

• a copy of at least one advertisement placed in a national professional journal or magazine, containing the name and place of the publication, and description of the opening, job title, duties, and salary;

• evidence of any other recruitment sources used by the school (Web sites, on-campus recruiting, etc.);

• written statement attesting to the degree of the worker's educational and professional qualifications and academic achievements.

(6) Sheepherders—evidence that the sheepherder has been lawfully employed by his or her employer for at least thirty-three of the last thirty-six months is required. Sufficient evidence would be a signed, written statement from the employer attesting to this.

Note that if the USCIS makes a determination that the Application 9089 based on Schedule A or Sheepherder sections does not meet the necessary requirements for approval, the employer must go through the regular labor certification process.

2. Labor certification procedure

If the alien does not fall under one of the lucky exception categories discussed above, the employer needs to obtain a labor certification before filing I-140 Petition for Alien Worker. There are a number of steps which must be taken by the employer before the Application ETA 9089 is filed with the DOL. Filing of the 9089 Application is technically the last step. Each step taken must be documented. The documents do not have to be sent with the application; however, they must be kept in the employer's file for five years. If the employer is one of those unlucky ones to be audited by the DOL, he or she will have to provide the entire documentation to the DOL.

Within 180 and 30 days before the Application 9089 is filed, the employer must either give a notice of a job opening to the bargaining representative for the employer's workers, or post a notice of the job opening at the employer's place of work (see discussion below under 4., Notice to Workers). In addition, the employer must conduct two mandatory steps, post a job order with a state workforce agency and publish two print advertisements. These two mandatory steps must be done at least thirty days, but no more than 180 days before the Application 9089 is filed. Therefore, an employer effectively has 150 days to perform the mandatory steps.

A) JOB ORDER

The employer must place a job order with the state workforce agency (SWA) covering the area of employment. Individual states usually do not call those agencies "state workforce agencies," and you will have hard time finding them under this description. They are usually listed under "Department of Employment Security"; for example, the Illinois Department of Employment Security or "IDES." The job order must be placed with the SWA for thirty days.

What is a job order? A job order is a job description of the position the employer is seeking to fill. In other words, it generally contains the name of the employer and location of work, job duties and responsibilities, education and work experience required and the salary or wages for the job. The Web site *onetcenter.org* will give a general job description for a particular occupation. The Web site online.onetcenter.org allows occupation and skill searching, so that an employer can create a general job description. Of course, the employer should also add any particular job duties specific to this particular job. Here is an example of a job description prepared for a medical research assistant:

_____ Hospital is in need of a Research Assistant who will assist with the performance of laboratory experiments in investigations of the physiology of preterm labor. Research Assistant will utilize techniques in molecular biology and animal model experimentation. Other duties include preparing material and specimens to be used in the conduct of complex experiments, including biological essays and quantitative and qualitative analysis; preparation of results for presentation at meetings and in print; performance of scientific literature searches; and general laboratory maintenance. Research Assistant will not have a contact with patients. Medical degree required, and two years of laboratory experience. Legal proof of eligibility to work in the United States. Salary is $_____ per year, plus benefits.

How does an employer place a job order? Once the employer has created a description of the job order, it must be posted with a SWA. Depending on where the employer is located, the employer should contact that state's Department of Employment Security. Go to *www.doleta.gov* and click on "Regions and States."

B) ADVERTISEMENTS

Two advertisements must be placed on two different Sundays in a newspaper of general circulation in the area where the alien will work. For example, if the alien will work in Chicago, the ad should be placed in the *Chicago Tribune* or the *Sun Times*.

If the alien will work in a rural area where there are no newspapers with a Sunday edition, the employer can use the newspaper edition with the widest circulation in that area. The advertisement must satisfy the following conditions. It must contain:

- employer's name and address;
- direction to applicants for the job to send resumes to the employer for review;
- a detailed job description, including educational work experience requirements;
- the location where the work will be performed;

- the salary or wage to be paid, which cannot be less than the prevailing wage for the area where the work will be done;
- the same requirements as indicated on the Application 9089.

It cannot contain work terms or wages which are worse than those offered to the alien.

If the position the employer is seeking to fill requires experience and an advanced degree, and there are professional journals or magazines which generally advertise openings for the professionals in those occupations, the employer may place an advertisement in one of those journals, instead of placing it in a Sunday paper.

C) ADDITIONAL RECRUITMENT STEPS

In addition to the two mandatory steps described above, the employer must choose three additional steps. All three additional steps must be done within the 180 days of filing the Application 9089, however, only one of the steps may be done within the thirty-day period before the Application 9089 is filed. The additional steps from which three must be chosen are the following:

- Job fairs— Look for potential employees at job fairs, as evidenced by brochures advertising the job fair, or newspaper advertisements where the employer is named as a participant.
- Employer's Web site — If the employer has a Web site, the job can be posted there. Employer should print out the Web pages showing the job opening.
- Other job search Web sites— There are numerous job Web sites on the Internet (monster.com, etc.). If the employer is using any of those sites to look for prospective employees, Web pages with the job posting should be printed out.
- On-campus recruiting — If the employer is trying to recruit on campus, the employer should ensure that its job posting is posted in the school's placement office. The job posting should have the name of the employer and the date of interviews. Also send a copy of the report prepared after interviews with students.
- Trade or professional organizations— Provide copies of the trade journals or newsletters where the job posting was placed.

- Private employment firms— Send a copy of the contract with the private recruitment firm, copies of any advertisements posted by the firm on their Web site, other Web sites, newspapers or journals.
- Employee referral program with incentives— Provide copies of the employer's notices and memorandums to existing employees asking for a potential referral, and outlining the incentives.
- Campus placement offices— Provide copies of the employer's notice of a job opening given to the school placement office for a posting.
- Local and ethnic newspapers— Provide a copy of the page containing the job opening advertisement.
- Radio and television advertisements— An actual recording is not necessary as long as the employer sends a copy of the text of the advertisement along with a letter from the TV or radio station confirming the airing of the ad.

D) RECRUITMENT REPORT

After the period of recruitment is over, the employer must prepare a recruitment report. The report should describe the steps taken to find appropriate U.S. workers, results of the recruitment process, the number of people accepted, the number of people rejected, and the reasons why they were rejected. Copies of all resumes, job applications, and rejection letters should be kept in the employer's file.

Keep in mind when rejecting an applicant that the DOL considers a U.S. worker to be qualified for a position offered if the worker can acquire the necessary job skills by having on-the-job training for a reasonable time.

E) JOB DUTIES AND REQUIREMENTS

Generally, job duties and requirements cannot be different from the ones required for a particular occupation and cannot be above the Specific Vocational Preparation (SVP) level listed on *www.onetcenter.org* (see discussion on SVP levels in chapter 5, section A). The employer may state that he or she requires other or additional duties and requirements for a particular position, but only if the employer has a specific "business necessity."

To show that the employer has a business necessity, he or she must show that those other or additional duties and requirements are reasonably related to the occupation, taken in context of the employer's business, and are necessary and reasonable in order to perform work in an effective manner.

Frequently, an employer trying to get an employment visa for an alien will state fluency in a foreign language as a requirement for a position. Generally, foreign language requirement cannot be included, unless the employer can prove that the requirement is a business necessity. To prove business necessity in this context, the employer must show that the foreign language requirement is necessary because:

- the nature of the occupation calls for fluency in a foreign language (translator, for example);
- a majority of the employer's customers, contractors, or employees, cannot communicate effectively in English. This can be documented by providing a statement from the employer showing the percentage of the employer's business with businesses and customers from a foreign country, marketing efforts in that country, and percentage of employees, contractors or customers who do not speak English. Also, the employer should explain why this particular position requires constant contact with the customers, employees or contractors who do not speak English. Finally, an explanation is required as to why it is reasonable to believe that those customers, employees and contractors do not speak English well.

F) COMBINATION OF OCCUPATIONS

If a position normally involves a combination of occupations, the employer must demonstrate that the workers engaged in this particular position generally perform a combination of occupations, that the employer has previously been employing workers for this position which requires a combination of occupations, or that the employer has a business necessity. To prove that this particular position requires a combination of occupations, the employer should provide copies of payrolls, letters or statements from other employers in the same field stating that they similarly employ workers for positions that require a combination of occupations, or any documents showing a business necessity.

G) MINIMUM JOB REQUIREMENTS

The employer always creates a minimum job requirement for a particular position he or she is trying to fill. Once this minimum job requirement is established, the employer cannot hire a worker who does not satisfy the minimum job requirements. Please note that if the worker for which a labor certification is being sought is already employed by the employer, the minimum job requirements will be judged at the time the employment started.

H) CONDITIONS OF EMPLOYMENT

Working conditions for a particular position must be the same or mostly the same as the general work conditions in that industry.

I) LAYOFFS

If the employer laid off workers in the preceding six months who were employed in the same position which the employer is now trying to fill, or a similar position, the employer must document that it notified in writing all laid-off workers qualified for the position about the job vacancy, and the result of the notification. Prepare copies of the notifications sent, responses from the laid-off employees, and the reason why a laid-off worker has not been rehired for the position, if he or she applied.

J) ALIEN WITH INTEREST IN THE COMPANY (OWNERSHIP OR FAMILY)

If the worker for whom a labor certification is being sought is actually one of the owners of the company, or the worker has a family relationship with the corporate officers, stockholders, owners or partners, the employer must be ready to show, if the employer is being audited by the DOL:

- copies of the partnership agreement, articles of incorporation, operating agreement, or business license;
- a list of all corporate officers, relations to each other and their relationship to the worker, plus copies of any shareholder's agreements;
- dollar amount of each owner's investment in the company, including any investment by the worker (copies of stock certificates, bank ledgers, bank accounts);
- the name and position of the company's authorized hiring official.

If the company has less than ten employees, it must document the existence of a family relationship between the worker and any of the employees.

3. Live-in household domestic workers

Applications for a labor certification for a live-in domestic worker must satisfy all of the requirements of the preceding paragraphs outlined in Section 2, Labor Certification Procedure; however, there are additional items which must be taken into consideration. The following should be prepared in advance of any anticipated audit from the DOL:

A letter is required describing the living accommodations in the employer's household, including whether the place is a house or a condominium or apartment, the number of rooms, the number of adults, and the number of children (and their ages) in the employer's residence. The letter must include a statement that the room provided to the worker would be free and not shared with anyone else.

The employer must have an employment agreement with the domestic servant, signed by both and dated before the Application 9089 is filed, outlining the wages paid to the worker; hours of work per day and total hours per week; a statement that the worker is free to leave the employer's residence when not working, unless he or she works overtime for compensation; that the worker will reside at the employer's residence; that both the employer and the worker are not required to give more than a two weeks notice to each other of termination of employment; that the room and board are provided at no cost; and that a duplicate signed and dated contract was given to the worker.

The employer must be also prepared to provide references and letters from the worker's previous employers. The letters from previous employers must include a job description, specific job duties, dates of employment, wages paid, hours worked per day and week, and specific appliances or equipment used in the performance of the duties. The total work experience must be equal to one full year of permanent employment.

Finally, the employer must explain why he or she needs a live-in domestic servant. The explanation must include the employer's current living, employment and financial condition. An example situation might be parents with small children where both parents work full time at various times during the day, and both travel for work or must report to work on short notice (such as doctors on call). Sufficient evidence would be a work schedule, travel itineraries and tickets, and letters from the employer's employer outlining his or her work requirements.

4. Notice to workers

In the beginning of the discussion on the Labor Certification, I mentioned that an employer must either give a notice of the job opening to a bargaining representative of the employer's workers in the occupation the employer is seeking to fill, if there is a bargaining representative, or post a notice at the employer's place of work.

If there is no bargaining representative, the employer must post a notice. The notice must be posted for ten business days and be clearly visible, placed in an area at work where the employees usually congregate and where it will be easily seen by the employees (food court, rest area, human resources, etc.). Appropriate locations for posting are the locations where other notices are usually posted, for example, notices regarding wages and hours, occupational safety and health, etc. The notice must contain the following information:

- statement that the notice is being posted as a result of the filing for an application for permanent alien labor certification, Form 9089 for a specific job opening;
- statement that any person may provide documentary evidence bearing on the application to the certifying officer of the Department of Labor, along with the address of the certifying officer;
- all information required for an ad in a newspaper, stating the rate of pay.

5. Attestations

The final part of the labor certification process is the filing of the 9089 form. Note that the form contains certain statements on the signature page. By signing the form, the employer is certifying that the statements are true. Read the statements before signing and make sure that they are true and correct.

CHAPTER 5

Obtaining Permanent Resident Status Through Immigration Lottery

In October of each year, the United States awards 50,000 visas to lucky persons who had submitted an application for the immigration lottery. The USCIS calls it the Diversity Visa Lottery Program. Why "Diversity"? Because the 50,000 visas are spread over a number of countries in the world with a low rate of immigration to the United States. Essentially, no visas are awarded to countries from which more than 50,000 immigrants have immigrated to the United States in the previous five years. The visas are not evenly divided among the selected countries; each country selected gets a certain number of visas. There are some countries which do not get any visas. The list of countries selected for 2009 is posted at *www.dv lottery.state.gov*.

A. Eligibility Requirements

If you decide to participate in the lottery program, you have to satisfy only two requirements.

First, you must be a citizen of one of the selected countries. Note, however, if you are a citizen of one of the countries not selected for lottery, and your spouse is a citizen of a selected country, your spouse may apply. Also, if you were born in a country which was not selected, but neither of your parents was born in or resided in that country at the time of your birth, you may claim nativity in the country of birth of one of your parents, if the country is selected for the immigration lottery.

Second, you must have a high school diploma or the equivalent of a high school diploma (GED in the United States). In the United States, that means that you have completed twelve years of elementary and secondary education. If you do not have a high school diploma, you must have two years of work experience in the last five years in an occupation which requires at least two years of training or experience to perform. Occupations under this requirement are classified as Job Zone 4 or 5 in a Specific Vocational Preparation (SVP) range of 7.0 or higher. I know you are confused now.

How do you find out if your occupation qualifies? Qualifying occupations are listed on the O*Net Web site, *www.onetcenter.org*. O*NET maintains a comprehensive source of job descriptions for more than 900 key occupations. The job descriptions include the skills and knowledge required, work activities, experience level required, work needs, and work styles. Go to the Web site and follow these instructions: click on "Find Occupations"; click on "Job Family"; click on the link for the specific occupation; then click "Job Zone" to find the zone number and the SVP rating range.

B. Application Process

If you are a citizen of a selected country and you have a high school diploma or the equivalent, or have the required work experience, you may send your lottery entry. The immigration lottery is done exclusively through the Internet; mailing is no longer accepted.

The entry form can be obtained by accessing *www.dvlottery.state.gov*. The registration period usually runs from the beginning of October through the beginning of December. One person can send only one entry. If multiple entries are sent, all entries will be rejected. Nevertheless, if you are married, each of you may send one entry. There is no fee for the immigration lottery.

Once you have accessed the Web site and have the entry form on your screen, you must provide the required information:

(1) your full name — Family Name, First Name, Middle Name;

(2) your date of birth — (month/day/year — 00/00/0000, remember, in the United States, the month goes first);

(3) your gender — male or female;

(4) your city of birth;

(5) your country of birth;

(6) country of eligibility or chargeability for the DV Program (this is your country of birth, it is not where you live; if you live in a country that is selected for lottery, and you were born in a country that was not selected for lottery, you do not qualify);

(7) photographs — one photograph for each family member, unless your child is already a U.S. citizen or a permanent resident of the United States;

(8) your mailing address;

(9) country where you live now;

(10) your telephone number;

(11) your e-mail address;

(12) your highest level of education (check the appropriate box);

(13) your marital status ("legally separated" means that a court has entered a judgment of legal separation, it does apply to situations when you and your spouse live at different places);

(14) number of your children — you must give the name, date and place of birth for your spouse, and for all of your children not married and under twenty-one, and your spouse's children, including stepchildren and adopted children. Children over twenty-one and married children are not eligible. If you fail to disclose all children, you will be disqualified.

(15) your spouse's information — name, date of birth, gender, city of birth, country of birth, photograph (if you do not list your spouse you will be disqualified);

(16) child information — name, date of birth, gender, city of birth, country of birth, photograph for each child listed in paragraph 14.

C. Special Instructions for Photographs

Because the only way to send an entry for the immigration lottery is via the Internet, you must also send the photographs the same way. There is absolutely no mailing involved. Each photograph must be either a new digital photograph or you can scan an existing photograph. Color photographs are preferred.

The image must conform to the following requirements:

- the person must directly face the camera; the head cannot be tilted up, down or to the side; and the head must cover 50 percent of the area of the photograph;
- the background behind the person should be in white or other light neutral color; no dark colors are accepted;
- the image must be focused, not blurred;
- the person cannot wear sunglasses, a nonreligious hat, earrings, tribal gear or similar items;
- head coverings and hats may be acceptable if they are related to the person's religious beliefs and they do not obscure any portion of the person's face.

If a new digital photograph is taken, it must be of course downloaded from the camera into the computer. The digital image must be in the JPG format; the maximum image file size is 62,500 bytes (62.5K); the image resolution must be 320 pixels high by 240 pixels wide; and the image color depth must be in 24-bit color mode. If you send a black-and-white image, note that it must be also scanned in a 24-bit color mode (monochrome images are not accepted).

If an existing photograph is being scanned, it must be scanned at a resolution of 150 dpi (dots per inch); the image must be in the JPG format; the maximum image size is 62,500 bytes (62.5K); image resolution must be 300 by 300 pixels; and image color depth must be 24-bit color mode (for both color and black-and-white photographs).

Winners are randomly computer-selected each year from the submitted entries. If a person is selected, he or she will receive a notification in the mail with instructions and a request for payment of fees. The letter will arrive from the Kentucky Consular Center. The fee is currently $375 per person. That means that if you were selected and you are married with two children, the fee would be $375 times four. You should pay the fee as soon as possible because by sending a payment you put the Kentucky Consular Center on notice that you are indeed interested in getting a visa. The Kentucky Consular Center sends more notifications than the number of available visas because not every person who receives a notification decides to continue the process. Getting a notification does not guarantee that you will get a visa. Therefore, as soon as you send the fee and receive a paid receipt, either file for adjustment of status in the United States, if you are eligible, or commence visa processing at the U.S. Consular Department in your country. Please note that you must finish the adjustment of status or visa processing by the end of the fiscal year, September 30, or you will lose your lottery visa.

CHAPTER 6

Asylum and Refugees

A. General Information

The concept of helping persons who are being discriminated against based on race, religion, nationality or political beliefs is the essence of modern American democracy and the immigration policy. There is a reason why people from all over the world have continued to regard the United States a promised land. The United States gives everyone hope for the right to be left alone, to make a living, and to live with dignity, no matter one's color, religion, nationality, social group or political belief.

A person may apply for asylum if he or she is already in the United States, or is requesting admission in the United States at a border. A person applies for refugee status while residing outside the United States. A person who is granted asylum or refugee status is eligible to apply for adjustment of status one year after being admitted in the United States as an asylee or refugee.

In order to be eligible for asylum or refugee status, a person must be found to fit the description of a refugee. A refugee is described as a person who is outside the country of that person's nationality, or — if the person does not have a nationality — is outside the country where he or she last habitually resided; and he or she is unable or unwilling to return to such country, and is unable or unwilling to get protection in such country for himself or herself, based on past persecution or well-founded fear of future persecution based on race, religion, nationality, membership in a social group, or political opinion.

A person is not considered a refugee if he or she participated in the persecution of others on account of race, religion, nationality, membership in a social group, or political opinion.

A person will not be allowed to apply for asylum if:

(1) the USCIS determines that the person may be removed to a country where the person's life and freedom would not be threatened and where the person would be afforded full and fair procedure for determining a claim for asylum, based on international agreements between the United States and such countries. A person shall not be returned to the country of a person's last habitual residence if he or she has no current nationality;

(2) he or she filed the asylum application more than one year after arriving in the United States. The one-year period starts with the date of arrival in the United States. The application may be considered after the expiration of the first year in the United States if the person demonstrates either:

(a) "changed circumstances" allowing for filing of the application. Changed circumstances could be changes in the conditions in the person's country of nationality or last habitual residence, or changes in the U.S. law, or if the person's activities outside the person's country would place him or her at risk or persecution; or

(b) "extraordinary circumstances" which precluded the person from filing the application timely. Extraordinary circumstances may be a serious illness or mental or physical disability, death or serious illness of a member of the person's immediate family, or if the application was timely filed but was returned for improper filing or for corrections, and was refiled within a reasonable time;

(3) the person participated in persecution of any person based on race, religion, nationality, membership in a social group or political opinion;

(4) the person was convicted of an aggravated felony and it presents a danger to the United States;

(5) there are serious reasons to believe that the person committed a serious crime prior to arriving in the United States;

(6) there are reasonable grounds to believe that the person is a danger to the security of the United States;

(7) there is evidence that person actually firmly resettled in another country before arriving in the United States.

A person is considered "firmly resettled" if he or she, prior to arriving in the United States, entered into another country as a citizen or permanent resident, or was offered citizenship or permanent residency in such country. A person will not be considered firmly resettled if his or her entry into such country was a necessary act during the escape from persecution, and the person remained there as long as it was necessary to arrange further travel, or the conditions of his or her stay in that country were so restricted that he or she was not really resettled. Factors considered are the type of housing given, the availability of employment, travel, education, public relief and other rights.

B. Asylum and Withholding of Removal Application

A person may apply for asylum at the time he or she is requesting admission in the United States, after his or her admission in the United States, or during a removal or deportation proceeding. The application for asylum is made on Form I-586, Application for Asylum and Withholding of Removal. A person filing for asylum should list his or her spouse and all his or her children in the application. If the spouse and the un-

married children under twenty-one are in the United States, they will receive asylum as well, if the primary applicant's application is approved. However, they will not be able to get asylum if the person filed an application in the immigration court (during deportation proceeding, for example) and the spouse and children are not a part of the court proceeding.

For each additional person included in the application, the applicant must make extra copies of the application. Therefore, send the original and two copies, and one additional application for each family member listed in the application. For each person in the application, send a passport-size photograph. Also, send three copies of each person's passport. The applicant must send three copies of the marriage certificate if a spouse is included, and three copies of the birth certificate for each child under twenty-one years of age. If the applicant is lacking these documents, he or she must provide affidavits, or sworn statements, from relatives and friends with personal knowledge of facts contained in those documents. People making a statement do not have to be U.S. citizens or permanent residents. The statements must include:

- the name and address of the person making a statement;
- attestation that the person's knowledge is based on his or her personal knowledge;
- description of a specific event or facts (marriage, baptism, etc.);
- an explanation as to how this person acquired the knowledge; and
- an explanation of the relationship between the applicant and the person making a statement.

If the applicant is providing sworn statements instead of providing the original marriage and birth certificates, he or she must explain why the originals (or even copies) are not available.

The bases of an asylum application are the negative experiences (persecution) that a person has encountered in the past or well-founded fear that persecution against him or her would occur in the future. It is of utmost importance that the applicant present in writing, on a separate piece of paper, all of his or her experiences which have led the applicant to believe that he or she may be eligible for asylum in the United

States. Details are essential, explaining the events, including dates, places, names of witnesses; always remember "the five Ws" when describing a story: who, where, why, what, when. Write as much as you can remember. Try to keep the story in chronological order, starting with the first occurrence and going forward in time. The application's Part D must be signed by the applicant; parts F and G should be signed later when instructed by a hearing officer.

1. Past persecution

To prove past persecution, the applicant must provide evidence that he or she was persecuted in the past in the applicant's country of nationality, or, if the applicant does not belong to a country, then the country of his or her last habitual residence. The applicant must prove that the past persecution was based on the applicant's race, religion, nationality, membership in a social group, or political opinion. Any documentary evidence is extremely helpful, and the applicant must be creative. Evidence of arrest, detention, imprisonment, court documents, photographs of injury or mutilation, membership cards, and applicant's published articles, would all be helpful. Also important are newspaper and magazine articles from the country where the applicant was persecuted, and from other world newspaper organizations, about specific instances of persecution in the applicant's country, or about the general conditions in the country showing a pattern of persecution. These newspaper articles may shed light on the persecution going on in a particular country against members of a group to which the applicant belongs.

It is also helpful to consult country reports from the U.S. State Department (issued every year) and the reports made by Amnesty International. See *www. state.gov/g/drl/rls/hrrpt* and *www.amnesty.org*.

If a person was subject to past persecution, then he or she will be presumed to have a well-founded fear of future persecution. However, this could be rebutted by the USCIS. Note that the hearing officer or immigration judge may deny an application even if the applicant proves past persecution if:

(1) there has been a fundamental change in circumstances in the applicant's country of nationality or the applicant's last habitual country of residence, such

that the applicant does not have a well-founded fear of persecution in such country anymore; or

(2) any future persecution could be avoided by sending the applicant to another part of the applicant's country of nationality, or the country of the applicant's last habitual residence, and it would be reasonable to expect the applicant to relocate. Factors for determining whether a relocation is reasonable are: any ongoing civil unrest or war; judicial, administrative and economic infrastructure; geographical limitations; age, gender, health, and social and family ties.

Note that in cases where the government of a country is actually the perpetrator of a persecution, it shall be presumed that any internal relocation of the applicant in such country would not be reasonable.

2. Well-founded fear of future persecution

To prove that the applicant would be likely subject to persecution in the future if he or she were to return to the applicant's country of nationality, or the applicant's last habitual residence, the applicant must provide similar documentary evidence as suggested for past persecution. The applicant does not have to show that he individually would be subject to future persecution if the applicant can establish:

(1) that there is a pattern of practice in such country of persecution of people based on race, religion, nationality, membership in a social group or political opinion; and

(2) the applicant can establish that he or she belongs to a group being persecuted.

C. Asylum Procedure

If a person is an arriving alien, he or she may request asylum at the border, as discussed later in Part IV. If a person is already in the United States, the application is either filed with a USCIS service center, or with the Immigration Court (during deportation proceeding, for example). For these cases, the USCIS will strive to finish all cases within 180 days of filing of the application.

After an application is filed, the applicant will be required to have his or her fingerprints taken, and to appear before a hearing officer at the Office of International Affairs. If the applicant does not appear at the interview, or does not show up for the fingerprinting, the application may be dismissed.

During the interview, the asylum officer will ask questions, interview any witnesses, and review the documentation presented. After the interview, the asylum officer will ask the applicant to return at another time to receive a decision in person. If the application is granted, the applicant is granted asylum in the United States, and has to wait one year before applying for adjustment of status and permanent residence. If the application is denied, two things may happen.

If a person entered the United States on a valid visa (B2, visitor visa, for example) and applies for asylum, the person will revert to the status he or she had before applying for asylum if the application for asylum is denied and the original entry visa has not expired. If the asylum application is denied and the original entry visa had expired, the person will not have a legal immigration status and will be referred to the immigration court for a deportation proceeding. Of course, the person may reapply for asylum and withholding of removal before the immigration judge.

D. *Withholding of Removal*

If an application for asylum is denied, the applicant for asylum may request withholding of removal. This is generally requested during a deportation proceeding. The basis of this request is the applicant's claim that his or her life or freedom would be threatened in the country where the applicant is supposed to be removed to, because of the applicant's race, religion, nationality, membership in a particular social group or political opinion. If the request is granted, the applicant shall be given deferral of removal to a particular country.

1. Past threats to life and freedom

If the applicant maintains that he or she has suffered past threats to life and freedom in a country to which he or she is to be removed, it will be presumed that he or she will suffer similar threats in the future if the person was removed to such country. The USCIS can attempt to rebut this presumption by demonstrating that either there has been a fundamental change of circumstances such that the applicant's life or freedom would not be threatened, or any future threats may be avoided by relocating the applicant to another part of the same country if it is reasonable to do so.

If the applicant has proven past prosecution, the USCIS may present evidence of either fundamental change of circumstances or a possible relocation as discussed in the previous paragraph.

2. Future threats to life and freedom

An applicant who has not suffered any past persecution may attempt to persuade the immigration court that his or her life and freedom would be threatened in the future if he or she was to be removed to a particular country. Importantly, the applicant does not have to provide any specific evidence if he or she can demonstrate that in that particular country there is a pattern of persecution of people based on race, religion, nationality, membership in a particular social group or political opinion, and the applicant belongs to one of those groups.

3. Withholding of removal under the Convention Against Torture

This subsection refers to protections under the United Nations Convention Against Torture and Other Cruel, Inhuman, or Degrading Treatment or Punishment. To be eligible for withholding of removal, the applicant must prove that it is more likely than not that he or she would be tortured if removed to a particular country. Torture is considered an extreme form of intentional cruel and inhumane treatment, causing severe mental or physical pain and suffering.

E. *Spouse and Children*

As explained earlier, an applicant's spouse and unmarried children under twenty-one will obtain the asylum status at the same time as the applicant if they are in the United States. If the spouse and children are outside the United States, the asylee (person granted asylum status) or refugee may file Form I-730, Refugee/Asylee Relative Petition for each family member. This form must be filed within two years of the time the asylee or refugee was admitted in the United States. Note that for a spouse to be eligible for asylum status, the marriage must have existed at the time the asylee or refugee was admitted in the United States, and it must not have been dissolved. For children to be eligible, the children must have been at least conceived at the time the asylee or refugee was admitted in the United States. Relatives who are not eligible are:

(1) spouse if each was not present at the marriage ceremony;

(2) spouse if it is determined that the marriage was fraudulent, entered into for the sole purpose of getting legal immigration status;

(3) adopted child if the adoption took place after the child's sixteenth birthday, or if the child was not in legal custody living with his or her parents for at least two years;

(4) stepchild, if the marriage that created the stepchild relationship took place after the child turned eighteen years of age;

(5) parent, sister, brother, grandparent, grandchild, nephew, niece, uncle, aunt, cousin or in-law.

Documents which must be sent with the petition include evidence of your asylee or refugee status, a photograph of each relative, and the evidence of the spousal or parent child relationship.

To show a spousal relationship, send a marriage certificate, and copies of all death certificates and divorce judgments for previous marriages.

To demonstrate a parent-child relationship, if the petitioner is the child's mother, send a copy of the child's birth certificate, and any legal documents evidencing a name change if the last names of the mother and child are different.

To demonstrate a parent-child relationship if the petitioner is the father, send a copy of the child's birth certificate, marriage certificate if married to the child's mother, and copies of all divorce judgments and death certificates for previous marriages. If the father is not married to the child's mother, evidence that the child was legitimated by father by civil authorities and ev-

idence of a real father-child relationship. Evidence could be money receipts, school, church, social-services records, medical records, income-tax returns where child was listed as a dependent, and sworn statements by persons with knowledge of the relationship.

For a stepchild relationship, send child's birth certificate, marriage certificate with the child's parent, and copies of all divorce judgments and death certificates for previous marriages.

For an adopted child relationship, send certified copy of the adoption decree and evidence that the child resided with the petitioner for at least two years before the adoption became final.

If the above documents are not available, then send church records, school records, census records or at least two affidavits (sworn statements) by people with knowledge of the facts and events. Each affidavit must include the name and address of the person, date and place of birth, relationship to the petitioner, information regarding the event (marriage or birth), and details as to how the person acquired such information.

F. Work During Asylum Proceedings

A person applying for asylum will be allowed to work, but must file Form I-765, Application for Employment Authorization. However, the applicant must submit the application for work not earlier than 150 days after the asylum application was filed. The work authorization will not be issued before the expiration of 180 days after the asylum application was filed.

G. Travel During Asylum Proceedings

A person applying for asylum may be able to obtain a travel document by filing Form I-131, Application for Advance Parole. However, if the applicant goes back to the country where he or she was supposedly persecuted in the past, the asylum application will be considered abandoned, unless the applicant shows compelling reasons for return to such country.

H. Temporary Protected Status

Temporary Protected Status (TPS) allows nationals of certain countries to legally remain and work in the United States. The secretary of the Department of Homeland Security may designate countries whose nationals will gain Temporary Protected Status. Reasons for TPS designation include the existence of an ongoing armed conflict in a particular country, an environmental disaster, or other extraordinary conditions existing in a country. TPS designation is effective for a minimum of six and a maximum of twelve months.

As of May 2008, countries subject to this program are Burundi, El Salvador, Honduras, Nicaragua, Somalia, Sudan, and Liberia. TPS may be requested by filing Form I-821, Application for Temporary Protected Status. Applicants may also apply for a work authorization by filing Form I-765. Importantly, TPS does not lead to permanent resident status.

To be eligible for TPS, an applicant must show that he or she is a national of a country selected for TPS, that he or she has continuously resided in the United States from the time a particular country was selected for TPS, and that he or she is otherwise admissible in the United States. To prove citizenship in a particular country, send a copy of the passport or birth certificate. To show entry in the United States and continuous residence in the United States, send copies of the I-94 card, employment records, medical records, school records, leases, mortgages, bank records, etc.

CHAPTER 7

Useful Forms and Tips

This chapter will cover several simple forms which may be used by either persons in the process of preparing documents in support of adjustment of status application, persons who have already obtained permanent resident status, and persons with nonimmigrant visas. I will also discuss E-Verify, a web site of importance for employers to check if their employees are authorized to work in the United States. In addition, this chapter will discuss INFOPASS, a way to communicate with USCIS and make an appointment with USCIS.

A. How Do I Obtain a Replacement I-94 Card?

You must use Form I-102, Application for Replacement of Initial Nonimmigrant Arrival-Departure Record. The initial arrival and departure document, Form I-94, is the document which is filled out (usually on a plane or boat) by travelers before entering the United States; the I-95 is used for crewmembers. (The I-94 card is usually white, or green if the traveler is from a country belonging to the Visa Waiver Program.) At the border, the USCIS official will tear off a portion of the form and staple it to a page in the alien's passport. The I-94 is stamped, and a notation of the nonimmigrant visa number (B2, K1, etc.) and the visa expiration date is written on the card.

It is extremely important to have this card when applying for adjustment of status, or when leaving the United States as a nonimmigrant. This card conclu-

sively proves that the person legally and lawfully entered the United States. This is very important if a person intends to file for adjustment of status because proof of legal entry into the United States is essential. Second, it is also important for persons with nonimmigrant visas to have I-94. When leaving the United States, this card is given to the airline officials at the border. It conclusively proves that a person did not overstay his or her nonimmigrant status in the United States.

If a person's I-94 card is lost, stolen or damaged, if one was not issued for some reason when the person entered the United States, or the card contains incorrect information, such person must file Form I-102 in order to get a new card. Documents which must be sent with the form are the following:

- Lost or Stolen — for a lost or stolen card, send a copy of the card, if available, biographical page from the passport (page with the photograph), and a copy of the page where the USCIS stamped the passport upon arrival into the United States. If documents are not available (stolen), provide a written explanation and a copy of the police report.
- Damaged/Mutilated — send the original form (make a copy for your records);
- Never Received — if a person did not receive an I-94 card upon entry into the United States, provide evidence that you legally entered the United States (stamp in the passport);
- Incorrect Information — send the original form and a statement with available documentary evidence

showing that the card contains incorrect information.

If you leave the United States and forget to turn in your I-94 card, you will have a very hard time getting back in the United States. Whether you are applying for a new nonimmigrant visa at a consulate or at the border under the Visa Waiver Program, you probably will not be approved.

To make sure that the USCIS records indicate that you did not overstay your visa in the United States, send the original I-94 and any documents proving that you left the United States to: ACS-CBP SBU, 1084 South Laurel Rd., London, KY 40744. Send also a letter explaining why you did not turn in your I-94 card, along with a copy of your airline ticket, boarding pass, stamps in your passport from other countries after departure, employer records, bank records, and other evidence showing that you left the United States within the allowed time period in your visa.

B. How Do I Obtain a Replacement Green Card?

You must use Form I-90, Application to Replace Permanent Resident Card. This form is used when the original permanent resident card is lost, stolen or destroyed, damaged or mutilated, has incorrect information because of the USCIS error, to update information on the card, or if the card was never received.

This form is also used to renew the permanent resident card, replace the old edition card, replace a card issued to a child before child's fourteenth birthday (one must file within thirty days of the person's fourteenth birthday), for a permanent resident taking up the commuter status, or taking up actual residence in the United States after being in commuter status. Commuter status refers to persons with permanent resident status who live in Mexico or Canada, but also maintain residence and a job in the United States and work in that position for at least six months per year.

Once the application is filed, a person will receive a notice to go to the USCIS local office for processing. The petitioner should bring the old card, or a copy of the old card, and any identity documents.

C. Why Have I Not Received My Green Card?

You must use Inquiry About Status of I-551 Alien Registration Card. This form should be used by a person whose visa processing or adjustment of status application has been approved, but has not received the actual card in the mail yet. This form should be filed sixty days after the person entered the United States, or ninety days after the adjustment of status was approved. Send a self-addressed, stamped envelope.

D. How Do I Report a Change of Address?

You must use Form AR-11, Alien's Change of Address Card. It is extremely important to send this form within ten days of an address change, every time a person changes an address. This applies to persons in the process of adjustment of status, permanent residents and nonimmigrants holding nonimmigrant visas. Failure to comply may be punishable by fine or imprisonment and removal from the United States.

For persons who filed an Affidavit of Support, Form I-864, the form used to report change of address is I-865. There is no fee but the form must be filed within thirty days of address change.

E. How Do I Get My Original Documents Back?

You must file Form G-884, Request for the Return of Original Documents. If a person sends an original document with his or her application or petition, once the application or petition is approved, he or she may request the return of the original documents, if needed. This is accomplished by filing Form G-884. Send copies of the actual original document being sought (marriage certificate, birth certificate, judgment for dissolution of marriage, etc.). In addition, send copies of two forms of identification, such as the green card (Form I-551), driver's license, state ID, employment authorization card, Certificate of Naturalization or Citizenship, and U.S. or foreign passport.

If a person is seeking original documents for someone else, submit proof of the relationship between the two of you. If the person whose documents are sought is deceased or incapacitated, send a copy of the power of attorney or a court document showing that you are the executor or administrator of the person's estate (letters of office).

The form should be mailed to the last USCIS center which processed the person's case. If the case is still pending, the form should be sent to the USCIS center currently processing the case. The form should be signed in front of USCIS official before being mailed. Make an appointment by using INFOPASS (see discussion on INFOPASS below).

F. How Do I Get Advance Permission to Reenter the United States If I Believe I May Be Inadmissible?

If you are a permanent resident alien, and you believe you may be denied reentry into the United States after a travel abroad because of a ground of inadmissibility (see Part IV on inadmissibility and deportability), you must use Form I-191, Application for Advance Permission to Return to Unrelinquished Domicile. Of course, you must file this form and get an approval before you leave the United States. Note, however, that if you advise the USCIS that there may be grounds for inadmissibility or deportability, the USCIS may commence a deportation action against you once you reenter the United States.

G. E-Verify—How Can I Determine Whether an Employee Can Legally Work in the United States?

E-Verify is an Internet tool designed for employers to determine if a prospective employee may legally work in the United States. Employers who wish to use this service must first register with E-Verify; however, participation is voluntary, not mandatory. Go to *www.vis.dhs.com/EmployerRegistration*. You can also go directly to *www.uscis.gov* and click on "E-Verify."

Regardless of whether an employer wishes to participate in E-Verify or not, every employer must ask every prospective employee to fill out and sign Form I-9, Employment Eligibility Verification and provide acceptable documents showing eligibility to work in the United States. This form is not filed with the USCIS but it should be kept in the employer's file.

Once I-9 form is ready, the employer can go on E-Verify to check if the employee is indeed eligible to work in the United States. E-Verify will ask for information the employee has given in Sections 1 and 2 of Form I-9. After the information is submitted, a response will come back immediately. This query must be initiated within three business days after the employee has started work.

H. INFOPASS—How Do I Make an Appointment with USCIS or Check the Status of My Case?

If you need to check the status of your case, go to *www.uscis.gov*. In the lower right-hand corner you will see a prompt for case status. Enter your case number — this is the number on the receipt you received when you filed a case, I-793. The number is located in upper left-hand corner of the receipt. Enter the entire number including any preceding letters; do not use spaces.

If you need to make an appointment with your local USCIS office and inquire about your case or any other questions you may have, you need to go to *www.uscis.gov* and click on "INFOPASS." INFOPASS may be used in several different languages; pick the one that suits you the best. Enter your zip code, and then explain the reason for the appointment. For example, it may have been more than 90 days since you filed I-765 form for a work authorization and you may have not received a card yet. The next screen will ask you to enter certain personal information (name, address, birth date, etc.). Finally, you can pick any available date and time. You should print out the notice because you will be asked to present the notice at the local USCIS office. If you cannot make the appointment, please cancel your appointment online as well.

I. How Do I Apply for Reentry Permit If I Am a Permanent Resident and My Trip Will Last More Than Twelve Months?

If a person is a permanent resident of the United States and he or she plans to leave the United States for twelve months or more, a reentry permit is a must. The application is made on Form I-131, Application for Travel Document. The permit is valid for two years.

PART II

—⁓—

Obtaining Citizenship

A person can become a U.S. citizen by birth or by naturalization. Some persons who obtain permanent resident status in the United States never apply for U.S. citizenship. Nevertheless, being a citizen of the United States brings certain benefits which permanent residents do not have. For example, there are no backlogs for family applications by U.S. citizens for their spouses, parents and unmarried children under 21. United States citizens can vote, purchase and own guns, serve as jurors, and live abroad if they wish without any travel or residence requirements.

Citizenship by Birth

A person is considered a born U.S. citizen if he or she was born in the United States, or was born to a United States citizen.

Just as a person born in the United States is a U.S. citizen, so are children born in Puerto Rico, Guam and the Commonwealth of Northern Mariana Islands. However, children of foreign-born diplomats will not be considered U.S. citizens even if they were born in the United States.

A person born abroad to parents who are U.S. citizens is considered a U.S. citizen if at least one of the parents lived in the United States during his or her life.

A person born abroad will be considered a U.S. citizen if one parent was a U.S. citizen at the time of his or her birth; the U.S.-citizen parent lived for at least five years in the United States before the child was born; and at least two of those five years occurred after the fourteenth birthday of the U.S.-citizen parent.

In all cases of birth abroad, proof of U.S. citizenship may be obtained by applying for a U.S. passport, filing Form N-600, Application for Certificate of Citizenship, or by getting a record of birth abroad from the U.S. consulate, Form FS-240.

The Child Citizenship Act (CCA) grants automatic U.S. citizenship to certain children with at least one parent who is a U.S. citizen if they can satisfy certain requirements. Children who qualify under the CCA are: biological or legitimated children if they were legitimated before the age of sixteen while in legal custody of the parent; orphans born abroad with the final adoption decree, or orphans born abroad and adopted in the United States; children born out of wedlock whose mother becomes a naturalized U.S. citizen; and adopted children satisfying the two-year residence requirement (living with the adopting parents for at least two years before adoption).

A. Child Residing in the United States

If a child is residing in the United States the child will automatically become a U.S. citizen if:

- one parent is a U.S. citizen either by birth or naturalization;
- child has been admitted to the United States as a permanent resident;
- child is under eighteen and is not married;
- the child was adopted and, the adoption is final;
- the child was legitimated and, the child was legitimated before the child's sixteenth birthday;
- child is residing in the United States in legal and physical custody of the U.S.-citizen parent.

Proof of U.S. citizenship may be obtained by applying for a U.S. passport or by filing Form N-600, Application for Certificate of Citizenship. However, foreign orphans adopted abroad will receive a Certificate of Citizenship within forty-five days of their arrival in the United States—no need to file Form N-600.

B. Child Residing Outside the United States

For children who reside outside the United States, there is no automatic U.S. citizenship. Even if they satisfy the requirements for citizenship, they will have to enter the United States to complete the naturalization processing and take the oath of allegiance to the United States. To be eligible for U.S. citizenship the child must be under eighteen years of age, and the following also must be true:

- at least one of the child's parents is a U.S. citizen;
- the U.S.-citizen parent has been physically living in the United States for at least five years, and two of those five years occurred after the person's fourteenth birthday; or the U.S.-citizen parent has a U.S.-citizen parent who has physically lived in the United States for at least five years, two of which had occurred after the person's fourteenth birthday;
- the child is residing abroad in the legal and physical custody of a U.S.-citizen parent; or in the legal and physical custody of a U.S.-citizen grandparent or legal guardian if the U.S.-citizen parent is deceased;
- the child is temporarily in the United States in a lawful, unexpired status;
- the parent-child relationship is established by either birth, including legitimated children, or adoption (no stepchildren). If the child was legitimated, this must have occurred while the child was in the parent's legal custody prior to the child's sixteenth birthday. If a child was adopted, the adoption requirements must be satisfied; there must be a final adoption decree, the child must have been adopted before his or her sixteenth birthday, and the two-year residency requirement must have been satisfied, or — if the child was adopted abroad — there must be an approved Form I-600 (see Part I).

To obtain proof of U.S. citizenship, Form I-600K, Application for Citizenship and Issuance of Certificate Under Section 322, must be used. If the application is filed by a U.S.-citizen grandparent or legal guardian, if the U.S.-citizen parent has died, the application must be filed within five years of the parent's death.

CHAPTER 2

Citizenship by Naturalization

Naturalization is a process through which a permanent resident of the United States becomes a U.S. citizen. In order to become a U.S. citizen, a permanent resident must satisfy certain residency requirements, be a person of good moral character, and pass a test of English and civics. A form which must be used is Form N-400, Application for Naturalization. A person who belongs to any of the following categories is ineligible for U.S. citizenship:

- advocates or teaches anarchism, or is a member of any group or organization opposed to all organized government (anarchist);
- one who is a member of, or affiliated with, the Communist Party of the United States or of any state in the United States, or a foreign country; the Communist Political Association, or any other totalitarian party of the United States, any state in the United States, or a foreign country, or a successor or direct predecessor of such party, unless the person demonstrates that the person did not have knowledge when he or she joined, or had no reason to believe, that such organization or party was a Communist-front organization.
- advocates, or is a member of a group which advocates, the economic, international and governmental doctrines of world communism or the establishment in the United States of a totalitarian dictatorship;
- advocates, teaches or is a member of any organization or a group which advocates the overthrow of the United States government by force, killing of officers of the United States government, damage and destruction of property, or sabotage;
- writes or publishes matter advocating the overthrow of the United States government by force, killing of officers of the United States government, damage and destruction of property, sabotage, or the economic, international and governmental doctrines of world communism.

A. Residency Requirements

The first residency requirement is that an applicant has resided at least three months within a particular USCIS district. In addition, a person who has filed an Application for Naturalization must maintain U.S. residence until the taking of the oath.

1. Five years

A permanent resident who is at least eighteen years of age may apply for U.S. citizenship if he or she has had permanent resident status for at least five years and has resided in the United States for at least thirty months in those five years. However, for citizenship purposes, the applicant must not have taken a trip outside the United States which lasted six months or more in any year in the past five years. In other words, a person may have thirty months of residence total in the United States in the past five years, but he or she may not be eligible to obtain citizenship if he or she spent between six and twelve months in any of those five years outside the United States. Why? Because there is a presumption, which may be rebutted, that a continuous residence is broken if a person spends more than six months outside the United States in any calendar year.

Let me give you an example. A person is a permanent resident of the United States. She became a permanent resident on January 1, 2003 (that is the date on the approval letter and her green card). She may apply for naturalization on or after October 1, 2007. After becoming a permanent resident, she had not traveled outside the United States until 2007. In 2007 she spent eight months outside the United States and returned on September 1, 2007. For purposes of citizenship, although she has been a resident for more than five years at this time, and although she has resided in the United States for more than thirty months in the last five years, she may not eligible to obtain U.S. citizenship. Why? Because she cut the continuity of residence in the last five years. She will now have to wait until June 1, 2012, to apply again, because the continuity will have to start from the time of her return to the United States after the travel abroad. She cannot "jump over" 2007 and use months of residence in the United States from the previous years; she has to start all over again.

2. Three years

If a permanent resident became a permanent resident by marrying a U.S. citizen, the residency requirement is three years. Again, the applicant must have at least six months of continuous residence in the United States in each of the three years to be eligible. Additional requirements:

(1) person is still married to the U.S.-citizen spouse;

(2) person has been living with the U.S.-citizen spouse for the last three years;

(3) person's U.S.-citizen spouse has been a U.S. citizen for the past three years.

For both the 5-year and 3-year residency requirement, the application may be filed not earlier than ninety days before the fifth or third anniversary of obtaining the permanent resident status. For refugees, the required time period (five years) starts from the time the refugee was admitted in the United States, not when he or she became a permanent resident.

3. Application to preserve residence for naturalization purposes

In certain situations, a permanent resident may be able to preserve the residency requirements (five or three years) for naturalization purposes even though he or she did not reside at least six continuous months in a calendar year in the United States. An application is made by filing Form N-470, Application to Preserve Residence for Naturalization Purposes.

Those who may be eligible are:

- a person who is or will be employed by the U.S. government;
- a person who will perform scientific research on behalf of an American institution of research;
- a person employed by an American company who will engage in the development of foreign trade and commerce on behalf of such company;
- a person employed by an international organization of which United States is a member;
- a person in the capacity of a clergyman, clergywomen, missionary, or member of a religious order with organization in the United States.

4. Reentry permit

If a permanent resident knows that he or she will spend at least twelve months outside the United States, he or she must obtain a reentry permit before any travel. The Form needed is I-131. The permit will allow the person to reenter the United States, however, it will not negate any disruption of continuous residence. In fact, if a person lives the United States for one year or more with a reentry permit, any time before the departure from the United States will not be counted towards the time in continuous residence in the United States. Note that if a person returns to the United States with a reentry permit within two years after departure, the last 364 days of the time outside the United States may be counted toward continued residence requirement.

B. "Good Moral Character"

In order to be eligible for U.S. citizenship, the applicant must be deemed a person of "good moral character" during the required residency period. It is generally considered that "good moral character" means a character which is up to standards of an average citizen in the community where the applicant resides. It is very important to reveal any and all criminal records and provide a certified court copy of any arrest, conviction or other court disposition. For traffic related incidents, unless the person was fined $500 or more, or the incident was drug- or alcohol-related, no reporting is necessary. A person convicted of murder or an aggravated offense which occurred on or after November 29, 1990, is not considered a person of good moral character.

The following are examples of a behavior which is not considered to represent "good moral character":

- any crime against a person with intent to injure (battery, for example);
- any crime against property or government involving fraud;
- two or more crimes for which the total court sentence was five years or more;
- violation of any controlled-substances law (drugs);
- illegal gambling;
- prostitution;
- drunk driving or alcoholism;
- polygamy (having more than one spouse at the same time);
- failure to pay child support or alimony per court order;
- terrorist acts;
- lying to obtain immigration benefits;
- jail time for 180 days or more in the past three or five years, depending on the residence requirement;
- failure to complete any probation, parole, or suspended sentence before applying for citizenship;
- persecution of any person based on race, religion, national origin, political opinion or social group.

Remember that if you committed any crimes which are discussed in Part IV on deportability, think very hard before you apply for citizenship. You must know that if the offense falls under one of the deporta-bility grounds, the USCIS may commence a deportation proceeding.

C. English and Civics Test

Every person applying for U.S. citizenship must demonstrate that he or she has an understanding of the English language and can read, write and speak simple words and phrases in English. In addition, every applicant must also pass the civics test, which is a series of questions on the principles of the U.S. government and history of the United States. Please note that starting October 1, 2008, the test on the civics will be somewhat changed. New material can be found by going to *www.uscis.gov*; click on "Services and Benefits," then click on "Citizenship," then click on "Citizenship Information."

There are certain applicants who may be excused from taking the tests or who are allowed to take the civics test only. These exceptions are allowed if:

- applicant is over fifty years of age and has lived in the United States as a permanent resident for at least twenty years; he or she does not have the take the English test; the civics test must be taken, but it may be taken in the person's native language;
- applicant is over fifty-five years of age, and has lived in the United States as a permanent resident for at least fifteen years; he or she does not have to take the English test; the civics test must be taken, but it may be taken in the person's native language;
- applicant is over sixty-five years of age, and has lived in the United States as a permanent resident for at least twenty years; he or she does not have to take the English test; the civics test must be taken, though this is a simpler version and it may be taken in the person's native language;
- applicant has a physical or mental disability so severe that it effectively prevents the person from learning the required information or demonstrating the knowledge of the English language and civics. The disability must have existed for at least one year, and must not be a by-product of illegal drug use.

A request for exception based on a physical or mental disability is made by filing Form I-648, Medical

Certification for Disability Exception. The first part of the form is completed by the applicant for citizenship. The second, most-important part of this form must be completed by a doctor, doctor of osteopathy or licensed clinical psychologist. The medical professional must provide a clinical diagnosis and description of the applicant's disability, show a connection between the disability and the inability to learn and demonstrate the required knowledge of the English language and civics, and a professional certified opinion that the applicant is unable to learn/demonstrate knowledge of the English language and civics.

D. Naturalization Procedure

The application must be filed with two passport-size photographs and some additional documentation. Documents, depending on the basis for citizenship, may include:

- copy of divorce judgment, marriage certificate or other document showing the name change if the applicant's name is different on the application then on the green card;
- evidence that the U.S.-citizen spouse has been a U.S. citizen for the last three years, such as birth certificate, Certificate of Naturalization, copy of the U.S. passport biographical page, etc.;
- evidence that the applicant and the U.S.-citizen spouse have been living together for the past three years, such as federal income tax returns, bank statements, leases, mortgages, children's birth certificates, etc.;
- applicant's current marriage certificate and copies of all divorce judgments and death certificates for previous marriages;
- if the applicant is required to pay child support or alimony, either a letter from the other spouse confirming that the payments are current, or an official letter from a state's Department of Health and Family Services, or equivalent, showing that the child support payments are current;
- if the applicant was ever arrested and no charges were filed, a certified copy from the arresting agency or court that no charges were filed;
- if the applicant was ever arrested and charges were

filed, a certified copy of the complete arrest record and court disposition (conviction, acquittal, dismissal);
- if the applicant was ever convicted, or placed in an alternative sentencing program or rehabilitative program, a certified copy of the sentencing record and evidence that the sentence was completed;
- if the applicant's arrest or conviction was vacated, set aside, sealed, expunged or otherwise removed from the applicant's record, a certified copy of the order vacating, expunging, setting aside the arrest or conviction;
- if the applicant ever failed to file a federal income tax return, copies of the correspondence with the IRS, or, if any taxes are due, a signed agreement with IRS showing arrangements to pay taxes.

Once the application is filed with the appropriate fee, the USCIS will send a receipt acknowledging the receipt of the application. The applicant will shortly thereafter receive a request for fingerprinting. The next step is the interview. If the applicant passes the interview, the final part of the process is taking the oath of allegiance before a U.S. judge. After the oath is taken, the new citizen will receive a Certificate of Naturalization. Make sure that the information in the Certificate is correct. If your name is misspelled, let the authorized person know right away, because they may be able to correct it on the same day.

If the application is denied, the applicant has the right to appeal the negative decision by filing Form N-336, Request for a Hearing on a Decision in Naturalization Proceeding. The form must be filed within thirty days after the denial was entered and it should be supported with a written statement or brief as to why the applicant believes the denial was inappropriate.

E. Selective Service

Very few new immigrants have knowledge of the existence of the Selective Service. In the United States, every male, excluding males in a valid nonimmigrant status (visitors, students, etc.) between eighteen and twenty-six years of age, must register with the Selective Service. The Selective Service is a governmental agency that maintains a list of males in the United States in case of a need for a military draft. Note that the U.S. military is currently made up of enlisted personnel and commissioned graduates of service academies. There is no draft in the United States at this time.

For males born in the United States, registration generally takes place during high school years. However, for other males in the United States, especially for those who immigrated to the United States after their eighteenth birthday, this could pose a problem. If the applicant is still under twenty-six, he must register. If he is over twenty-six, he will need to obtain a so-called "Status Information Letter" from the Selective Service. The easiest way is to go to the Web site *www.sss.gov* and print out the form. This Status Information Letter should be sent along with the actual application.

F. Obtaining a Replacement Certificate of Naturalization

If your certificate is lost, mutilated or destroyed, or you change your name after becoming a naturalized U.S. citizen, you may ask for a replacement certificate by filing Form N-565, Application for Replacement Naturalization/Citizenship Document.

Send a copy of the certificate if you have it, along with two passport-size photographs.

CHAPTER 3

Losing Citizenship

United States citizenship may be lost by persons who were born in the United States and also by persons who are naturalized U.S. citizens. It is of course clear that the citizenship may be lost if a person obtained U.S. citizenship by fraud. Other grounds for losing citizenship are:

- voluntarily obtaining citizenship in another country after reaching the age of eighteen;
- taking the oath or making a formal declaration of allegiance to a foreign state after reaching the age of eighteen;
- serving in the armed forces of a foreign state if those forces are engaged in hostilities against the United States, or serving as an officer in such forces;
- serving in any office of the government of a foreign state after the age of eighteen, if being a citizen of that state is required for the post, or if a formal oath of allegiance is required for such post;
- formally renouncing the citizenship before a consular officer at a U.S. consulate or embassy;
- committing an act of treason against the United States, conspiring to overthrow the U.S. government, or wage a war against it, if and when convicted of such act by court martial or other court.

PART III

—⚬—

Obtaining Nonimmigrant Visas

Visa is a permission to enter the United States. Every person who wishes to enter the United States must have some type of visa. In this section I discuss nonimmigrant visas, as opposed to immigrant visas. An immigrant visa gives a person permanent resident status in the United States. Nonimmigrant visas are visas of temporary duration and they give a person permission to spend a limited time in the United States. Each kind of visa carries different conditions and rights.

Every person who wishes to obtain a nonimmigrant visa must apply at a U.S. consulate or embassy abroad if he or she is residing abroad. If he or she is currently residing in the United States in a valid nonimmigrant status, then any change of status is made in the United States. For some nonimmigrant visas, a U.S. sponsor is required, for example an employer or an organization. If a sponsor is required, the sponsor will initiate the process by filing an appropriate form in the United States.

If a person is residing abroad, the application process always starts with the filing of Form DS-156, Nonimmigrant Visa Application, along with the appropriate fee and the necessary documents, with the U.S. consulate of the applicant's residence. The U.S. consulate of every country has specific documentary requirements for each type of visa; these vary from country to country. Please refer to the "Embassy Consular" section at *www.usembassy.gov* and click on the appropriate country. In addition, Form DS-157, Supplemental Nonimmigrant Visa Application, is required for all male applicants between the age of 16 and 45, and for all applicants over the age of 16, regardless of gender, from North Korea, Cuba, Syria, Sudan and Iran.

Each applicant must produce a valid passport with an expiration date of at least six months beyond the applicant's intended length of stay in the United States. One passport-size photograph (two inches by two inches) is also required.

Getting a visa at a U.S. consulate or embassy abroad does not guarantee that one will actually be let through at the U.S. border. The final decision whether to let someone enter the United States lies with the USCIS and the U.S. Customs and Border Protection.

Visitor Visa/Business Visa (B1/B2)

Most people who visit the United States come here for either business or pleasure. They come as tourists, or to visit family and friends. Others may come for business purposes, to obtain training, to attend educational or professional conferences or conventions, to talk with business partners and associates, to negotiate a contract or settle an estate. Some come to the United States to obtain medical treatment.

Business people coming to the United States for business purposes need a B1 nonimmigrant visa — a visa to enter the United States temporarily for business. Other visitors require a B2 nonimmigrant visa — a visa to enter the United States for pleasure or medical treatment. Regardless of whether one needs a B1 or B2 visa, the following requirements must be satisfied:

- the purpose of the trip must either be business, pleasure, or medical treatment; if the purpose of the trip is purely pleasure, just visiting the United States as a tourist, the applicant should produce tourist brochures, trip itinerary, and information about hotels where he or she intends to stay. If the applicant is visiting friends and family, he or she should produce letters from friends and family inviting the applicant to visit. If the trip is for medical reasons, the applicant should produce letters from doctors from his or her country and letters from doctors from the United States con-

firming that the applicant is coming to the United States for a medical procedure or diagnosis. If the purpose of the trip is business, the applicant should produce appropriate documents showing that he or she will be booked for a seminar, conference or training, including brochures for those events, letters from business associates or business partners, an invitation to negotiate a contract, etc.

- if the traveler plans to stay for a specific, limited time period in the United States, the applicant must produce a travel itinerary showing that his or her trip will last from a certain date to a certain date. A nonrefundable travel ticket should not be booked before a visa is obtained. However, the applicant must make a reservation with dates certain.

- the traveler must have evidence of sufficient financial ability to cover expenses of the stay in the United States; the applicant should produce letters from his or her employer showing that the trip is covered by the employer, or bank statements showing deposits in the bank. The applicant may also be able to satisfy this requirement if the applicant's friend or family prepares Form I-134, Affidavit of Support.

- the person has a residence and employment outside United States, as well as other ties binding this person to his or her residence, which will guarantee that the person will return to his or her country after the visit to the United States is over, the applicant should produce a letter from his or her employer showing that he or she is currently employed, school papers showing that he or she is still attending school, and evidence of residence, mortgage, lease or ownership papers. Business B1 visa is appropriate if the reason for the trip is to:

— consult with business associates;
— attend a training, educational or business conference or seminar;
— negotiate a contract, take orders, participate in litigation;
— settle an estate (when a person dies, his or her heirs must probate the deceased person's estate in court in order to receive inheritance).

The essence of the activity is that it does not involve employment in the United States or receipt of funds from a U.S. employer in exchange for work.

To facilitate easier entry of businesspeople into the United States and provide B1 visa information to U.S. businesses with frequent contacts with foreign businesspeople, the United States Department of State has established a Business Visa Center. The purpose of this is to provide information about the B1 visa application process. The center cannot speed up the application process or make sure that a visa is granted. For any questions regarding business visas, you can call the Department of State at 202-663-3198 or 202-663-1225.

The duration of B1/B2 status may be up to one year. Extensions can be granted for up to six months. Request for an extension is made by filing Form I-539, Application to Extend/Change Nonimmigrant Status. For any extensions, the applicant must be prepared to produce evidence that he or she really intends to return to his or her home country, such as a copy of a plane ticket with a certain date, and evidence that he or she still has available funds to support himself or herself in the United States.

CHAPTER 2

Visa Waiver Program

The Visa Waiver Program allows citizens of some countries to travel to the United States for either business or pleasure, and stay in the United States for up to ninety days, without first having to obtain a B1 or B2 visa at a U.S. consulate abroad. It is designed to allow citizens of "approved" countries to enter the United States without having to go through the regular visa application process. The down side is that the ninety-day period cannot be extended, and visitor status cannot be changed to either immigrant or other nonimmigrant visa. Therefore, if a person wishes to stay more than ninety days or plans to change his or her status in the United States, he or she should apply for a regular B1 or B2 visa at a U.S. consulate. Also note that, a person with a criminal record or a person whose previous visa application was denied must apply for a visa at a consulate.

Currently, countries which participate in the Visa Waiver Program are: Andorra, Australia, Austria, Belgium, Brunei, Denmark, Finland, France, Germany, Iceland, Ireland, Italy, Japan, Liechtenstein, Luxemburg, Monaco, the Netherlands, New Zealand, Norway, Portugal, San Marino, Singapore, Slovenia, Spain, Sweden, Spain, Switzerland, United Kingdom.

The main requirement for citizens from the above countries is to present at the border a machine-readable passport for each person seeking entry in the United States. If a passport was issued or renewed after October 26, 2006, the passport must have an integrated chip with information from the biographical page of the passport. Machine-readable passports issued or renewed between October 26, 2005, and October 25, 2006, must have a digital photograph printed on the biographical page or an integrated chip with information from the biographical page. For machine-readable passports renewed or issued before October 25, 2005, above requirements do not apply.

In addition, every traveler must fill out I-94W card (green I-94W) and present it at the border. This card will be provided to all travelers in the plane or on the boat. At the border, a portion of the card will be detached and stapled to the passport. This card must be returned when leaving the United States.

CHAPTER 3

Canadian and Mexican Citizens as Visitors

Generally, citizens of Canada are exempt from visa and passport requirements. In other words, as long as they can prove that they are Canadian citizens they will be allowed entry in the United States. To prove Canadian citizenship, a citizen of Canada must have a birth certificate, a citizenship certificate, or a Canadian passport.

For citizens of Mexico the requirements are different. Citizens of Mexico must produce a passport and a nonimmigrant visa or a Border Crossing Card, Form DSP-150. This Border Crossing Card is a laminated, credit-card style document which lasts ten years (called a "laser visa"). The card is in essence a B1/B2 visa.

To acquire a "laser visa," the applicant must satisfy the same requirements needed for a regular B1 or B2 nonimmigrant visa. For those applying for the first time, a Mexican passport is a must. For those applicants replacing the old cards, they need the old card and a current photo identity card. Go to *www.ciudad juarez.usconsulate.gov*.

For Canadian or Mexican citizens seeking entry as business visitors, in addition to the above requirements, they must show the purpose of the trip, and demonstrate that they are engaged in one or more of the following occupations as listed in the North American Free Trade Agreement (NAFTA):

• Research and design (technical, scientific or statistical researchers conducting research for a business located in Canada or Mexico);

• Growth, manufacture and production (this might apply to a harvester owner supervising a crew, or purchasing and production management employees conducting business for a company located in Canada or Mexico);

• Marketing (market researchers and analysts conducting marketing and analysis for a company in Canada or Mexico, or trade fair and promotional employees attending a trade convention);

• Sales (sales representatives and agents taking orders or negotiating contracts for goods or services in the United States for a company in Canada or Mexico, or buyers purchasing goods for a company in Canada or Mexico);

• Distribution (transportation operators transporting people and goods from Canada and Mexico to United States and vice versa; customs brokers; after-sales service people, including installation, repair, and maintenance employees and supervisors working for a company from Canada or Mexico, possessing specialized knowledge and performing work in the United States during the warranty period for the industrial equipment and machinery, including computer software, manufactured outside United States).

• General service professionals; management and supervisory employees; financial services employees—bankers, insurers, investment brokers; public relations and advertising employees; tourism employees—tour guides and travel agents; translators and interpreters; tour bus operators, if the bus tour started with a group of passengers in Canada or Mexico and will return to Canada or Mexico, or to pick up passengers in United States and drive them to Canada or Mexico, or to unload passengers in United States from a tour in Canada or Mexico.

A. FAST (Free and Secure Trade)

FAST is a border-accord initiative between the United States, Canada and Mexico. It allows commercial participants who have been determined to be a low security risk to receive expedited border crossing. It applies to importers, carriers, drivers and southern border manufacturers. To be able to participate, an applicant must register. Go to *www.cbp.gov* to register.

B. NEXUS and SENTRI

NEXUS allows citizens and permanent residents from United States and Canada, and citizens of other countries who plan to temporarily reside in United States or Canada, and who pass the Interpol criminal-history check, prescreened, faster processing at the border. Go to *www.cbp.gov* to register. SENTRI is the same program applicable to Mexico. Go to *www.cbp. gov* to register.

CHAPTER 4

Exchange Visitor Program (J1/J2)

A. Categories

The essential purpose behind the Exchange Visitor Program is to foster better understanding between the United States and other countries by facilitating educational, cultural and business exchanges between the United States and other countries. Designation J1 is for a person qualifying for an exchange program, J2 designation is for the spouse and children (under twenty-one years of age) of the principal applicant. If a person is outside the United States, the application process is done at a U.S. consulate. If a person is already in the United States and seeks a change of status to J1, a request is made by filing Form I-539, Application to Extend/Change Nonimmigrant Status.

In order to be eligible for this visa type, a person must first apply to participate in a program sponsored by a number of private, or academic or public sponsors. A list of sponsors can be found at *www.exchanges.state.gov/education/jexchanges*. Click on "Designated Sponsor List," and then choose a sponsor in your category. Note that the list contains almost four thousand sponsors. Program categories are separated based on whether the sponsor is a private sponsor, or an academic or public sponsor.

1. Private sponsors

For private sponsors, program categories are:

- Alien Physician. For alien physicians who wish to come to the United States for graduate medical training (residence) including clinical training activities, the Educational Commission for Foreign Medical Graduates (ECFMG) (*www.ecfmg.org*) is designated as the sponsor for all J1 applicants. The applicant must satisfy the following requirements for acceptance:

  — must have passed Step 1 and Step 2 Clinical Knowledge of the United States Medical Licensing Examination;
  — must have a valid Standard ECFMG certificate;
  — must have a contract or an official letter offering a position in a program of graduate medical education or training which is affiliated with a medical school;
  — provide a Statement of Need from the Department of Health from his or her country of residence; this letter should advise that this particular medical specialty is needed in the applicant's country.

  Duration of status is up to seven years, but depends on the actual duration of a particular program.
- Au Pair or EduCare. The Au Pair program is a famous program for young people who wish to travel and temporarily live in another country.

Young people between the age of eighteen and twenty-six are eligible to apply. Participants live with a host family and provide childcare services to the family for the duration of stay. Each participant must be proficient in English and most complete at least six hours of academic credit at an accredited U.S. college or university, and the host family is required to provide up to $500 toward tuition. Each participant receives compensation for his or her work. They cannot work more than ten hours per day, nor for more than forty-five hours per week. Duration of the program is twelve months.

Each participant receives training in child development prior to being placed with a family. The training must be a minimum of eight hours, at least four of which relate to infants. In addition, each participant will receive twenty-four hours of child development instruction, at least four of which relate to children under two years of age.

Participants cannot be placed in a home with a baby three months old or less, unless there is an adult at home at all times. A participant cannot be placed in a home where there are children under two years of age unless the participant has at least 200 hours of documented infant child-care experience. Participants will not be placed with a family with a special-needs child unless the participant has special skills, experience and education for dealing with special-needs children and the host family has reviewed the participant's qualifications in advance and has agreed to participation.

EduCare places participants in families with school-age children which require child care before and after school hours. Maximum work is ten hours per day and thirty hours per week. Participants receive 75 percent of the compensation received by Au Pair participants. They must complete twelve hours of academic credit at a college or university, and the host family is required to pay up to $1,000 toward tuition.

- Camp counselor. Participants must be over eighteen and proficient in English. Participants interact directly with children at U.S. summer camps. They are not considered staff at the camps, such as cooks, dishwashers, janitors, etc.; rather, they organize activities with the kids (sports, plays, competitions, etc.). Maximum duration is four months, with no extensions.

- High school student. Participants must be between the age of fifteen and eighteen and a half, and they must not have finished more than eleven years of elementary and high school education. Participants may spend one year at a U.S. high school. During school, they stay with a participating U.S. family or at a participating U.S. boarding school. Participants may engage in sports and other extracurricular activities, but no work is permitted.

- Summer work. This category applies to post-secondary-school students. Most of the work is in non-skilled service positions at hotels, pools, resorts and amusement parks. It also includes summer internships at U.S. businesses and other organizations. Businesses may be engaged in law, architecture, scientific research, advertising, communications, graphic art, publishing, etc.

- Teacher. Participants must be of good reputation and character, must satisfy the teaching requirements for primary or secondary education in their home country, have at least three years of teaching experience, and must satisfy the requirements of the state where they will teach.

- Trainee. Participants engage in a training program designated to enhance their skills and give them knowledge of American techniques, methodology and expertise in their field. It applies to foreign nationals who are currently enrolled in a degree- or certificate-granting secondary academic institution outside the United States, or have graduated from such an institution no more than twelve months before the start of the exchange program. Each applicant must be proficient in English, and must provide evidence of sufficient financial support.

Allowed programs are: Agriculture, Forestry and Fishing, Arts and Culture, Aviation, Construction and Building Trades, Education, Social Sciences, Library Science, Counseling and Social services, Health-related Occupations, Hospitality and Tourism, Information Media and Communications, Management, Business, Commerce and Finance, Public Administration and Law, Sciences, Engineering, Architecture, Mathematics and Industrial Occupations.

2. Academic and public sponsors (public sponsors are federal, state or local government agencies)

- Government visitor. This category is reserved for U.S. federal, state, or local governmental organizations. Participants may be editors, business and other professional persons, government officials and labor leaders. Duration is up to eighteen months. Participants engage in workshops, conferences, seminars, travel, meetings and discussions.
- Professor and research scholar. This category is reserved for foreign professors and scholars (not foreign medical graduates), who engage in teaching, lecturing and researching with their American colleagues. Maximum duration is three years.
- Short-term scholar. Participants are professors and researchers who come to the United States for up to six months to lecture, observe, consult, train or demonstrate special skills at research institutions, museums, libraries, etc.
- Specialist. Participants are experts in a particular field who come to the United States to observe, consult or demonstrate special skills. Fields of work may be environmental services, mass-media communication, youth leadership, museum exhibitions, labor law, library science, public administration, etc. Duration is up to one year.
- College and university student. Participants are foreign students at a U.S. college or university, enrolled in either a degree or a non-degree program. To be eligible to participate, the program must be financed directly or indirectly by the U.S. government, the government of their home country, or an international organization of which the United States is a member. Duration of program for participants in a degree program is the time that they are enrolled in the program. For participants in a non-degree program, the duration is up to twenty-four months.

Participants must maintain a full course of study while in either program, except during school breaks and summer and winter vacations, time off due to an illness or medical condition, if they are engaged in authorized academic training, if they require less than a full course of study to complete their academic requirements, or if they are engaged full time in a prescribed non-degree program for up to twenty-four months.

Some participants may also participate in academic training during the studies or within thirty days after completion of the studies, whether or not they are paid wages, but this must be authorized in advance.

To be eligible for academic training, a student must be primarily in the United States to study and not to engage in academic training, the academic training must be directly related to the major field of study, and the student must maintain good academic standing. Academic training for undergraduate or doctoral students may be for up to eighteen months. For postdoctoral students, the limit is thirty-six months.

To be eligible for academic training, a participant must present a letter of recommendation from the student's academic dean stating the goals and objectives of the specific program, description of the program, relation to the student's field of study, and why it would be important for student to be engaged in such a program.

Participants may work part time during the studies, but the work must be pursuant to the terms of a scholarship, fellowship or assistantship, and must occur on the premises of the institution which the student is authorized to attend. Work outside campus will be authorized only for urgent, unforeseen financial circumstances. Approval is given in advance and for up to twelve months. The approval may be given if the student is in good academic standing, continues to engage in a full course of study, and employment is not more than twenty hours per week, except during school breaks and summer vacation.

B. Employment for J2 Visa Holders

For holders of a J2 visa, spouses and children of primary J1 visa holders, work may be authorized, however they must file Form I-765 with the USCIS. Work will be authorized if the primary reason is to support the family's recreational and cultural activities, including travel. It will not be approved if the income is needed to support the J1 visa holder. This employment may be authorized for the duration of J1 status, but for no longer than four years.

J1 and J2 visa holders may be readmitted in the United States with the original I-94 card if they are returning from a trip to Canada, Mexico, or adjacent islands and the trip lasted less than thirty days. Otherwise, a valid passport with an unexpired J1 visa and DS-2019 Form is needed for reentry. If J1 visa has expired, he or she will have to obtain a new J1 visa at a consulate abroad.

C. Procedure and Requirements for Visa Approval

To qualify for a J1 visa in general, any participant must have a valid passport with the expiration date of at least six months beyond the intended length of stay, and must show that he or she:

(1) intends to stay in the United States for a limited time, and will return to his or her home country after the expiration of the J1 stay;

(2) will have enough financial resources while in the United States;

(3) has enough ties with the home country insuring that he or she will indeed return to the home country.

The first thing to do is to search the database for sponsors. Once a potential sponsor is identified, that particular sponsor must be contacted. If a person qualifies, the sponsor must obtain Form DS-2019 from the Student and Exchange Visitor Information System (SEVIS). Go to the Immigration and Customs Enforcement Web site, *www.ice.gov*, click on "International Students" and log in to SEVIS. The DS-2019 will be sent to the potential participant who then must go to the U.S. consulate in his or her country. A separate DS-2019 is necessary for the spouse and each child of the principal applicant. The applicant must fill out Form DS-7002, along with the standard Visa Application DS-156 and Supplemental Nonimmigrant Visa Application DS-157, and DS-158, Contact Information and Work History. One two-inch-square photograph and the appropriate fee is required. Also, always check the Embassy Consular Section at *www.usembassy.gov* for additional documentary requirements for your particular country.

Once the visa is approved, the participant, spouse and children, if any, may enter no earlier than thirty days before the start of the program. If the spouse and kids are entering at a later date, they will need a copy of the visa approval, DS-2019, for each of them, proof that the applicant is still in his or her J1 status, proof of relationship to the principal applicant (marriage certificate, birth certificate), and evidence of sufficient funds to support themselves in the United States.

Note that every J1 and J2 visa holder is required by law to maintain minimum medical insurance while in the United States. Usually, the sponsor provides medical insurance; check with the sponsor first. If that is not the case, the participant must get insurance. Minimum insurance requirements are $50,000 per person per incident or illness, $7,500 for repatriation of remains, and $10,000 for medical evacuation. The deductible must not be greater than $500.

D. Two-year Foreign Residency Requirement

Some J1 participants are subject to the two-year foreign residence requirement. The two-year foreign residency requirement means that a holder of J1/J2 visa cannot change his or her status in the United States to another nonimmigrant visa or immigrant visa, unless he or she spends two years outside the United States after the expiration of the J1/J2 status. It applies in two situations and it is usually noted in the passport when a person obtains a J1/J2 visa:

• when the program is financed entirely or in part, directly or indirectly, by the U.S. government or the government of the participant's home country; or

• when the participant is a national of a country designated as one which needs persons working in a field with particular skills and knowledge, and the person was engaged in that field in his or her J1 status. Check the Association of International Educators Web site, *www.nafsa.org*, for the Exchange Visitor List to see if participant's skills are included for a particular country.

If a participant is not sure whether he or she is subject to a two-year requirement, he or she may request an advisory opinion from the U.S. State Department. The written request should include a copy of the participant's DS-2019 along with a stamped and self-addressed envelope, and should be sent to the address shown at *www.travel.state.gov/visa/temp/info/info_1288.html*.

E. Waivers to Two-year Residency Requirement

If a participant is subject to a two-year requirement, he or she may be eligible for a waiver. There are five possible waivers:

(1) "No Objection" statement. The participant's consulate or embassy in Washington, D.C. issues a "No Objection Letter." The letter states that the country has no objection to the participant's not returning to the home country and does not object to the possibility of the J1 participant becoming a permanent resident of the United States. This letter may also be issued by a designated ministry in the person's home country and forwarded to the U.S. Mission, Consular Section, in that country to be sent to the Waiver Review Division. A request for this letter is made directly by the J1 visa holder to his or her embassy in Washington, D.C. or the appropriate ministry in the home country. The letter should be sent directly by the Embassy to the Waiver Review Division address shown at *www.travel.state.gov/visa/temp/info/info_1296.html*. This waiver cannot be used by J1 foreign medical physicians.

(2) Request by an interested government agency. A U.S. interested government agency (IGA) may request a waiver for a person working on a project of interest to the United States. The IGA must be signed by the head of such agency and sent directly to the Waiver Review Division.

This waiver may be used for foreign physicians. Agencies which may apply for physicians are Appalachian and Delta Regional Commissions, Department of Health and Human Services, Department of Veterans Affairs, and Department of Interior for Indian Reservations. Documents which need to be sent are:

- physician's curriculum vitae and a copy of DS-2019;
- physician's statement which must read: "I, _____, hereby declare and certify, under penalty of the provisions of 18USC1101, that: (1) I have sought or obtained the cooperation of _____ (name of agency); and (2) I do not now have pending nor will I submit another request to any U.S. government department or agency or its equivalent, to act on my behalf in any matter relating to a waiver of my two-year home residence requirement";
- two self-addressed, stamped envelopes;
- letter of request from the agency stating why it is in the public interest to have the two-year requirement waived;
- copy of a signed contract for work, the duration of the work to be no less than three years and forty hours per week;
- evidence that the health facility is located in a designated Health Professional Shortage Area (see *www.hpsafind.hrsa.gov*) or Medically Undeserved Area (see *www.muafind.hrsa.gov*);
- statement from the head of the health facility stating that the facility is located in such an area, that it provides care to both Medicare and Medicaid patients, and poor uninsured patients. The statement should include the facility's zip code, a Bureau of Census tract or block numbering area number (see *www.census.gov*), and the Federal Information Processing Standards county code (see *www.itl.nist.gov*);
- evidence that the health facility has been unable to find an American physician for the position (ads in journals and newspapers, labor certification);

For VA Hospitals, which do not have to be in an underserved area, the package must include a signed memorandum of agreement between the hospital and physician instead of an employment contract.

(3) Request by a designated state department of public health. A state public health department may request a waiver for a foreign medical school graduate. The doctor must have received an offer of full-time employment at a health-care facility in an area with a shortage of doctors, must begin work within ninety days of receiving a waiver, and must sign a contract to work forty hours per week for no less than three years

in that facility. This waiver applies only to foreign medical doctors who have received their J1 status to pursue graduate medical education or training. Documents needed are:

- physician's curriculum vitae and a copy of DS-2019;
- two self-addressed, stamped envelopes;
- a letter from the facility which wishes to hire the physician;
- evidence that the facility is in a designated HPSA or MUA;
- signed contract for no less than three years and forty hours per week;
- letter from the designated state health department official explaining why it would be in the public interest to grant the waiver; this must include physician's name, county of his or her residence, name and address of the medical facility, and the HPSA ID number of the medical shortage area.

(4) Persecution. A waiver may be granted if the participant can prove that he or she would be persecuted on basis of race, religion, or political opinion if he or she had to return to the home country.

(5) Exceptional hardship to a U.S. citizen or permanent resident spouse or child. A waiver may be granted if the participant can show that his or her departure from the United States would cause extreme hardship to his or her U.S.-citizen or permanent resident spouse or unmarried child under twenty-one.

For the first three waivers, a request is made on Form DS-3035 J1, Visa Waiver Recommendation Application. This could be done via the Internet: *www.travel.state.gov/visa/temp/info/info_1296.html*. This is preferred and much faster, than regular mail. If using the Internet, upon submission of the form a case number will be issued with further instructions. After the form is submitted the rest of the necessary documents must be sent. A person requesting a waiver via regular mail should send the form along with the following documents to the Waiver Review Division:

- passport biographical page;
- fee in form of a cashier's check or money order;
- a copy of DS-2019;
- two self-addressed, stamped envelopes; and
- statement explaining why a waiver may be applicable.

Once this form is submitted, a person will receive a case number and can check the status of the waiver application at the above Web site. After the form is submitted, the person must contact appropriate entities for a letter requesting a waiver, as explained in the first three waivers. If the Waiver Review Division recommends approval, the recommendation will be forwarded to USCIS which will make the final determination and send the result.

For waivers four and five, the process is different. The J1 participant must use USCIS Form I-612, Application for Waiver of the Foreign Residence Requirement. The form and the appropriate fee should be sent directly to USCIS at the address listed in *www.uscis.gov* (click on "Forms").

CHAPTER 5

Cultural Visitors (Q1/Q2/Q3)

There are a number of cultural visitor programs in the United States (see *www.exchanges.state.gov* for a list of various programs), the main purpose of which is the sharing of culture, history and traditions between the United States and different countries in the world. This is accomplished by bringing cultural visitors to the United States, people who through their work and training in the United States reveal cultural traditions in their native countries. The essence of every program is this "cultural component," or aim to explain the history, culture, art, philosophy, heritage or traditions of a foreign country.

The program under Q1 visa may run up to fifteen months. Each participant is given an extra thirty days after the end of the program to make travel arrangements.

This type of exchange program requires an actual employer, and any employment or training must be done in a school, museum, business or other establishment where the American public may be exposed to a particular foreign culture. Examples are seminars, language camps, lectures, or classes. In other words, the employment itself must be a vehicle for cultural exchange.

The employer sponsor must file Form I-129, Petition for a Nonimmigrant Worker. Premium Processing Service is allowed (Form I-907). The employer must demonstrate that the potential participant in the program:

- is at least eighteen years of age;
- is qualified to perform the work or services or receive training as stated in the petition;

- speaks English well enough to be able to communicate with the public and express ideas;
- has resided outside the United States at least one year prior to filing of the petition if he or she was previously a Q1 visitor;
- will be paid at least at the level of the wages paid to American workers for the same type of job with the same or similar qualifications and experience.

The Walsh Visa program (Q2/Q3 visas) is aimed at young individuals from the Northern Ireland and the six counties bordering the Republic of Ireland (Louth, Monghan, Cavan, Litrim, Sligo and Donegal). The purpose of the program is to afford young individuals an opportunity to enhance their personal and professional skills which they can put to use in their native country once they return.

Duration of the program is twenty-four months. As with Q1 visas, there must be an actual employer. Go to *www.walshvisa.net* for more information.

The minimum age of participants is twenty-one and the maximum age is thirty-five. Participants must demonstrate that they have been unemployed for at least twelve months, and that they have been residents of Northern Ireland or the six counties bordering the Republic of Ireland for at least eighteen months. Participants cannot be graduates of higher educational institutions (colleges and universities.) Examples of job titles in this program include

- audio service technician;
- front desk agent;

- security officer;
- direct care residential worker;
- professional moving specialist trainee;
- delivery person;
- credit card collector;
- label printer;
- factory utility person;
- residential counselor.

Visas are obtained at the United States consulate. Participants seeking a Q2 visa and their spouse and dependents under twenty-one years of age seeking Q2 visas, must have valid passports and a certification letter issued by the Department of State Program Administrator.

CHAPTER 6

Student Visas (F1/F2 and M1/M2)

There are two types of student visas. The first type, F1, is for applicants seeking to study in the United States at a college, university, or other academic institution. Students wishing to study at a vocational or other non-academic institution need an M1 visa. F2 and M2 designations are for corresponding spouses and children under twenty-one years of age. Note that F1 students cannot attend a public high school for more than twelve months and must pay the full tuition for the school year.

Before applying for a student visa, a student must first be accepted by a U.S. school approved by USCIS. There are a couple of excellent Web sites which will guide you through the process of choosing the right school and being accepted by such a school. Go to *www.educationusa.state.gov* and *www.exchanges.state.gov* for important information on approved schools, requirements for admission to each school, financial considerations, and other valuable information.

A. F1/F2 Visas

Once a student is accepted by an approved school, the school will send Form I-20 to the student. This form is generated by the school through the SEVIS system (see *www.egov.ice.gov/sevis*). The student then must apply for an F1 visa at the U.S. consulate in his or her country of residence. If a student is already in the United States in some other nonimmigrant status, then the student must file form I-539, Application to Extend/Change Nonimmigrant Status. Documents needed are:

- original I-20 issued in his or her name;
- evidence that the student has sufficient financial support to attend the school and support himself or herself in the amount listed in the I-20 Form;
- for students attending a public high school, evidence that the full tuition was paid;
- any other documents needed by the consulate in that particular country (see *www.usembassy.gov*).

The spouse and dependents under twenty-one of an F1 student can apply for an F2 visa at the same time that the principal applicant is applying, or at a later date. The spouse and each child will all have a separate I-20. If they are applying after the principal F1 holder is admitted to the United States, they need to show the consular officer that the F1 visa holder has been admitted in a full course of study.

1. Duration of status

A student whose F1 visa application is approved may enter the United States no earlier than thirty days before the start of the school year. Duration of F1 visa depends on the length of the school course. Ordinarily, an F1 student is admitted for the duration of the school course, as long as he or she is pursuing a full course of study. A student who has completed the course of study and any authorized practical training after completing the studies is allowed sixty days to finish his or her affairs in the United States and leave the country. A student who has been authorized to withdraw from school will have only fifteen days to depart the United States. Note that a student who fails to maintain a full course of study or otherwise fails to maintain his or her student status (unauthorized work, does not attend school, etc.) does not get any additional time for departure. A student is considered to be maintaining his or her status if he or she is making a normal progress toward completion of the course of study.

2. Full course of study

Full course of study is considered:

- a postgraduate study or postdoctoral study at a college or university, or undergraduate or postgraduate study at a conservatory or seminary;
- undergraduate study at a college or university, certified by a school official to consist of at least twelve semester hours, where all students enrolled in such a study are considered full-time students;
- study in a postsecondary school which gives its graduates associate or other degrees, in liberal arts, fine arts, or other non-vocational program;
- any other school with a non-vocational program in liberal arts, fine arts, or other non-vocational training, which program consists of at least eighteen hours of attendance per week if it is mainly classroom instruction, or twenty-two hours if it is mainly laboratory work;
- private elementary or middle school or public or private high school in a curriculum certified by the school official to have a certain minimum number of hours leading to normal graduation;
- on-campus employment pursuant to a scholarship, fellowship or assistantship.

A maximum of one class or three semester hours may be taken online or in any other way which does not require attendance in class.

3. Reduced school load

A student may be allowed to reduce the full course of study in limited circumstances. Generally, the school load may not be reduced to less than six semester hours. Each reduced course load must be approved by the designated school official.

A reduced school load may be authorized if the student has initial difficulties with the English language or reading requirements, or unfamiliarity with U.S. teaching methods. The student who was authorized for a reduced school load must resume a full load in the next semester.

A reduced school load may be authorized due to a temporary illness or medical condition, but not for longer than twelve months. Of course, the student must provide medical documentation demonstrating the medical condition.

A reduced school load may also be authorized during the student's final semester if fewer semester hours are needed to complete the course.

The designated school official must report any proposed reduced course of study to USCIS and update the SEVIS file before the school load is reduced.

4. School transfer

A student may transfer from one approved school to another approved school. He or she must obtain a new I-20 from the new school, and I-20 must be returned to the old school within fifteen days of beginning attendance. A student transferring to a new school may not wait in the United States if it will take more than five months to start a program at a new school.

5. Employment in F1 Status

On-campus limited employment is allowed during the school session. The employment must be an integral part of the student's educational program. "On-campus employment" is allowed either on campus, or off campus if the location is educationally affiliated with the school. Employment may be authorized for not more than twenty hours per week during school in session, or full time when school is not in session, including summer vacation.

Off-campus work may be authorized if the student is dealing with severe economic hardship. The severe economic hardship must be based on unforeseen circumstances beyond the student's control. Examples include loss of financial aid, fluctuation in the currency exchange rate, large increases in tuition, books and living costs, medical bills, etc. Such a student cannot work more than twenty hours per week, and full time is allowed only when the school is not in session, including summer vacation.

A student who needs off-campus work must first request permission from the designated school official. The school official will recommend work in one-year intervals if:

- the student has been in F1 status for one full year;
- the student is in good standing academically;
- the student has demonstrated that the acceptance of work will not interfere with the student's school requirements;
- the student has demonstrated that he or she is experiencing a severe economic hardship.

If a permission is granted, the student must apply for a work permit by filing Form I-765 with USCIS.

6. Practical training

Practical training refers to work in a position which is directly related to the student's major area of study. There are two types of practical training for which employment authorization may be issued, "curricular practical training" and "optional practical training."

Curricular practical training refers to a training which is an integral part of the school program curriculum. It could be an internship, work/study, cooperative education, or any other program offered by a sponsoring employer in agreement with the school. Note that a student who receives one or more years of this training will not be eligible for optional practical training after the completion of study.

As with any other employment for students, designated school official must first authorize the work.

Optional practical training refers to temporary employment directly related to the student's major area of study. It may be authorized during times when school is not in session, including summer vacation;

while school is in session, but not more than twenty hours per week; or after the completion of the course of study.

Optional practical training should be requested before the end of the course of study, but no later than thirty days after the end of school program. A student may apply within 180 days of the start of work but not earlier than ninety days before the end of the first school year. Total duration of optional practical training cannot be more than twelve months, including time during school, and the training will not be authorized fourteen months beyond the end of the school program. This means that if a student applied for a work authorization at the end of the school program, and received approval in ninety days (it takes up to ninety days for approval), his or her work authorization will be for only eleven months. The student must apply for a work permit by filing Form I-765 with USCIS.

Note that if a student is taking optional practical training during the regular school program, the time spent in those programs will reduce or eliminate the time in optional practical training after the school program ends.

7. Reinstatement

A student who is out of status may be able to reinstate his or her student status under certain conditions:

- if the student has been out of status for not more than five months;
- does not have a record of willful violations of immigration status;
- has not been working without proper work permit;
- is not otherwise deportable under any of the deportability grounds; and
- demonstrates that the violation of his or her status resulted from either circumstance beyond the student's control (such as serious illness or medical condition, natural disaster, oversight or neglect by the designated school official) or that the violation of status relates to the reduction of the school load which the school official could have authorized, and where the denial of reinstatement would result in extreme hardship to the student.

Reinstatement must be requested by filing Form I-539, Application to Extend/Change Nonimmigrant Status with USCIS. The form must be accompanied by a new I-20 with a recommendation to reinstate by the designated school official.

8. Spouse and children under twenty-one (F2 visa holders)

The spouses and children of F1 visa holders cannot work.

B. M1/M2 Visas

The M1 visa is limited to students who wish to study in vocational and other non-academic schools. The procedure is very similar to the procedure for F1 students. The first step is to find an appropriate school approved by the USCIS (see the Web sites named above in the discussion of F1 visas). If accepted, the school will send a SEVIS-generated I-20 to the student. The student then needs to go to the U.S. consulate in his or her country and apply for a visa. If the student is in the United States in some other nonimmigrant status, the student must file Form I-539, Application to Extend/Change Nonimmigrant Status.

The spouse and unmarried children under twenty-one years of age may apply for M2 visa at the same time as the principal visa holder, or at a later time. Each of them will need a separate I-20 form from the school. If they apply at a later time, they will need to show the consular officer that the M1 visa holder has been admitted and is currently enrolled in a full course of study.

1. Visa duration

An M1 student may stay in the United States for up to one year, plus thirty days after the end of the program to depart the United States. An M1 student may be admitted in the United States not earlier than thirty days before the start of the program. Any extensions may be requested on Form I-539.

2. Full course of study

Full course of study for the M1 visa means study at a community college or junior college, carrying at least twelve semester hours, where all students at that school who take at least twelve semester hours are considered full-time students; or a postsecondary vocational or business school, other than a language-training program, which gives its students associate or other degrees; or a school with a vocational or other nonacademic curriculum with at least eighteen hours of classes per week if the primary study is in a classroom, or twenty-four hours of classes per week if the primary study is in a shop or laboratory; or a vocational or other nonacademic high school curriculum with weekly class attendance necessary to normally progress towards a degree.

No online instruction is allowed.

3. Reduced course load

Reduced course load may be authorized in case of the student's illness or medical condition documented by letters from doctors. Reduced course load may not be for more than five months.

4. Extension of stay

The M1 student may be granted extensions up to three years from the school start date in order to finish the program. An extension may be granted if the student is maintaining his or her current nonimmigrant status, compelling educational or medical reasons have caused the delay in the student's study (suspension or academic probation are not acceptable) and the student is able to continue the M1 status for the period of extension.

The extension of stay must be requested by filing Form I-539, Application to Extend/Change Nonimmigrant Status with USCIS. The form must be filed at least fifteen days, but not more than sixty days before the end of the school program. The applicant can include spouse and children in the application. The student and the spouse and children all need separate I-20s.

5. School transfer

An M1 student will not be allowed to transfer to another school after the first six months. Otherwise a student will be allowed to transfer if he or she is still maintaining nonimmigrant status, has been pursuing full course of study, intends to pursue a full course of study at the transfer school, and is financially able to attend the new school.

Application for transfer is made by filing Form I-539 with the USCIS.

6. Reinstatement

A student who has lost his or her M1 status may be able to be reinstated to M1 status by filing Form I-539 with the USCIS. The student will need a new I-20 with a recommendation for reinstatement from the designated school official.

A student may be reinstated if he or she has not been out M1 status for more than five months; does not have a record of willful immigration violations; is currently pursuing or intends to pursue a full course of study; has not worked without a work permit; is not otherwise deportable; and the violation of status occurred because of circumstances beyond the student's control, such as serious illness, closure of school, nat-ural disaster, neglect on the part of the designated school official, or because of the reduced school load which the designated school official could have authorized, in cases where the denial of reinstatement would result in extreme hardship to the student.

7. Employment

An M1 student is allowed to engage in practical training only. Practical training starts after the completion of a school program and may last for up to six months (one month of practical training for each four months of full-time school). Application for practical training must be requested by filing Form I-765 with the USCIS. The application must be requested no earlier than ninety days before the end of the school course.

To be eligible, the designated school official must certify that the proposed employment is recommended for the purpose of practical training, that the practical training is related to the student's course of study, and that such training is not available in the student's home country.

Spouse and children holding M2 visas are not allowed to work. A spouse may not engage in full-time study; a child may engage in full-time study only if the study is in elementary or high school.

CHAPTER 7

NAFTA Professional Workers (TN and TD Visas)

The North American Free Trade Agreement (NAFTA) allows certain professionals from Canada and Mexico to come to the United States and work in their professions for a U.S. employer for up to one year. All professions require a Baccalaureate or Licenciatura Degree. Some require work experience as well. For the complete list of professions, and requirements for each profession, go to: *www.nafta-sec-alena.org*, and look at Appendix 1603.D.1. All applicants must be citizens of Mexico or Canada; an applicant's profession must be on the list; an applicant must have a prearranged job in the United States with a U.S. employer; and an applicant must have the required qualifications.

The procedure is different for Canadian professionals and Mexican professionals. A Canadian professional applying for a TN visa does not have to apply at a U.S. consulate. Rather, the applicant may request admission at a U.S. port of entry showing to the immigration officer at the border:

- an employment letter evidencing the existence of a job for a United States employer; the letter should contain detailed job duties and responsibilities, and describe the activity in which the applicant will be engaged; state the purpose of entry and anticipated length of stay in the United States; note educational requirements for the position; give evidence of compliance with any federal and state laws; describe arrangement for pay; and if re-quired, give proof of appropriate licensure for a particular position;
- proof of professional qualifications, transcripts of grades, certificates, diplomas, degrees, record of previous employment, letters from former employers, etc.;
- proof of ability to meet license requirements for a profession, if any;
- proof of Canadian citizenship (passport is enough, or a birth certificate).

Spouses and children of Canadian applicants generally do not need visas before applying for admission at the U.S. border. They will receive TD visas upon proving their relationship to the TN visa holder (marriage certificate, birth certificate), evidence of Canadian citizenship, and photocopies of entry documents of the TN visa holder if they are applying after the admission of the TN visa holder. Work is not allowed for TD visa holders.

Mexican professionals, on the other hand, have to apply for a TN visa at a U.S. consulate. Regular forms are required, DS-156, DS-157, a valid passport, one passport-size photograph (two-inch square), letter of employment, proof of professional qualifications, and ability to meet license requirements for the profession, if any. Spouse and children of a Mexican TN visa holder must apply for a TD visa at a U.S. consulate.

The TN visa may be extended in one-year increments. If the visa holder is in the United States, the employer should file Form I-129, Petition for Nonimmigrant Worker with the USCIS. Premium Processing Service is allowed, Form I-907. If the visa holder is not in the United States, a Canadian visa holder may apply at the border. Mexican citizens must apply at a U.S. consulate. Extensions of TD status for spouse and children are accomplished by filing Form I-539.

Chapter 8

Specialty Visa (H1B)

This is a popular visa as it allows young individuals with bachelor's degrees to come to and work in the United States for a U.S. employer for up to six years. Even better, frequently, the same or another employer files a petition for the holder of an H1B visa for permanent resident status through employment.

The actual H1B visa can be divided into three separate parts as it can be used for three different purposes. It can be used by individuals in specialty occupations, H1B1 visa, for individuals who will perform services of exceptional merit and ability for a project administered by the Department of Defense, H1B2, or fashion models of distinguished merit and ability, H1B3.

Before attempting to apply for an H1B visa, however, the employer must have a job description for a position (see *www.onetcenter.gov* for helpful hints, or *www.bls.gov*). The employer must also determine the prevailing wage for this position. See Part I, Chapter 4 for discussion of the Prevailing Wage.

Duration of an H1B visa is three years, plus an extension of three additional years, plus ten days after the expiration of the six-year period. For aliens working on a project for Department of Defense (DOD), the total length of stay may be up to ten years. A person cannot be reaccepted as a H1B visa holder unless he or she spends at least one year outside the United States after the end of the three-year stint. However, if a holder of an H1B visa is also a beneficiary of an I-140 petition for an immigrant worker, the H1B status may be extended even after the expiration of the six-year period, if more then 365 days have passed since the filing of the foreign labor certification (necessary for employment immigrant petition) or the employment immigrant petition. The extensions are granted in one-year increments by filing Form I-129, Petition for Nonimmigrant Worker. For spouses and dependents of principal H visa holders, H4 visa holders, requests for extensions are done by filing Form I-539, Application to Extend/Change Nonimmigrant Status.

Note that there are only 65,000 H1B visas allocated each year, plus 20,000 H1B visas for holders of a master's or higher degree. In addition, citizens of Chile and Singapore are awarded 5,800 H1B visas each year, based on the free-trade agreements between the United States and those two countries, which number counts against the 65,000 limit.

The I-129 form may not be filed earlier than 180 days before a job will start. Since the new federal fiscal year starts usually on October 1, or the next business day if October 1 falls on a weekend, if an employer wants to submit a petition in a timely fashion, the USCIS must receive that application on April 1, or the first business day after that if April 1 falls on a weekend. Even if the employer files in a timely fashion and the application is not rejected, the employer may be out of luck, as there are many more applications than available visas. Keep in mind that we are talking about the federal fiscal year, not calendar year. Therefore, if you need workers starting the first day of 2009 federal fiscal year, October 1, 2008, you must file your application on April 1, 2008.

A. Persons in Specialty Occupations (H1B1)

1. Specialty occupations

What is a specialty occupation? It is an occupation which requires at least a baccalaureate or a higher degree, or its equivalent, as a minimum for entry into the occupation in the United States. Examples of fields with specialty occupations are architecture, engineering, mathematics, physical sciences, social sciences, medicine and health, education, accounting, law, theology, and the arts.

What are the criteria for classifying a particular position as a specialty occupation? To qualify, a position must satisfy the following requirements:

- the minimum requirement for the position is a baccalaureate or higher degree;
- the degree requirement is common in this particular industry for this particular position, or the employer must show that the position is so complex and unique that it can be performed only by an individual with a degree;
- the employer seeking this classification normally requests such a degree for the position, or the nature of the duties is so specialized that the knowledge to perform the duties is usually associated with attainment of a baccalaureate or higher degree.

2. Qualifications for a specialty occupation

A person applying for an H1B1 specialty occupation must:

- hold a U.S. baccalaureate or higher degree;
- hold a foreign degree determined to be equivalent to a U.S. baccalaureate or higher degree (there are a number of companies performing this type of evaluation; go to the Internet and search under "credentials evaluations service"; they all charge a fee, but a report from an evaluator is a must);
- hold an unrestricted state license, registration or certification necessary to perform the required duties in a particular state, or
- have education, training and experience equal to completion of a U.S. baccalaureate or higher degree, and present evidence of holding positions in the specialty; in this situation, the individual must provide one of the following in order to show that he or she possesses the required qualifications:

  — an evaluation from an official who has authority to grant college-level credit for training and/or experience in a specialty from a college or university with a program for granting such credit;
  — results of college-level equivalency examinations, such as the College Level Examination Program (CLEP), see *www.collegeboard.com*, or the Program on Noncollegiate Sponsored Instruction (PONSI), see *www.nationalponsi.org*;
  — evaluation of education by a credentials evaluation service specializing in evaluating foreign educational credentials;
  — certification or registration from a nationally recognized professional association or society for a particular specialty, which requires a certain level of competence in the field;
  — determination by the USCIS that the combination of education and experience in the field is equivalent to a baccalaureate or higher degree. Three years of work experience in a specialty equals one year of college. Five years of work experience after the baccalaureate degree equals a master's degree. To prove that he or she has a meaningful work experience in a specialty occupation, the individual should provide at least two letters recognizing his or her expertise from recognized authorities in the field; evidence of membership in a U.S. or foreign association or society in the specialty occupation; evidence of published material in journals, professional publications or books; and evidence of a license or registration to practice in a specialty occupation in a foreign country.

3. Necessary documents and forms

The necessary forms are I-129, Petition for Non-immigrant Worker, H Classification Supplement to Form I-129 and H1B Data Collection and Filing Fee Exemption Supplement. Most employers also use the Premium Processing Service, Form I-907. The benefit is the speed of processing. For an additional $1,000, the USCIS will make a determination in about fifteen calendar days.

The required documents are:

- a copy of the filed Labor Condition Application, Form 9035. This form is filed directly, online, with the Department of Labor (see *www.foreignlabor cert.doleta.gov*). A copy of this form, or an abbreviated version, must be posted at the employer's place of business within thirty days of filing of the form. It must be given to a bargaining representative, if any, or if there is no bargaining representative, it should be posted in two conspicuous places at the employer's place of work for ten consecutive days (bulletin board, web page, via e-mail, etc.). Employers must review "Additional Labor Condition Statements" before they sign, and make sure that those statements are accurate.
- a copy of the prevailing wage determination by an SWA;
- school records, transcripts, degrees, diplomas, certifications, etc., to show that the individual has the required degree;
- letters, affidavits, statements from present and former employers describing the duties performed and skills, knowledge and experience needed for the occupation;
- copy of any employment contract between the employer and the prospective employee describing the job and duties, wages paid and other consideration, if any;
- a copy of any license to engage in work in a particular specialty in a state, if a license is required in that particular state (if only a temporary license is available to the worker, petition may be approved if the worker will work under supervision; a petition may also be granted if a particular state does not require a license if a person will work under supervision);
- copy of I-94, I-20, DS-2019 or any other document

issued by the USCIS to the worker demonstrating legal status in the United States, if the worker is residing currently in the United States in a different status.

4. Spouse and dependents (H4 visa)

Spouse and children under twenty-one of the principal H1B visa holder are eligible to receive the H4 visa, which allows them to stay in the United States as long as the primary visa holder's H1B visa is valid. They are not allowed to work, though study is permitted. If the spouse and children are located abroad, they will need to obtain a H4 visa at a U.S. consulate. If they are lawfully in the United States on a different temporary visa, the will need to file Form I-539, Application to Change/Extend a Nonimmigrant Status.

5. Change in employment/loss of job

If an H1B visa holder gets a better opportunity for work at a different company, a transfer is possible, however, the new employer must file a new I-129 petition. If a visa holder is laid off or loses a job, he or she should generally attempt to find a new job as soon as possible to stay legally in the United States; the rule of thumb is that this should be done within thirty days after the job is lost. If a person stays without a job more than thirty days after losing a job, he or she may be deemed to be out of status by the USCIS.

6. Dependent employers and willful violators

The Data Collection and Filing Fee Exemption Supplement for H1B visa asks questions regarding whether the employer is a "dependent employer" or a "willful violator." In case the employer falls under one or both categories, the employer must satisfy two additional attestations before filing the labor condition application.

A "dependent employer" is an employer which:

- employs twenty-five or less full-time employees, and more than seven of those employees are H1B employees;
- employs between twenty-six and fifty full-time

workers, and more than twelve of those workers are H1B employees;

- employs more than fifty-one full-time workers, and at least 15 percent of those workers are H1B employees.

A "willful violator" is an employer found to have made a misrepresentation of a material fact on an LCA within the last five years, by either the Department of Labor or the Department of Justice.

Dependent employers and willful violators are subject to addition attestations regarding the LCA unless the H1B nonimmigrant is considered "exempt." An exempt H1B nonimmigrant is a worker who will receive at least $60,000 per year in salary, or has a master's or higher degree in a particular specialty.

Employers subject to the two additional attestations are required to take good-faith steps to recruit U.S. workers prior to filing the LCA. In addition, the employer is prohibited from displacing any U.S. workers either directly or indirectly.

The additional recruitment requirement puts an obligation on the employer to actively and passively look for U.S. workers who may be qualified for the same position the employer is trying to fill with H1B workers. Active recruitment includes participation in job fairs; making inquiries with the appropriate unions, trade associations, and professional organizations; contacting placement offices at colleges and schools; and use of private recruitment companies. Passive recruitment includes placing advertisements in newspapers, trade and professional journals, or placing them in-house at work sites, etc. Documentation of any recruitment must be kept at the employer's place of business.

Displacement of a U.S. worker essentially means a layoff of a worker, other than a discharge for poor performance, a voluntary departure, retirement, or the expiration of a contract or grant. "Layoff" applies here to workers in the same position the employer is seeking to fill with H1B workers. Direct displacement applies to the employer's own workers. The employer is prohibited from discharging an employee ninety days prior and ninety days after the employer files an H1B petition for a H1B worker. This applies only to workers who are working in the same jobs the H1B workers would be employed. Indirect or secondary displacement occurs when the employer places H1B employees with another employer where there is a relationship between the H1B employee and the other employer.

7. LCA code and NAICS code

These two codes are required for the I-129 petition. The LCA code may be found in Appendix 2 to LCA (see Appendix B of this book for forms). The NAICS code may be obtained from the Department of Commerce, Census Bureau (see *www.census.gov/naics/*).

8. Australians in specialty occupations (E3 visa)

The E3 visa category is reserved for nationals of Australia. There are 10,500 E3 visas available each year. The requirements are essentially the same as for "specialty occupation." Maximum duration is twenty-four months, and it may be renewed indefinitely. The spouse and children under twenty-one are eligible for E1D visas. Spouses are allowed to work in the United States, but must first apply for a work authorization by filing Form I-765 with the USCIS.

B. Persons Providing Services to the Department of Defense (H1B2)

The H1B2 visa is reserved for persons who are hired to perform services of exceptional nature relating to projects associated with the Department of Defense. A baccalaureate or higher degree is required, or its equivalent. Importantly, filing of a labor condition application is not required.

The I-129 petition must contain the following documents:

- verification letter from DOD project manager stating that the person will be working on a project for DOD; job requirements and duties should be explained, however, no details are needed;
- a statement from DOD whether they are currently employing any other foreign workers on a project,

including their names, and the number of foreign workers whose duties ended in the past year;
- copies of relevant documents giving evidence that the person has the required qualifications for the job, including diplomas, degrees, certificates, letter from current and past employers, etc.

The duration of this type of visa is up to ten years, including a five-year extension, plus ten days to depart. A new H1B2 status may be obtained if a person spends at least one year outside the United States after the maximum allowed time in H1B2 status ends.

A spouse and dependents may receive H4 status. If they are in the United States, change of status to H4, or extension of H4 status is done by filing Form I-539. Study is allowed, work is not.

C. Distinguished Fashion Models (H1B3)

This visa is reserved for fashion models of distinguished merit and ability. A labor condition application is required.

Initially, documents required include certifications, writings, reviews, affidavits, statements, and letters of former and current employers or recognized experts in the field, establishing that the applicant is a fashion model. In addition, a copy of the employment contract is needed.

The employer must also show in a letter that the model will perform services at events (usually fashion shows) which have a distinguished reputation, or for an organization or establishment with a distinguished reputation. The model must provide evidence through documentation that he or she is a distinguished fashion model. Evidence may include:

- copies of reviews in magazines, journals, TV and radio shows, the Internet, etc.;
- evidence that he or she is currently working or has worked for an employer of distinguished reputation in the fashion field;
- evidence of the recognition of significant achievements in the fashion industry from organizations, critics, fashion houses, modeling agencies, etc.

- evidence that he or she commands a high salary or compensation for fashion modeling (copies of contracts, for example).

A spouse and dependents may receive H4 visa. If they are already in the United States, any change of status to H4, or extension of H4 status, is made by filing Form I-539. Study is allowed, work is not.

D. Physicians (H1B)

Foreign physicians, meaning graduates of medical schools outside the United States and Canada, may use an H1B visa to teach, do research, or engage in clinical practice or graduate medical training (residence).

A foreign physician requesting an H1B visa must produce evidence that he or she has a required license or other authorization for practicing medicine in a state of intended employment if he or she will perform direct patient care, unless exempt by law, and evidence that he or she holds a license to practice medicine in a foreign country or has graduated from a U.S. or foreign medical school.

A petitioner filing for a foreign physician must show that the physician will be employed at a public or nonprofit private educational or research institution or agency to teach or conduct research, where no patient care will be involved; or, if the physician will be engaged in patient care, that the physician has passed the Federation Licensing Examination (FLEX), parts 1 and 2 (see *www.ecfmg.org* and *www.ama-assn.org*); National Board of Medical Examiners (NBME), exam parts 1, 2 and 3 (*www.NBME.org*), or the United States Medical Licensing Examination (USMLE), parts 1, 2 and 3 (*www.USMLE.org*), or is a graduate of a U.S. medical school. The petitioner must also show that the physician is competent in oral and written English, by showing that he or she has passed the test given by the Educational Commission for Foreign Medical Graduates (ECFMG), or that he or she is a graduate of a school of medicine accredited by the Secretary of Education.

CHAPTER 9

Temporary Agricultural Workers (H2A)

The H2A visa allows agricultural employers to hire foreign agricultural workers for temporary or seasonal work. The basic premise for seasonal work is that the work is needed during certain time of the year (planting, sowing, harvesting) and that the employer needs work for a period of time not to exceed one year.

An employer may file petition I-129 for a named worker or a number of unnamed workers. In any event, the employer must show that the potential workers are qualified to do the job. To prove that, the employer should attach letters from previous employers who hired the worker, copies of payroll and tax records for the worker, or affidavits of fellow workers.

Before the petition is filed, the employer must determine the prevailing wage if the workers are to be paid hourly (see discussion on prevailing wages in Part I), and the employer must obtain a temporary foreign agricultural certification from the Department of Labor. The process is the following. The employer must fill out and file Form ETA 750A, Application for Alien Employment Certification with the National Processing Center visa via e-mail (at *www.h2a.doleta.gov*), or by regular mail (go to *www.foreignlaborcert.doleta.gov*, and click on "National Processing Centers"). There are two centers, one in Atlanta and one in Chicago. Each center processes applications for a number of different states. The ETA 750A form should be filed at least forty-five to sixty days before the actual work is to start. The form must be ac-companied with a job offer, and an agreement to abide by certain legal requirements (see below for details on both). The employer should file an original and a copy of ETA 750A with the National Processing Center and send a copy to the state workers agency (SWA) in the state of intended employment. Go to *www.foreignlaborcert.doleta.gov*, and click on "Regions and States" for your particular state.

When the National Processing Center receives the ETA 750A, it will notify the employer within seven days whether the application is accepted for processing or denied. If denied, the employer has five days to correct any deficiencies. If the application is accepted for processing, the labor certification must be granted or denied no later than twenty days before the start of actual work.

If the application is accepted for consideration, the National Processing Center will notify the employer and SWA of the acceptance. The notice to employer will direct the employer to engage in recruitment of U.S. workers in that state and other states where there is a potential source of agricultural workers. Upon receipt of this notification, the SWA will prepare a local job order and start recruiting U.S. workers for the position. The SWA will also prepare an Agricultural Clearance Order, ETA 790, which will allow recruitment of U.S. workers from that and other states.

A. Job Offer

A job offer must contain certain minimum provisions regarding wages, benefits and working conditions, and it cannot contain less-favorable conditions than the ones offered to foreign workers.

- Housing. Employer must provide housing at no charge to those workers who are not reasonably able to return to their residence after a day's work.
- Worker's compensation. Employer must provide worker's compensation for the workers, covering injury and disease arising out of work. The employer will have to provide the insurance policy number and effective dates before the application is approved.
- Tools and equipment. Employer shall provide tools and equipment to workers, at no extra charge.
- Meals. Employer shall either a have a cooking and eating facility for the workers, or provide three meals to workers per day at a charge set by the National Processing Center (go to *www.foreign laborcert.doleta.gov* and click on "Adverse Effect Wage Rates").
- Transportation. Employer shall either provide transportation to workers to the place of work or pay them the transportation cost to work.
- Three-fourths guarantee. Employer shall guarantee to workers employment for at least three-fourths of the work days for the period of employment. If the employer cannot guarantee work for three quarters of each work day, the employer shall pay the difference.
- Records retention. Employer shall keep accurate records on the employees, such as work hours, wages paid, payroll records, and any deductions from wages.
- Hours and earnings statement. Employer shall give to each worker before each pay day a statement stating the total earning per pay period, hourly rate, hours of employment, hours actually worked by worker, itemizations of deductions from the paycheck, and, if piece rates are used, the units produced daily.
- Rates of pay. Employer shall pay the prevailing wages if the worker will be paid per hour.
- Frequency of pay. Employer shall state how often the worker will be paid.
- Abandonment of employment or termination for cause. Employer shall not be responsible for paying any transportation expenses or the three-quarters guarantee if it notifies the local office of such abandonment or termination.
- Contract impossibility. If the work cannot be finished for reasons beyond the employer's control, such as so-called acts of God, the employer may terminate the contract.
- Deductions. Employer shall specify deductions which the employer shall deduct from a worker's paycheck.
- Copy of work contract. Employer shall provide each worker with a copy of the employment contract, no later than on the day the work is to start.

B. Statement of Assurances

The employer must include a statement in the job offer that the employer will abide with the conditions set forth in 20 CFR 655.103. The employer makes the following assurances:

- the job opening does not exist due to a previous worker being on strike or being locked out because of a labor dispute;
- the employer shall abide by all applicable state, federal and local employment-related laws;
- no U.S. worker will be rejected or terminated unless for a lawful, job-related reason;
- the employer shall independently engage in recruitment until the foreign workers have left their residence to join the employer;
- from the time the foreign workers have left to join the employer, the employer shall provide employment to any qualified U.S. worker who applies for a job until 50 percent of the work contract period for foreign workers has elapsed;
- the employer shall perform any specific recruitment requested by the National Processing Center;
- the employer shall not discriminate or retaliate against any person who with a just cause institutes a proceeding, files a complaint, testifies, or consults an attorney in connection with these provisions;

• the employer shall file any applicable fees in a timely manner.

C. Duration of Status

The period of status is the period of approval plus seven days before the beginning of the approved period and up to ten days after the end of the approved period. This status may be extended for a total of three years by filing I-129. Each extension may be up to one year; however, after the three years, the individual must spend at least six months outside the United States before applying for H2A visa again.

A spouse and unmarried children under twenty-one may obtain H4 status. If they are already in the United States they may request a change to H4 status or an extension of H4 status by filing Form I-539. Study is allowed, work is not.

CHAPTER 10

Nonagricultural Temporary Workers (H2B)

This visa is used for temporary nonagricultural workers. "Temporary" means that the employer's need for work is one year or less. The employer's need for services must be a one-time occurrence, seasonal need, peakload need or intermittent need. The need should not be for more than ten months for seasonal, peakload or intermittent work. Part-time work does not qualify; it must be full-time work.

- One-time occurrence. The employer must establish that his or her temporary need for more workers did not happen in the past and will not occur in the future, but is based on an specific event requiring more workers now.
- Seasonal need. The employer must demonstrate that the work needed by the employer is tied to a season of the year by a certain event or pattern which occurs every year. The employer should state the dates when such need occurs every year. The employment is not considered seasonal if it is due to regular employees taking vacations, or is unpredictable or subject to change.
- Peakload need. The employer, in this case, needs extra workers to help his permanent employees due to a seasonal or short-term demand. The employer must demonstrate that the temporary staff will not become permanent employees.
- Intermittent need. The employer, in this case, needs extra workers occasionally or intermittently for short periods. The employer must demonstrate

that he or she did not previously employ workers permanently for those positions.

There are only 66,000 visas available each federal fiscal year, from October 1 to April 30. The visas are divided into two groups, 33,000 each, one for winter and the other for a spring work period, for the time period from October 1 through March 31, and April 1 through September 30. The cap does not apply to returning workers. However, at the time of the writing of this book, Congress had not reauthorized H2B visas for returning workers for the year 2009.

Petitions are done on Form I-129, Petition for Nonimmigrant Worker. A petition may be for one known worker or a number of unnamed workers as long as they all do the same job under the same conditions for the same duration. Because of the 66,000-visa cap, the employer should apply as soon as possible to ensure that he or she will have enough workers.

As with any other similar visa, the employer must formulate a job description, and the employer must pay prevailing wages for this type of work in the location of the intended employment. See Part I on prevailing wages and a job description.

A. Procedure

The employer first must file an application for temporary labor certification, form ETA 750A, with the state workforce agency (SWA) in the state of intended employment. Go to *www.foreignlaborcert.doleta.gov* and click on "Regions and States" to find your state. The employer should apply not earlier than 120 days before the start of work, but not later than 60 days before the start of work. The purpose of the labor certification is to make sure that there are no available U.S. workers who are ready, willing, and able to work in this position. The employer must send:

- two originals of form 750A;
- a temporary need statement on the employer's letterhead explaining why the need for more workers is temporary (the letter should explain the employer's business operations, schedule of activity, and why the employer's need falls under one of the four situations when temporary workers may be approved);
- for a seasonal or peakload occurrence, copies of the signed contracts for services or products requested to be delivered during those times; letters of intent from clients in relation to those time periods; invoices from previous years for those time periods; or annual or multi-year work contracts showing the dates for work which match the dates for the relevant time period when workers are needed; or monthly payroll for a minimum of one previous year showing the total number of workers, total hours worked and total earnings received;
- documentation of any efforts to recruit U.S. workers before filing the labor certification, including any advertising.

Once the application is received by an SWA, the SWA will review the application and, if incomplete, will return it to the employer for corrections. If everything is fine, the SWA will prepare a job order based on the information given in the application and post it in the SWA job bank system for ten consecutive days. During those ten days, the employer shall advertise the job in a newspaper of general circulation for three consecutive calendar days. If there is no newspaper of general circulation, then in a local, ethnic or professional publication, which is determined by SWA to most likely elicit a response from prospective workers.

The advertisement must have the following information:

- employer's name, location, and a directive for prospective applicants to send resumes to the local SWA, including SWA contact information and job order;
- a job description with specific details about duties, hours of work, days of work, rate of pay and job duration;
- employer's minimum job requirements, including education and work experience;
- a statement that the job is temporary.

After the ads are run, the employer must send copies of the newspaper ads to the SWA. In addition, the employer shall also prepare a written, detailed recruitment report showing the source of recruitment (SWA job base, ad in a newspaper, etc.), name, address and telephone number of every person who sent a resume or applied for a job, and the reasons why any person was not hired. The employer must also contact any union covering the workers in that particular position, and provide documentation showing that the union was contacted, and that the union either did not respond or was unable to refer any available U.S. workers to the employer.

After the end of the recruitment period, the SWA will send the entire package to the National Processing Center (NPC) for that particular state (either Chicago or Atlanta). The application may be granted or denied or referred back to SWA for additional recruitment. The NPC may also send a request for evidence to the employer. The employer will have seven days to respond.

If the certification is granted, the employer may file I-129 with the USCIS. The I-129 petition should be filed with the certification and any evidence showing that the worker has satisfied the required minimum educational and work experience. Note again that there are only 66,000 available visas, and they go quickly. If you want a shot at getting some workers, you have to be one of the first ones in the line. Keep in mind, we are talking about the federal fiscal year, not calendar year. That means if you need workers to start in the first part of the 2009 fiscal year, let's say from October 1, 2008, through March 31, 2009, you need to file your temporary labor certification with the DOL 120 days before October 1, 2008, and then file I-129 as soon as the certification is granted. For work which is to start between April 1, 2009, and September 30, 2009, temporary labor certification must be filed 120 days before April 1, 2009, and I-129 as soon as the certification is granted. Premium Processing Service is allowed, Form I-907.

A spouse and dependents may obtain H4 status. If they are already in the United States they may request a change to H4 status, or an extension of H4 status by filing Form I-539. Study is allowed, work is not.

B. Tree Planters and Entertainers

1. Tree planters

For tree-planting and related reforestation workers, the process is slightly different. First, the employer must register as a "Farm Labor Contractor" with the Department of Labor's Employment Standard Administration (see *www.dol.gov/esa*) for workers who will be performing temporary work for the employer. The applicable work is tree planting, brush clearing, and pre-commercial tree thinning. The employer must file an application for temporary labor certification, form ETA 750A, with SWA, and must describe in the application each housing facility to be used for the employees and the vehicles to be used to transport the workers. In addition, the employer must provide a written assurance that all applicable registrations, permits, licenses for the housing, vehicles and drivers will be valid for the duration of employment.

The employer may file one master application covering several work itineraries (places where work will be performed at different times), or file several applications for each itinerary with SWAs from different states, covering various places of work. The employer may file a master application including several itineraries if the master application is filed with the SWA with the most work locations, the application covers only crews working for a single employer, and the total range of days between work-start dates cannot be more than fourteen days.

The employer is allowed to file a single application with an itinerary with the SWA where the work will begin if the itinerary includes several locations for work covering different SWAs, but the states must be contagious or located close to each other. The itinerary must include:

- names, addresses, telephone numbers and wages offered at each location;
- the total number of crews and workers in each crew;
- estimated start and end date for each location.

2. Entertainment workers

There are only three SWAs that deal with entertainment workers, those of New York, Texas and California (no surprise). Go to *www.foreignlaborcert.doleta.gov*, click on "H2B" on the right-hand side under "hiring foreign workers," scroll down to Procedures for Entertainment Industry. You'll see that the New York, Texas, and California SWAs are designated "Offices Specializing in Entertainment" (OSE).

In addition to ETA 750A, the employer must include an itinerary of locations and duration of work at each location, if there will be multiple work locations. The employer must place an ad in a national publication looking for adequate U.S. workers and report to SWA the results of the recruitment. This could be done either before or after the application is filed. The OSE will also contact the appropriate union to determine if there are any available U.S. workers for the position. If any workers are referred to the employer, the employer must document why none of them were hired.

CHAPTER 11

Trainees (H3)

This type of visa may be used for nonimmigrants seeking to enter the United States for the purposes of receiving training in a particular field. A trainee may receive training at a company or organization in any occupational field, such as agriculture, communications, finance, and government. It may not be used by physicians, but a medical student studying at a medical school abroad may use this visa to work as an extern at a hospital approved by the American Medical Association.

This visa may also be used by a nurse if it is established that the nurse will receive short training which he or she cannot get in his or her native country, and that the training will benefit the nurse and his or her employer in the native country. The nurse must either have a full, unrestricted nursing license in his or her country, or the nurse must have obtained nursing education in the United States. The petitioner must provide a statement that the nurse is fully qualified to receive training under the laws of the state where the training will take place.

For all H3 visas, the petitioner must demonstrate that:

- training is not available in the trainee's native country;
- the trainee will not be placed in any regular position occupied by the petitioner's employees;
- the trainee will not engage in productive employment unless the employment is a necessary part of the training;
- the training will benefit the trainee in his or her career outside the United States.

Each H3 petition must also include a statement from the petitioner:

- describing in detail the training and structure of the program;
- stating which portion of the training will be dedicated to employment;
- showing the number of hours of classroom instruction and on-the-job training;
- describing the trainee's career abroad for which the training is used;
- stating the reasons why such training cannot be obtained in the trainee's country;
- indicating any wages paid to trainee and any benefit to the petitioner from the trainee for providing the training.

A. Special Education Programs

The H3 visa may be used for trainees in special education programs giving practical training and experience to trainees in the education of children with physical, mental or emotional disabilities.

The petition must be filed by a facility with professionally trained staff and a structured program for children with disabilities. The petition must be accompanied with a statement describing the program and the facility, evidence that the trainee is close to getting his or her baccalaureate or higher degree in special education, or already has such a degree, or has extensive prior experience in dealing with children with disabilities.

There are only fifty available visas per year. Premium Processing Service is allowed. See Appendix A for Form I-907.

B. Duration

The duration of the H3 visa is up to two years. For trainees in special-education training, the maximum duration is eighteen months. For any reapplication for H3 status after the maximum allowed stay, the trainee must spend at least six months outside the United States before reapplying.

A spouse and dependents may obtain H4 status. If they are already in the United States they may request a change to H4 status, or an extension of H4 status by filing Form I-539. Study is allowed, work is not.

CHAPTER 12

Treaty Traders and Investors (E1/E2)

The E designation applies to two different situations, both of which are fairly similar. The E1 visa refers to "treaty traders," the E2 designation is for "treaty investors." For both visas, the underlying basis for a visa is the existence of a treaty between the United States and the country of alien's nationality. For the current list of treaty countries, see *www.travel. state.gov/visa/frvi/reciprocity/reciprocity_3726.html.*

If a treaty trader or a treaty investor is an employee of a foreign company, he or she must hold the executive or supervisory position in the company, or have specialized knowledge making his or her services essential for the company. Both the treaty trader or treaty investor and the company must be nationals of the same foreign country. In addition, the employer must be a person who is a national of a foreign country, and who is either currently in the United States in a E1 or E2 status, or is outside the United States and would be classified as a treaty trader or treaty investor if he or she applied for a visa. As an alternative, if the employer is an enterprise or organization (company), it must be owned at least 50 percent by nationals from the treaty country who are currently in the United States in E1 or E2 status, or if they are outside the United States, would be classified as treaty traders or treaty investors if they applied.

A. Treaty Traders (E1)

A treaty trader is a person who is a national of a foreign country, who is coming to the United States to engage in a substantial international trade, principally between the United States and the foreign country, on his or her own behalf, or on behalf of a foreign company for which he or she works.

Trade is defined as the international exchange of goods and services between the United States and a foreign country. Trade items could be goods, services, banking, insurance, transportation, communications, data processing, advertising, accounting, design, engineering, management consulting, tourism, and technology. The trade must be substantial, which basically means that the trade must be continuous and numerous. One trade transaction will not suffice. For a small business, the substantial trade requirement could be satisfied if it can be demonstrated that the income derived from the trade can support the trader and his or her family.

Trade is considered "principally" done between the United States and the foreign country if more than 50 percent of the international trade done by the trader is done between the United States and the foreign country.

B. Treaty Investors (E2)

A treaty investor is a person who has invested or who is in the process of investing a substantial amount of capital in an enterprise in the United States. The funds most be really committed, in other words, the investor may be at risk of losing the invested funds if the enterprise fails. The enterprise must be a real enterprise which produces services and goods for profit. The investor must demonstrate that he or she will develop and direct the enterprise. This can be proven by showing that the investor owns at least 50 percent of the enterprise or that he or she holds a managerial or executive position in the enterprise.

C. Documentation

If a person is located abroad, he or she will have to go through the regular process at a consulate abroad. The application is done on Form DS-156E. As for any other visa application, check the appropriate consular office for additional requirements (see *www. usembassy.gov*). If the person is in the United States in some other lawful status, the appropriate petition is I-129, Petition for Nonimmigrant Worker. Documents which are needed in support of an application or petition may include:

- evidence that that the applicant is a national of a foreign country, such as a passport and birth certificate;
- evidence that the applicant and a foreign employer are nationals of the same country, by producing corporate documents, articles of incorporation, etc.;
- evidence of ownership in a foreign company, such as corporate documents, certificates of stock, reports from accountants;
- evidence that a new enterprise was established in the United States or will be established in the United States (articles of incorporation, articles of organization, partnership agreement, commercial leases for business offices or warehouse, business license, office inventory, bank statements, statements from accountants, etc.);
- evidence of substantial trade (invoices, contracts, bills of lading, customs receipts, purchase orders, letters of credit, trade brochures, etc.);
- evidence that the applicant holds a managerial or executive position, or has specialized knowledge (diplomas; certificates; corporate resolutions; letter from employer explaining the duties, responsibilities and wages paid, and education and work experience needed for the job).

Premium Processing Service is allowed, Form I-907. It costs an extra $1,000 but you will receive an answer in fifteen days.

D. Duration, Spouse and Dependents

Initial visa duration is two years. The visa may be extended in two-year increments by filing Form I-129. Spouse and unmarried children under twenty-one are allowed to study, children are not allowed to work. Extensions of status are accomplished by filing Form I-539. Spouses are allowed to work but must file application for employment, Form I-765.

Fiancé/Fiancée Visa (K1/K2)

This visa may only be used by a U.S. citizen wishing to bring his or her foreign fiancé or fiancée to the United States to marry. A fiancé or fiancée is a person who is engaged to be married.

In order to be eligible, the U.S. petitioner and the foreign fiancé or fiancée must have met in person within the last two years. In other words, they must have spent some time together in person. Internet or telephone conversations do not suffice. There are exemptions, however, if the customs and traditions, and social practices in that particular country, prohibit man and women from meeting each other in person before marriage (arranged marriage), or if the petitioner would suffer extreme hardship if required to meet the fiancé or fiancée in person before marriage.

If the petitioner has filed two or more petitions for a fiancé or fiancée in the past, or a petition for a fiancé or fiancée has been approved in the last two years, the petitioner must apply for a waiver, a written request, signed and dated, with an explanation of why the waiver is appropriate. For example, the previous fiancé or fiancée died or never came to the United States.

The petition is done by filing Form I-129F, Petition for Alien Fiancé. If the petition is approved, the fiancé or fiancée will be given four months to enter the United States. Once in the United States the petitioner and the fiancé or fiancée must marry within ninety days of arrival. If the fiancé or fiancée has a minor child under eighteen years of age, the petition should include the child as well. The fiancé visa allows for a derivative status for minor children, and the children will receive a K4 visa to enter the United States with the fiancé or fiancée. Once the fiancé or fiancée is in the United States, after the marriage he or she and any children must file for adjustment of status in order to obtain permanent resident status in the United States. Keep in mind that the child, to be eligible, must be under eighteen when the marriage takes place.

A. Documentation

Documentation required includes:

- evidence of U.S. citizenship (birth certificate, certificate of naturalization, certificate of citizenship, report of birth abroad, FS-240, valid unexpired U.S. passport issued in the last five years);
- evidence that the petitioner and fiancé or fiancée have personally met in the past two years (notarized statements from parents, relatives, friends, dated photographs, etc.);
- evidence that the culture and tradition in the foreign country prohibits meeting of man and a woman before marriage (statements from parents, religious authorities, civil authorities, articles and books on the subject);
- evidence that both parties are currently single (divorce judgments, annulments, death certificates);
- G-325 Form for each party, and one color, passport-size photograph for each party;
- a waiver, if applicable.

B. International Broker Regulation Act

If the petitioner and fiancé or fiancée have met each other by using the services of an international marriage broker, the petitioner must satisfy additional requirements. If the petitioner was convicted of any of the following crimes, the petitioner must provide copies of any police reports and court records. Crimes which require reporting are:

- domestic violence, sexual assault, child abuse and neglect, dating violence, stalking;
- homicide, murder, manslaughter, rape, abusive sexual conduct, sexual exploitation, incest, torture, trafficking, peonage, holding hostage, involuntary servitude, slave trade, kidnapping, abduction, unlawful criminal restraint, false imprisonment, or attempt to commit any of these crimes;
- crimes relating to controlled substances or alcohol on three or more occasions.

A petitioner may seek a waiver from the filing requirements under the act. A waiver is filed with the petition. It should be in a written form, signed and dated, explaining why a waiver would be appropriate.

For a petitioner who has committed a serious offense, the petitioner must show the existence of extraordinary circumstances. For example, that the petitioner was subjected to extreme cruelty by a spouse, parent or adult child when he or she committed the crime, or if the petitioner was not the primary perpetrator of violence in a relationship, and he or she was acting in self defense. Another example would be if the petitioner was convicted of a crime which did not involve serious bodily injury and where there was a connection between the crime and the petitioner's being subjected to battery or extreme cruelty.

Documents needed for this type of waiver may be police records, court records, news articles, trial transcripts, etc.

Work may be authorized; the visa holder must file I-765, Application for Employment Authorization. Travel may be authorized; the visa holder must file form I-131, Application for Travel Document.

CHAPTER 14

Spouse of U.S. Citizen (K3)

If a U.S. petitioner is already married to a foreign spouse, the petitioner may try to bring the spouse and his or her minor children to the United States to finish the process of gaining permanent residency. This is accomplished by filing Form I-129F.

There are two different ways this can be accomplished. First, if a petitioner has already obtained an approval for I-130 Petition for Alien Relative for the spouse, the approval notice from USCIS is sent with the I-129F. Second, if the I-130 petition is only filed and the petitioner has received a receipt from the USCIS, the petitioner may file I-129F along with a copy of the receipt for I-130 form. The I-129F will be approved if the I-130 is approved. After the approval, the USCIS will send the approval to the National Visa Center which will forward the file to the appropriate consulate for further processing.

After the spouse arrives in the United States, he or she will have to file for adjustment of status. The length of stay under a K3 visa is up to two years. Employment is authorized, but the visa holder must file I-765, Application for Work Authorization. Travel is also authorized, but only if the visa holder obtains advance parole by filing form I-131, Application for Travel Document.

CHAPTER 15

Religious Worker (R1/R2)

Foreign religious workers who belong to a religious denomination with a nonprofit religious status in the United States may apply for a temporary religious visa, R1. The R2 designation applies to the R1 visa holder's spouse and unmarried children under twenty-one.

Religious denomination is defined as a religious group or community of believers which has a form of religious government, a statement of faith, form of worship, formal or informal code of discipline, religious services and ceremonies, and established places of warship. A religious nonprofit organization in the United States is exempt from taxation by the Internal Revenue Service.

The R1 visa may be used for ministers of a religious denomination, persons invited to work in a professional capacity for the religious organization or an organization affiliated with the religious denomination, or individuals invited to work in a religious vocation or occupation. A person applying for an R1 visa must have been a member of such religious denomination for at least two years prior to applying for a visa.

"Minister" means a religious worker who is authorized by a religious denomination to conduct religious worship and other religious duties. It does not include a lay preacher. "Religious worker in a professional capacity" means a position in a religious vocation or occupation for which a baccalaureate degree is required. Religious workers in a religious vocation include individuals with a calling and commitment to a religious life, usually by taking of vows, such as nuns, monks and religious brothers and sisters. "Religious

workers in a religious occupation" refers to individuals who are engaged in traditional religious activities, such as liturgical workers, religious instructors, religious counselors, cantors, catechists, workers in religious hospitals, missionaries, etc.

The process in seeking an R1 visa usually starts when a church, mosque or other type of a religious organization in the United States invites a religious worker to work for the organization in the United States. Most frequently, the religious worker will obtain a visa at a U.S. consulate. If, however, the religious worker is already in the United States on some other nonimmigrant visa, the church must file form I-129, Petition for Nonimmigrant Worker, to change his or her status. Premium Processing Service is allowed, Form I-907.

Every application should include a letter from the Internal Revenue Service showing that the organization is exempt from taxation; and a letter from the authorized official of the organization which will employ the religious worker showing that:

- the individual has been a member of the religious denomination for the two years immediately preceding the application;
- if the individual's membership in the religious denomination was maintained outside the United States, that the foreign and U.S. organizations belong to the religious denomination;
- if the individual is a minister, that he or she is authorized to conduct religious worship for the religious denomination;

- if the individual will be employed in a professional capacity, that he or she possesses a baccalaureate degree and that such degree is a prerequisite for such occupation (copies of diplomas, degrees, certificates, etc.);
- if the individual will work in a religious vocation or occupation, evidence that the person is a monk, nun, etc.;
- statement of salary or wages and other compensation to be paid, and whether the salary or wages and other compensation will be paid in exchange for the services to be performed by the individual;
- name and location of the religious organization; and, if the work is to be done for an organization affiliated with the religious organization, evidence of such affiliation.

Duration of the R1 visa is three years initially, with a possible two-year extension. The maximum is five years. A person may not reapply for an R1 visa after five years in R1 status unless he or she spends at least one year outside the United States.

Spouse and unmarried children under twenty-one years of age are allowed to study. They are not allowed to work in the United States. Extension of status for R2 visa holders is done by filing Form I-539, Application to Extend/Change Nonimmigrant Status, along with a copy of the receipt for the I-129 filed by the R1 visa holder, and evidence of the relationship (marriage certificate, birth certificate).

CHAPTER 16

Foreign Media: Press, Radio and Film (I)

The I visas are reserved for members of foreign media, such as newspapers, radio stations, or filmmakers. Individuals must be engaged in a news-gathering process and reporting of actual events. Examples are reporters, news crews, and editors.

Activities and individuals which may qualify for this visa may be the following:

- reporters for sporting events;
- crews filming an event or making a documentary;
- crews making a film in order to disseminate information or news;
- journalists holding credentials from a foreign press, working under an employment contract, sending reports abroad;

- representatives of tourist bureaus controlled and operated by foreign governments engaged in dissemination of tourist information about that country.

Please note that foreign journalists who are nationals of a country belonging to the Visa Waiver Program, and who are coming to the United States to report on an event, may not enter under the Visa Waiver Program, they must apply for an I visa. In addition, the following activities would not qualify for an I visa: making a film to be used primarily for entertainment or advertising purposes, reality television shows, and quiz shows. Proofreaders, librarians, and set designers would not qualify.

CHAPTER 17

Intracompany Transfers (L1/L2)

The L visa is reserved for employees of foreign corporations, firms or other legal entities (we will call them "companies") where the parent, branch, affiliate or subsidiary of the company is doing business in the United States and at least one foreign country. The employee must have worked abroad for the company for at least one year in the previous three years. The L1 visa is used only for employees in managerial or executive positions (L1A) and employees with specialized knowledge (L1B). The visa could also be used for employees coming to the United States to either open or work in a new office (an office doing business in the United States for less than one year).

"Employee in a managerial capacity" is an employee who:

- manages a department, subdivision, function or a component of the company;
- supervises and controls the work of other professional or managerial employees;
- has the authority to hire and fire employees;
- exercises discretion over day-to-day operations of the company.

"Employee in an executive capacity" is an employee who:

- directs the management of the company;
- establishes goals and policies of the company;
- has wide discretion in decision making;
- is supervised directly by a board of directors, stockholders of the company, or higher-level executives.

"Employee with specialized knowledge" is an employee with specialized knowledge of the company's product, services, research, equipment, techniques, management, processes and procedures.

An employer qualified to apply for this type of visa must be a parent, branch, affiliate or subsidiary of a corporation, firm or other legal entity doing business in the United States, and at least one foreign country directly or through a parent, branch, affiliate or subsidiary. "Doing business" means maintaining continued, regular flow of goods and services.

"Parent company" is a company having one or more subsidiaries. "Subsidiary" is a company where a parent company owns and controls more than 50 percent of it. A "branch" is an office or operating division of the same company at a different location. An "affiliate company" is either a subsidiary owned and controlled by a parent company, or one or more legal entities owned and controlled by the same group of individuals who own the same proportionate share in both companies.

A. Documentation

Documentation required includes evidence that the company doing business in the United States is a parent, branch, subsidiary or affiliate of a company from a foreign country. Evidence may include articles of incorporation, an annual report, financial reports, and certificates of stock.

Also required is a letter from the foreign

employer stating the dates of employment, specific job duties, wages or salary paid, and required qualifications. The letter must also state that the employee is going to work in a managerial or executive position or a position requiring specialized knowledge. If the employee is a professional with specialized knowledge, send copies of degrees, diplomas, certificates, etc.

Finally, evidence is required that the employee has worked for the foreign employer for at least one year in the past three years, and that the employee is a manager or executive, or has specialized knowledge.

If the employee is coming to the United States to open or work in a new office, the employer must present evidence that offices in the United States have already been secured and that the new U.S. operation will financially support the managerial or executive position within the year of visa approval. Alternatively, the employer must explain the financial goals of the new entity and its organizational structure, the size of the U.S. investment and ability of the foreign company to pay the beneficiary and start doing business in the United States, and the organizational structure of the foreign company.

The employer must file Form I-129, Petition for Nonimmigrant Worker, along with the L Classification Supplement. Premium Processing Service is allowed, Form I-907.

B. Blanket L Visa Petitions

"Blanket visa petition" refers to situations when an employer seeks a continuing visa approval for all of its companies. This can be done if:

- the principal company employer and each of its other entities are engaged in a commercial trade or services;
- the principal company has been doing business in the United States for one year or more;
- the principal company has three or more domestic and foreign branches, subsidiaries or affiliates;

- and the principal company has obtained at least ten L visas for its employees in the past twelve months, or have U.S. companies making at least $25 million, or have a U.S. workforce of at least 1,000 employees.

A blanket petition is filed on Form I-129 and the L Supplement; mark LZ on the form. If the petition is approved, then the company can get L1 visas for individual employees by filing I-129 if the employee is in the United States, to change the employee's status to L1. If the employee is abroad, the employer should file Form I-129S, Nonimmigrant Petition Based on Blanket L Petition. In both situations, include a copy of the approval receipt.

C. Duration and Dependents

Duration of the L1 visa is three years unless an employee is coming to a new office in the United States, in which case the duration is one year. Extensions are possible, up to two years; the employer must file Form I-129. For managers and executives, total allowed stay is seven years; for employees with specialized knowledge, five years. In order to reapply for an L1 visa, the employee must spend at least one year outside the United States after spending the maximum time allowed in the United States.

For blanket petitions, the duration is three years, and they may be extended indefinitely as long as the employer satisfies the general requirements.

Spouses and children of L1 visa holders are allowed to stay for the duration of the primary visa holder's stay, with applicable extensions. Extension requests are accomplished by filing Form I-539. Spouses and children are allowed to study, but children are not allowed to work in the United States. Spouses are allowed to work, but they must file for employment authorization on Form I-765.

CHAPTER 18

Aliens of Extraordinary Ability (O1/O2)

Generally speaking, if a an applicant believes that he or she might be able to get an O1/O2 visa, the applicant must be ready to present significant evidence that he or she is well known in his or her field. Extraordinary ability essentially means that an applicant has reached a high level of achievement, the top of his or her field, evidenced by his or her skills and recognition by other experts in the field. Note that there must be an employer sponsor for this type of visa. Self petitioning is not allowed. The employer must file Form I-129, Petition for Nonimmigrant Worker, along with O and P Supplement. Premium Processing Service is allowed, Form I-907.

The O1 visa classification is reserved for an applicant who has extraordinary ability in the sciences, arts, education, business, or athletics, demonstrated by national and international acclaim, and who is coming to the United States to work in a temporary position for an employer in the area of the extraordinary ability; or who has a demonstrated record of extraordinary achievement in motion picture or television productions and who is coming to the United States to work in a temporary position for an employer in the area of the extraordinary achievement.

The O2 visa classification is reserved for individuals who are coming to the United States to assist the O1 visa holder in an artistic or athletic performance. The O2 applicant must be an integral part of a performance or event and possess skills and experience with the O1 visa holder which others do not possess.

For O2 workers in a motion picture or television production, the O2 individual must have either critical skills and experience with the O1 visa holder which are based on a preexisting and longstanding relationship between them, or in case of a single production, a significant part of the production will take place both outside and inside the United States and the continuing work by the O2 applicant is essential for the success of the production.

Please note, O2 classification may not be used for people in the fields of science, business or education. This visa must be used in conjunction with the primary O1 visa; it cannot be used separately. However, a separate I-129 petition is required.

A. Evidentiary Requirements for O1 Arts and Motion Picture and Television Industry

To prove that the applicant has extraordinary ability in the arts, or in the motion picture or television industry, the employer must provide evidence demonstrating extraordinary ability. Please note that the term "arts" includes any field of creative ability. It may include visual arts, fine arts, culinary arts, and performing arts, among others. It does not include only the principal creators and performers, but also individuals whose work is essential to a performance.

Examples are directors, set designers, choreographers, lighting designers, conductors, orchestrators, coaches, arrangers, musical supervisors, costume designers, makeup artists, flight masters, stage technicians, and animal trainers.

Documentation necessary in support of the petition should include evidence that the person has been nominated or has received significant national or international prizes and awards (Academy Award, Grammy Award, Director's Guild Award, etc.), or if the person is not quite that significant, at least three of the following:

- evidence that the person has performed or will perform services as a lead or a starring participant in productions with a distinguished reputation (send advertisements, reviews, publicity releases, publication contracts, endorsements, etc.);
- evidence that the person has national and international recognition (send critical reviews about the person appearing in newspapers, magazines, trade journals, etc.);
- evidence that the person has performed in a lead or a starring role for organizations and establishments which have a distinguished reputation in the field (send articles from newspapers, trade journals, magazines, etc.);
- evidence that the person has achieved commercial and critically acclaimed successes in the field (send box office receipts, ratings, and other reports in newspapers, trade journals, magazines, etc.);
- evidence that the person has received significant recognition from critics, organizations, government agencies, etc. (send letters from critics, authorized persons from the organizations and government entities);
- evidence that the person commands or will command a high salary for his or her work (send copies of the employment contracts, letters from previous employers, income tax documents, etc.);
- affidavits from present and former employers or known experts describing the person's recognition and abilities and the source of such knowledge.

B. Evidentiary Requirements for O1 Science, Education, Business or Athletics

Documentation required for O1 applicants in the fields of science, education, business or athletics includes evidence of receipt of major international prizes and awards (a Nobel prize, for example); if this is not applicable, than send at least three of the following:

- evidence that the person has received national and international prizes and awards for his or her work in the field;
- evidence of the person's membership in national or international associations and organizations in his or her field which require outstanding achievements by its members (send copies of the membership rules and regulations, membership card, etc.);
- evidence that the person has published material in major trade publications, magazines, journals, books, etc.;
- evidence that the person has acted in a capacity of a judge on a panel evaluating the work of others in the same field (send the invitation letter, brochure, articles about the event, etc.);
- evidence of the person's original scientific, business, or scholarly contribution to the filed;
- evidence that the person has been employed by organizations and establishments with distinguished reputations (send letters from employers);
- evidence that the person commands or will command a high salary for his or her services (send income tax records, letters from employers, employment contracts, etc.).

C. Consultation with "Peer" Group or Union

Before an O1 or O2 visa may be approved, the employer petitioner must obtain a written advisory opinion from the appropriate peer group, or labor or management organization covering the particular field. A list of the groups and organizations can be found at *www.uscis.gov*. Click on "Laws and Regulations," then click on "Immigration Handbooks, Manuals and Policy Guidance," and then click on "Adjudicator's Field Manual, Appendix 33.1." A waiver of an advisory opinion may be obtained when a person seeks readmission in the United States in a similar position within two years from the previous consultation. In lieu of an advisory opinion, the organization may provide a no-objection letter.

D. Duration, Spouse, and Dependents

The duration of an O1 visa is three years. The duration of an O2 visa must be the same as that of O1, since it is dependent on, and connected to, the principal O1 visa. Extensions in one-year increments are possible. Extensions are requested on the I-129 form.

Visa holders are given ten extra days after the visa expiration to depart the United States.

Spouses and unmarried children under twenty-one may be admitted in O3 status. The duration of an O3 visa must be the same as the duration of the principal O1 visa. Study is allowed, but work is not. Extensions are accomplished by filing Form I-539.

E. Traded Professional Athletes in O1 Status

If a professional athlete is traded from one organization to another, the O1 status will still be considered valid and employment will be authorized for thirty days after the trade is finalized. However, the new organization must file a new I-129 for the athlete within the thirty-day period. Otherwise, the athlete will lose his or her O1 status.

Artists, Athletes, and Entertainers (P1/P2/P3/P4)

The P visa can be divided into three separate parts. The P1 visa is reserved for individual athletes or athletes belonging to a team, or an internationally recognized entertainment group. The P2 visa is reserved for artists and entertainers under a reciprocal exchange agreement. The P3 visa is reserved for individual artists or entertainers coming to perform in a culturally unique program. The P4 visa is reserved for the spouse and unmarried children under twenty-one of the principal visa holder.

"Arts" includes fields of creative activity such as fine arts, visual arts, and performing arts. "Competition, event or performance" means an athletic tournament, competition, season, tour, exhibition, or engagement, or an entertainment event. "Culturally unique" means a style of artistic expression which is unique to a particular country, nation, society, class, ethnicity, religion, or tribe.

For any P visa there has to be a sponsor, an employer, or a sponsoring organization. The petition is filed on Form I-129, Petition for a Nonimmigrant Worker, plus O & P Supplement. Premium Processing Service is allowed, Form I-907. An advisory opinion from a "peer" group or union is required (see discussion on O visas). The petition may include multiple beneficiaries if they are a part of the same group, but all must be named in the petition. If a petition includes several beneficiaries belonging to a group, a beneficiary may be substituted if the sponsor files a letter asking for a substitution, including a copy of the approval letter from USCIS with the appropriate consulate. Essential support personnel may not be substituted. If a group is to perform at several locations, the petition must be accompanied by an itinerary with the exact locations and dates of the performances.

Each petition must include a copy of the contract between the sponsor and beneficiary, and a description of the performance or event, including the start and end dates.

A. Athletes and Entertainers (P1)

For the P1 visa for athletes, "athlete" means an internationally recognized athlete or a member of an internationally recognized group or a team, coming to the United States to perform at a specific athletic event or competition with a distinguished reputation.

The P1 entertainment visa can be used by individuals who perform with, or are an essential part of, an entertainment group recognized internationally as having been outstanding for a sustained and substantial amount of time, and where 75 percent of the members have had a sustained and substantial relationship with the entertainment group for at least one year. Individual entertainers cannot get this visa separately from a group, only if they are a part of a group.

"Essential personnel" means highly skilled individuals performing support services for the group.

The one-year relationship with the group may

be waived by the USCIS if, because of illness or an unanticipated situation, an essential member must be replaced by another essential member, or if an individual improves the group by performing a critical role for the group.

1. Documentary evidence for athletes

Documentary evidence required for athletes seeking a P1 visa include a contract with a major U.S. sports league or team, or individual sport; and at least two of the following:

- evidence of significant participation in a prior season with a major U.S. sports league;
- evidence of participation in an international competition with a national team;
- evidence of significant participation in a prior season for a U.S. college or university in intercollegiate competition;
- a written statement from the head of the governing body for a particular sport explaining how the individual athlete or the team is internationally recognized;
- a written statement from the sports media or a recognized sports expert explaining how the individual athlete or team is internationally recognized;
- evidence of ranking for the individual athlete or team, if the sport has rankings;
- evidence that the individual athlete or team has received significant honor in the sport.

2. Documentary evidence for entertainment groups

Entertainment groups seeking P1 visas are required to submit evidence that the group has been established and performing for at least one year; a statement from the petitioner listing the name of each group member and the length of time each member has been employed with the group; and evidence that the group has had international recognition for a sustained and substantial amount of time. Evidence must include at least three of the following:

- evidence that the group has performed in a leading or starring role in productions and events with distinguished reputations (send critical reviews, advertisements, publications, contracts, publicity releases, etc.);
- evidence that the group has international recognition and acclaim for outstanding achievements in the field (send news articles, reviews in trade journals, magazines, etc.);
- evidence that the group has performed for establishments with distinguished reputations (send copies of news articles, reviews in trade journals, magazines, etc.);
- evidence that the group has had commercial and critically acclaimed success (send box-office receipts, evidence of record, video, CD or cassette sales);
- evidence that the group has received significant recognition from organizations and government agencies (send letters from appropriate authorized officials from those organizations and agencies);
- evidence that the group commands or will command a high salary (send copies of the contracts, letters from previous employers, tax returns, etc.).

3. Documentary evidence for essential support

Evidence for essential support crewmember must show that there has been consultation with the appropriate union; it must also include a statement describing the person's skills and experience with the principal performers and a copy of the employment contract.

B. Reciprocal Exchange (P2)

The P2 visa may be used by artists or entertainers, individually or as members of a group, who will be performing in the United States under a reciprocal exchange program between an organization or organizations in the United States and an organization or organizations from one or more foreign countries. The exchange of artists and entertainers must be similar in terms of the notoriety and caliber of artists, length and conditions of employment, number of artists, etc. Similarly to P1 visa requirements, essential support personnel may be given P2 status based on their connection with the primary P2 visa holder.

1. Documentary requirements

Those seeking a P2 visa must submit a copy of the reciprocal exchange agreement between an organization from the United States and an organization from a foreign country; a statement from the sponsoring organization describing the exchange program; evidence that a labor union was involved in negotiating the contract, or is in agreement with the reciprocal program; and evidence that foreign artists and entertainers have adequate notoriety and skills, and that the length and conditions of employment are similar to that of U.S. artists when they go to a foreign country under the same program.

2. Documentary requirements for essential support

Those seeking P2 visas as support crew for primary P2 visa holders must show that a labor union covering the person's skills and occupation has been consulted.

In addition they must provide a statement describing the person's skills and experience, connection to the primary P2 visa holder, and why the skills are essential and critical; and a copy of the employment contract between the employer and the essential support worker.

C. Culturally Unique Programs (P3)

The P3 visa designation is used for artists and entertainers, individually or as members of a group, coming to the United States to perform in a culturally unique program. Performance is one aspect of this visa, but it may also cover teaching, coaching, developing, and interpreting. When you think of this visa, think of ethnic dances and songs limited to a particular country, region or people. Frequently, owners of ethnic restaurants or other establishments located in the United States apply for this type of visa to bring entertainers from their native countries to perform in their establishment for a limited length of time. But generally speaking the visa may be used to bring artists from a foreign country to participate in any culturally unique event or performance whose purpose is to further the understanding and development of an art form. The event may be commercial or non-commercial.

1. Documentary requirements for a primary P3 visa

Must include affidavits, statements, and testimonials from recognized experts demonstrating that the artist or group is authentic and culturally unique, attesting to the unique and special skills of the artist or of the group, and the source of knowledge for this information. Also send news articles, reviews, advertisements, etc.

A P3 visa also requires evidence that the event or performance is culturally unique (send reviews, ads, news articles, etc.).

2. Documentary requirements for essential support

Those seeking P3 visas as support crew for primary P3 visa holders must give evidence of a consultation with a labor union covering the person's skill's and occupation; a statement describing why his or her skills are essential and critical, and connection to the primary P3 visa holder; and a copy of the employment contract between the employer and the worker.

D. Duration of P Visas

For a P1 visa for athletes, the initial length of status is five years. It may be extended for an additional five years, not to exceed ten years in total. For a P1 visa for an entertainment group, the length is one year, and it may be extended in one year increments. For P2 and P3 visas, the length is one-year, and it may be extended in one year increments. For all visa types, the visa holder is given extra ten days after the end of visa period to depart the United States. Extensions are accomplished by filing Form I-129.

Spouses and unmarried children under twenty-one of the primary visa holder may be granted P4 status. No work is allowed, but study is okay. Extensions of status are accomplished by filing Form I-539.

CHAPTER 20

Spouses and Children of Permanent Residents (V)

The V visa is reserved for spouses and unmarried children under twenty-one of permanent residents. However, the following requirements must be satisfied. First, a family petition must have been filed for the spouse and children on or before December 21, 2000. Second, the petition must have been pending for at least three years, or the petition must have been approved but the beneficiary must have been waiting for an immigrant visa number for at least three years, and the number must still not be available.

The spouse and children under twenty-one will be eligible for this visa even if they entered the United States without inspection; if they do not have a passport, visa or other entry documents; or if they have been unlawfully present in the United States after the expiration of some other nonimmigrant visa for more than 180 days, then left the United States and now seek admission.

Request for a V visa must be filed on Form I-539, Application to Extend/Change Nonimmigrant Status, if the person is in the United States. If the person is outside the United States, the procedure is the same as for any other visa at a consulate. The I-539 form must be accompanied with Form I-693, Medical Examination of Aliens Seeking Adjustment of Status. The applicant must send a copy of the notice from the USCIS demonstrating that a family petition was filed on or before December 21, 2000.

The duration of this visa is two years, and it may be extended in two-year intervals. Keep in mind that a child may be granted this status only until the child is twenty-one years of age. Holders of a V visa are allowed employment, but must file Form I-765 to obtain employment authorization.

CHAPTER 21

Victims of Criminal Activity (U)

The U visa is reserved for victims of crime. Persons who are victims of a crime may be reluctant to report a crime if they are without legal status in the United States. In order to help those victims, and assist government officials in prosecuting the perpetrators of crimes, Congress created the U visa classification.

This visa applies to any victims of a crime, male or female, who have suffered substantial mental or physical abuse as a result of having been a victim of a crime, who have information regarding the crime, and who can assist government officials in the investigation and prosecution of such crimes. The crime must have violated U.S. law or occurred in the United States. Crimes whose victims qualify for a U visa are rape, torture, trafficking, incest, domestic violence, sexual assault, abusive sexual contact, prostitution, sexual exploitation, female genital mutilation, hostage holding, peonage, involuntary servitude, slave trading, kidnapping, abduction, unlawful criminal restraint, false imprisonment, blackmail, extortion, manslaughter, murder, felonious assault, witness tampering, obstruction of justice, perjury, or attempt, conspiracy or solicitation to commit any of those crimes.

There are 10,000 U visas granted per year. Visa duration is four years, and it may be extended. The form needed is I-918, Petition for U Nonimmigrant Status. In addition, the petitioner must also provide certification from a federal, state or local law enforcement official demonstrating that the petitioner has been helpful, is helpful, or is likely to be helpful in a criminal investigation. Please note that the petitioner does not have to be in the United States to apply. If the petitioner is outside the United States and believes that he or she may be inadmissible, he or she may request a waiver of inadmissibility by filing Form I-192, Application for Advance Permission to Enter as Nonimmigrant.

If the petitioner is over twenty-one, spouse and children may also apply. If the petitioner is under twenty-one, petitioner's spouse, children, siblings under eighteen, and parents may also apply.

CHAPTER 22

Premium Processing Service

Premium Processing Service (PPS) allows faster visa processing for certain nonimmigrant visas and immigrant employment petitions. The Form is I-907, Request for Premium Processing Service, and the fee is $1,000. The petitioner will receive an answer from USCIS in fifteen days.

Eligible nonimmigrant visas are H1B, H2B, H3, L1A, L1B, L-Blanket, O1, O2, P1, P1S, P2, P2S, P3, P3S, Q1, R1, TN1-Canada, and TN2-Mexico (in other words, I-129 petitions). Those in all employment categories for Form I-140, except for multinational executives and managers may request PPS.

CHAPTER 23

Waiver of Inadmissibility for Nonimmigrants

If a nonimmigrant believes that he or she may not be admissible in the United States (due to commission of a crime, a communicable disease, or membership in the Communist Party, for example), he or she may file Form I-192, Application for Advance Permission to Enter as Nonimmigrant. This application should be filed with the local USCIS office where the nonimmigrant is supposed to arrive in the United States.

If an application is made because the nonimmigrant is or was a member of the Communist Party or other totalitarian party or organization, the person seeking admission should send a letter, along with the application, explaining the person's history of the membership, with the applicable dates of membership, status in the organization and whether the membership was voluntary or involuntary.

If a person believes he or she may be inadmissible because of a disease, physical or mental defect, the application must include a description of the disease or physical or mental disability. If the person files an application because he or she will receive a medical treatment in the United States for such disease or disability, the application must include a statement that similar treatment is not available outside the United States, that arrangements have already been made for treatment at a medical facility in the United States, that person is financially able to pay for such treatment and that a cash bond will be posted by such person if required by the US CIS.

If a person believes that he or she may be inadmissible due to a commission of a crime, such person must send a statement explaining the crime, date and place of the crime, and sentence or other judicial disposition received. Official court record should be attached to the application.

PART IV

—∽—

Inadmissibility and Deportability

This chapter is divided into two sections, inadmissibility and deportability. Inadmissibility refers to grounds or reasons for denial of an application for a nonimmigrant visa, visa processing, or adjustment of status. Deportability refers to grounds for deportation — removal of aliens from the United States, including nonimmigrants and immigrants. Both areas are interconnected, as the grounds for inadmissibility are essentially also the grounds for deportability.

The areas of inadmissibility and deportability are very technical. I strongly suggest that anyone facing inadmissibility or deportability issues raised by the USCIS seek professional help from an immigration attorney specializing in these issues.

For some of the grounds of inadmissibility or deportability it is possible to obtain a waiver from the USCIS, and I will note when this is possible. Generally, a person may apply for a waiver on Form I-601, Application for a Waiver on Grounds of Inadmissibility. This waiver may be used by, among others, an applicant for an immigrant visa or adjustment of status, K1 and K2 (fiancé visa) and K3 and K4 (spouse and children of U.S. citizen) nonimmigrant visa applicants. If a person is in the United States, request for a waiver is sent to the appropriate USCIS center. If a person seeking a waiver is outside the United States, the waiver should be submitted to the appropriate U.S. consulate. In addition, there are certain defenses to deportability which may be available.

CHAPTER 1

Inadmissibility

A person may be ineligible to receive a nonimmigrant or immigrant visa in the following situations.

A. Health-related Grounds

1. Communicable diseases

Any person may be ineligible who has a communicable disease including infectious tuberculosis, HIV, infectious syphilis, gonorrhea, chancroid, granuloma inguinale, and lymphogranuloma venereum.

A waiver may be available for Section 1 situations for a person who is the spouse or the unmarried child under 21 of a U.S. citizen or a permanent resident, or a person whose son or daughter is a U.S. citizen or permanent resident, or a person applying as a battered or abused spouse or a battered child of a U.S. citizen or permanent resident.

2. Failure to vaccinate

A person seeking adjustment of status or seeking an immigration visa through visa processing, and who has failed to present adequate documentation of having been vaccinated against vaccine-preventable diseases, including at least mumps, measles, rubella, polio, tetanus and diphtheria toxoids, pertussis, influenza type B and hepatitis type B, may be ineligible.

A waiver may be available for Section 2 situations for a person who receives applicable vaccinations; for whom a civil surgeon, medical officer or panel physician certifies that a vaccination would not be medically appropriate; or if the vaccination would be against the person's religious or moral beliefs.

Please note that this Section 2 will not apply for a child under ten years of age seeking an immigrant visa as an immediate relative of a U.S. citizen, and whose U.S. parent signs an affidavit that it will vaccinate the child within thirty days of the admission to the United States.

3. Physical or mental disorder

Any person having a physical or mental disorder and behavior that may pose or has posed a threat to property, safety or welfare of such a person or others; and any person with a physical or mental disorder and behavior that may pose a threat to property, safety and welfare of such person or others, and whose behavior is likely to be repeated may be ineligible.

A waiver may be possible for Section 3 upon USCIS consultation with the U.S. Secretary of Health and Human Services.

4. Drug abusers and addicts

Any person who is a drug abuser or drug addict may be ineligible.

For any waiver of inadmissibility on health-related grounds, a person seeking a waiver should fill out and sign the first page of Form I-601 and submit the form, along with the appropriate fee, to either the appropriate USCIS center if the person is in the United States, or a U.S. consulate, if the person is residing abroad. The I-601 Form will be forwarded to the Center for Disease Control in Atlanta which will return the form, along with the supplemental form page outlining the conditions of any treatment required for the approval of a waiver. The person seeking a waiver then signs Part A agreeing to comply with the requirements. The person's sponsor/petitioner completes Part C of the form. The medical doctor who will see this person upon arrival into the United States completes and signs Part B. If the medical doctor is a private physician, a local or state health official must sign Part D of the form.

B. Criminal and Related Grounds

A person who was convicted of — or has admitted committing — the following crimes may be ineligible to receive a nonimmigrant or immigrant visa.

1. Moral turpitude

A person who is convicted of, or has admitted committing a crime of "moral turpitude" may be ineligible. "Moral turpitude" is a catch-all term which may include a number of different offenses. For example, a person caught for the first time driving under influence (DUI) may not fall under the category of moral turpitude. However, getting more than one DUI, or getting a DUI while driving on a suspended license could be considered a crime of moral turpitude.

Some of the other offenses falling under the category of moral turpitude are: aggravated battery, murder, rape, armed robbery, evading income taxes, passing counterfeit money, mail fraud, perjury, and fraud. Note that a person may be inadmissible even if a conviction is from a foreign country.

A waiver may be available at the discretion of the USCIS for Section 1 if the crime occurred more than fifteen years before applying for a visa; if the admission would not be contrary to the welfare, safety and security of the United States; and if the person has been rehabilitated.

A waiver may also be available if the person seeking a waiver is a spouse, parent, or child of a U.S. citizen or permanent resident, and if it is established that a visa denial would result in an extreme hardship to the U.S. citizen or permanent-resident alien.

A waiver is not available to a person convicted of — or who has admitted to committing — a murder or criminal acts involving torture, or an attempt or conspiracy to commit murder or torture.

2. Controlled substances

A person who is convicted of — or has admitted to — violating any law of the United States or a foreign law relating to controlled substances (illegal drugs) may be ineligible. However, this will not apply to a person who has committed only one crime, if the crime was committed when the person was under eighteen, if the crime was committed more than five years before applying for a visa, if the maximum penalty for the crime did not exceed one year of imprisonment, and if the person was not sentenced to more than six months of imprisonment.

A waiver may also be available at the discretion of the USCIS for Section 2 if the crime was a single offense of possession of thirty grams or less of marijuana; if the crime occurred more than fifteen years before the person applied for a visa; if the admission would not be contrary to the welfare, safety and security of the United States; and if the person has been rehabilitated.

A waiver may also be available if the person seeking a waiver is a spouse, parent, or child of a U.S. citizen or permanent resident, and if it is established that a visa denial would result in an extreme hardship to the U.S. citizen or permanent-resident alien.

A waiver may also be available to a self-petitioner battered spouse or a child of a U.S. citizen or a permanent-resident alien.

A waiver is not available to a person convicted of — or who has admitted to — committing murder or criminal acts involving torture, or an attempt or conspiracy to commit murder or torture.

3. Multiple crimes

A person who is convicted of two or more offenses whose aggregate prison sentences were for five years or more may not be eligible.

A waiver may be available at the discretion of the USCIS for Section 3 if the crime occurred more than fifteen years before applying for a visa; if the admission would not be contrary to the welfare, safety and security of the United States; and if the person has been rehabilitated.

A waiver may also be available if the person seeking a waiver is a spouse, parent, or a child of a U.S. citizen or permanent resident, and if it is established that a visa denial would result in an extreme hardship to the U.S. citizen or permanent-resident alien.

A waiver may also be available for a self-petitioner battered spouse or a child of a U.S. citizen or a permanent-resident alien.

A waiver is not available to a person convicted of—or who has admitted to—committing murder or criminal acts involving torture, or an attempt or conspiracy to commit murder or torture.

4. Traffickers in controlled substances

A person who is trafficking in controlled substances (illegal drugs) or aiding, abetting, assisting or conspiring to traffic controlled substances may not be eligible.

The spouse or child of a trafficker in controlled substances who has in the last five years obtained a financial benefit from the trafficking, and knew or should have reasonably known that the money came from this activity, also may not be eligible.

5. Prostitution

A person who is entering the United States mainly to engage in prostitution, who has been engaged in prostitution within the ten years before applying for a visa, and who procures or attempts to procure prostitutes or receives proceeds from prostitution may be ineligible.

A waiver may be available at the discretion of the USCIS for Section 5 if the crime occurred more than fifteen years before applying for a visa; if the admission would not be contrary to the welfare, safety and security of the United States; and if the person has been rehabilitated.

A waiver may also be available if the person seeking a waiver is a spouse, parent, or a child of a U.S.

citizen or permanent resident, and if it is established that a visa denial would result in an extreme hardship to the U.S. citizen or permanent-resident alien.

A waiver may also be available for a self-petitioner battered spouse or child of a U.S. citizen or a permanent-resident alien.

A waiver is not available for a person convicted of—or who has admitted to—committing murder or criminal acts involving torture, or an attempt or conspiracy to commit murder or torture.

6. Aliens with immunity

A person involved in a serious criminal offense, such as a felony, crime of violence, or driving while intoxicated, who has exercised immunity from criminal prosecution (diplomats with immunity, for example), who has left the United States because of the offense and the exercise of immunity, and has not submitted himself or herself to a court in the United States to answer for such offence, may not be eligible.

A waiver may be available at the discretion of the USCIS for Section 6 if the crime occurred more than fifteen years before applying for a visa; if the admission would not be contrary to the welfare, safety and security of the United States; and if the person has been rehabilitated.

A waiver may also be available if the person seeking a waiver is a spouse, parent, or a child of a U.S. citizen or permanent resident, and if it is established that a visa denial would result in an extreme hardship to the U.S. citizen or permanent-resident alien.

A waiver may also be available for a self-petitioner battered spouse or child of a U.S. citizen or a permanent-resident alien.

A waiver is not available for a person convicted of—or who has admitted to—committing murder or criminal acts involving torture, or an attempt or conspiracy to commit murder or torture.

7. Foreign government officials who committed religious freedom violations

Government officials of foreign countries who are responsible for carrying out severe violations of religious freedom in their countries may not be eligible.

8. Trafficking in persons

Any person trafficking in persons, or who is engaged in aiding, assisting or conspiring in trafficking of persons, may be ineligible. So may the spouse and children of a trafficker in persons who have received a benefit from the activity in the last five years. This does not apply to sons or daughters who were children at the time the benefit was received.

9. Money laundering

Any person engaged in money laundering, or who has been aiding, abetting, assisting or conspiring in the offense of money laundering, may be ineligible.

C. Security Grounds

Any person seeking to enter the United States in order to engage in the following activities is ineligible to receive a nonimmigrant or immigrant visa to the United States.

1. Espionage or sabotage

Any person is ineligible who seeks to enter the United States to commit espionage, sabotage, or violate any law prohibiting the export of U.S. technology, goods or sensitive information.

Any person is ineligible who would engage in activities for the purpose of opposing or overthrowing the government of the United States by force.

2. Terrorist activities

Any person is ineligible who is engaged — or is likely to be engaged — in a terrorist activity after entering the United States, or who has incited terrorist activity in the past.

Any member of a terrorist organization is ineligible, unless he or she can prove by clear and convincing evidence that he or she did not know and should not reasonably have known that the organization was a terrorist organization.

Any representative of a terrorist organization, or any political or social group that endorses terrorist activity, is ineligible.

Any person endorsing terrorist activities or persuading others to endorse terrorist activities is ineligible. The inadmissibility does not apply to a spouse or child of such a person if they did not know or should not have reasonably known that the person was engaged in the activity, or if the person has renounced the activity.

Any person receiving military-type training from a terrorist organization is ineligible, as is any spouse or child of a person whose terrorist activity occurred within the past five years.

Note that any official or representative of the Palestinian Liberation Organization (PLO) is considered to be engaged in a terrorist activity.

3. Danger to United States foreign policy

Any person whose entry or proposed activities in the United States would have an adverse effect on U.S. foreign policy is ineligible.

An exception exists for officials of foreign governments and candidates for office in a foreign government. Also, a person may be admitted if his or her beliefs, statements or associations would be lawful in the United States, unless there is a compelling foreign-policy reason not to admit such person.

4. Membership in totalitarian party

Any person who is or was in the Communist Party or any other totalitarian party is ineligible. Such person will be admissible, however, if he or she can prove that the membership was terminated at least two years before applying for a visa, or, in case of membership in a party controlling the government, at least five years before applying for a visa, if the person would not be a threat to the security of the United States.

A waiver may be available for a spouse, parent, son or daughter, brother or sister of a U.S. citizen or a spouse, son or daughter of a permanent-resident alien for humanitarian purposes or to ensure family unity, when the person is not a threat to the security of the United States.

An exception also exists for a person who can establish that his or her membership was involuntary, entirely while the person was under sixteen years of age, or required by law or for the sole purpose of obtaining employment, food rations, living quarters, or other necessities of life.

5. Participants in Nazi persecution, genocide, or commission of act of torture or extrajudicial killing

Any person is ineligible who participated in Nazi persecutions between March 23, 1933, through May 8, 1945, under the Nazi government of Germany, any government of a country occupied by Nazi Germany, any government established by Nazi Germany, or any government which was an ally of Nazi Germany.

Any person is ineligible who ordered, incited, assisted or participated in a genocide outside the United States, or who committed, ordered, incited, assisted or participated in any act of torture or extrajudicial killing of another person.

D. Public Charge

Any person who is found to be likely a public charge if admitted into the United States is not eligible to receive a nonimmigrant or immigrant visa. "Public charge" means that the person will likely become a burden on the state or federal government. As mentioned in the discussion on Affidavit of Support in Part I, if a petitioner submits a proper Affidavit of Support in context of family immigration, the issue of public charge will not be raised. This section is also not applicable to self-petitioning battered or abused spouses and children of U.S. citizens or permanent residents and self-petitioning widows or widowers of a U.S. citizen.

Receipt of public benefits that can raise a red flag are Social Security Disability (SSI) benefits, long-term nursing home or mental-care institution Medicaid benefits, and state and local assistance. Some of the benefits which do not warrant consideration are school lunch, food stamps, housing benefits, emergency disaster relief, and child-care benefits.

E. Labor Certification

For discussion on labor certification, refer to Part I. This issue will generally arise if a labor certification is required for a particular occupation, but has not been supplied with a petition for immigrant worker.

F. Illegal Entrants and Immigration Violators

Any person who is found to belong to one of the following categories may be ineligible to receive a nonimmigrant or immigrant visa.

1. Illegal entry

Any person may be ineligible for visa who enters the United States without being properly admitted (enters illegally). This section does not apply to a person who is a self-petitioning battered or abused spouse or child of a U.S. citizen or permanent resident, who was abused by a parent, spouse or member of the spouse's or parent's family residing in the same household, and the spouse or parent consented to such abuse, if there is a substantial connection between the abuse and the person's unlawful entry into the United States.

2. Failure to attend removal (deportation) proceeding

Any person who fails to appear at a deportation hearing is inadmissible if he or she attempts to reapply for admission within five years of such hearing.

3. Misrepresentation

Any person may be ineligible who fraudulently or willfully misrepresents a material fact in order to procure a visa or admission into the United States.

A waiver may be available for a spouse, son or daughter of a U.S. citizen or a permanent resident, if it is proven that the denial of admission would produce extreme hardship to the U.S. citizen or permanent resident. Also, in case of a self-petitioning battered spouse or child of a U.S. citizen or permanent resident, a waiver may be available if it is proven that denial of admission would produce extreme hardship to the petitioner, or the petitioner's U.S.-citizen or permanent-resident parent or child.

4. Falsely claiming United States citizenship

Any person may be ineligible who falsely represents himself or herself as a U.S. citizen. This section is inapplicable if a person's parents are U.S. citizens, the person permanently lived in the United States before his or her sixteenth birthday, and the person reasonably believed that he or she was a citizen of the United States.

5. Student visa abusers

Any person who was admitted as a student under a nonimmigrant student visa and who violates the terms of the student visa status is inadmissible unless such person spends at least five years outside the United States before applying for admission.

G. Lack of Documentary Requirements for Entry into the United States

Any person who falls under any of the following categories is ineligible to receive a nonimmigrant or immigrant visa:

- Any immigrant is ineligible who appears at the border without a valid, unexpired immigrant visa, permanent resident card, reentry permit, border crossing card, and a valid unexpired passport. A waiver may be available at the discretion of the USCIS if the person has an immigrant visa and is otherwise admissible, and can prove that the lack of the immigrant visa document was not known to him or her, or that the lack of the immigrant visa could not have been ascertained by reasonable diligence at the time of the person's departure.
- Any person is ineligible who at the border does not have a passport valid for at least six months after the expiration of the initial authorized stay in the

United States, or who does not have a valid nonimmigrant visa. A waiver may be available for a person applying for admission on the basis of an unforeseen emergency. See also Visa Waiver Program coverage in Part III.

H. Persons Ineligible for Citizenship

Any immigrant who is permanently ineligible for U.S. citizenship may be ineligible for a visa.

I. Draft Evaders

Any person may be ineligible who has departed the United States to avoid training or service in the armed forces in a time of war or national emergency.

J. Aliens Previously Deported

Any arriving nonimmigrant may be ineligible who has been previously deported from the United States if such person seeks admission within five years after deportation, or twenty years in case of a second removal.

Any other person may be ineligible who has been ordered removed from the United States, who departed the United States while the order of deportation was in force, and who seeks readmission within ten years of departure or removal, or twenty years in case of a second removal.

Exception exists for cases where the USCIS consents to person's reapplying for admission to the United States.

K. Aliens Unlawfully Present in the United States

Any person who falls under any of the following categories may not be eligible to receive a nonimmigrant or immigrant visa:

- Any person unlawfully present in the United States for more than 180 days but less than one year, who voluntarily departed the United States before the removal proceedings were commenced and is applying for a nonimmigrant visa within three years of departure;

- Any person who has been unlawfully present in the United States for more than one year and seeks admission within ten years of departure.

  Exceptions:

- Any period of time spent in the United States by a minor under eighteen years of age is not considered unlawful.
- Any period of time spent in the United States while the application for asylum was pending is not considered unlawful.

A waiver may be available if the person's U.S. citizen or permanent resident spouse of K visa petitioner would experience extreme hardship if the person was denied admission into the U.S.

L. Waivers for Refugees

Note that refugees have additional waivers available. First, grounds for inadmissibility based on public charge, labor certification and immigrant documentation requirements are inapplicable. For all other grounds, except the following, a waiver may be available for humanitarian purposes, to assure family unity and when it is otherwise in the public interest. A waiver is not available for:

- those who traffic in controlled substances;
- those ineligible on security grounds;
- those engaged in terrorist activity;
- those deemed a danger to U.S. foreign policy;
- those who participated in Nazi persecutions, torture and extrajudicial killing.

CHAPTER 2

Deportation or Removal from the United States

Deportation, also known as "removal," is an unhappy subject, but one which must be addressed. Note that any person subject to a removal proceeding by the USCIS should not attempt to defend himself or herself without outside help. Laws, regulations and proceedings concerning removal are complicated and the results could be disastrous for the person in removal proceeding and his or her family. You must get a lawyer specializing in removal proceedings.

This chapter will be divided into three sections. The first will discuss reasons for deportation. The second will discuss deportation procedure, including arrest and release on bond. The last will discuss defenses to deportation.

A. Grounds for Deportation

Any person who falls under any of the following categories may be deportable. This applies to both nonimmigrants and immigrants.

1. Inadmissible persons or violators of immigration status

A) INADMISSIBLE PERSONS

Any person may be deportable who at the time of entry into the United States, or at the time of adjustment of status was inadmissible. Inadmissibility refers to categories discussed in Part IV, Chapter 1.

B) LAW VIOLATORS

Any person may be deportable who violated any law of the United States and is currently present in the United States.

C) THOSE WITH NONIMMIGRANT VISA REVOKED

Any person may be deportable whose nonimmigrant visa was revoked.

D) NONIMMIGRANT VISA VIOLATORS

Any person may be deportable who violated the terms of a nonimmigrant visa, by either failing to maintain the nonimmigrant status (visa expired), or violating the conditions of the particular visa (worked while on tourist visa, for example).

E) THOSE WHO VIOLATED CONDITIONS OF ENTRY

Any person may be deportable who violated the terms and conditions of entry into the United States (failed to treat a health condition, for example).

F) THOSE WHOSE CONDITIONAL RESIDENT STATUS HAS BEEN TERMINATED

Any person may be deportable in conditional-resident status (through marriage or alien entrepreneur) whose conditional status has been terminated.

A hardship waiver may be available for a person who obtained conditional-resident status through marriage if it is determined that extreme hardship would result if the person was removed from the United States. The person seeking a waiver must prove either:

- that the marriage was a good-faith marriage (not marriage entered into for the sole purpose of getting a green card), that the marriage was terminated (divorce or annulment), and that the person was not at fault for failing to file for removal of the conditional-resident status; or
- that the person seeking a waiver, a spouse or a child of a U.S. citizen or permanent-resident alien, was battered or abused by such U.S. citizen or permanent-resident alien, and the person was not at fault for failing to file for removal of conditional permanent residence.

G) ALIEN SMUGGLERS

Any person may be deportable who has knowingly encouraged, induced, assisted, or helped another person to enter or try to enter the United States illegally.

A waiver may be available, for humanitarian purposes or to assure family unity, if the person was a permanent resident alien and he or she was helping his or her spouse, parent, son or daughter to enter the United States illegally.

H) THOSE ENGAGED IN MARRIAGE FRAUD

Any person may be deportable who obtained an immigrant visa through marriage if the marriage took place less than two years before the person entered the United States, and the marriage was terminated or annulled within two years after the person's entry into the United States.

2. Criminal offenses

Any person belonging to any of the following categories may be deportable from the United States.

A) CRIMES OF MORAL TURPITUDE

Any person may be deportable who was convicted of a crime of moral turpitude for which a sentence of one year or longer may be imposed, and which was committed within the last five years, or ten years for permanent residents. Note that the question is whether a particular crime carries a sentence of year or more, not whether the person was sentenced to a year or more. Whether a crime carries a sentence of one year or more depends on the state law covering such crime.

A waiver may be available if the person received a full pardon from the president of the United States or a governor of any state.

B) MULTIPLE CRIMINAL CONVICTIONS

Any person may be deportable who was convicted of two or more crimes of moral turpitude after being admitted in the United States.

A waiver may be available if the person received a full pardon from the president of the United States or a governor of any state.

C) AGGRAVATED FELONY COMMISSIONS

Any person may be deportable who committed an aggravated felony after being admitted in the United States. Aggravated felonies are:

- murder, rape, sexual abuse of a minor;
- illicit drug trafficking; illicit trafficking in firearms, destructive devices, explosives;
- money laundering in excess of $10,000;
- firearms offenses;
- a crime of violence for which the term of imprisonment is at least one year;
- a theft or burglary offense for which the term of imprisonment is at least one year;
- ransom;
- child pornography;
- racketeering;
- owning, controlling, or managing a prostitution business; slavery, trafficking in persons, involuntary servitude;
- treason, sabotage, gathering and transmitting national defense information, disclosure of classified information, divulging the identity of undercover agents;
- fraud and deceit where the damage to a person is over $10,000;
- alien smuggling;
- falsely making or altering a passport for which a term of imprisonment is more that twelve months;
- failure to appear to serve a sentence for a term of five years or more;
- failure to appear in court to answer charges on a felony carrying two years or more of imprisonment;
- obstruction of justice, bribery, forgery carrying a sentence of more than one year.

A waiver may be available if the person received a full pardon from the president of the United States or a governor of any state.

D) HIGH-SPEED FLIGHT

Any person may be deportable who escaped from an immigration check point.

A waiver may be available if the person received a full pardon from the president of the United States or a governor of any state.

E) FAILURE TO REGISTER AS A SEX OFFENDER

Any person may be deportable who is convicted as a sex offender and fails to register as a sex offender in his or her place of residence.

F) CONTROLLED SUBSTANCE VIOLATIONS

Any person may be deportable who has been convicted of a violation of any law of the United States, or a foreign law, relating to controlled substances, after being admitted into the United States. It does not apply to a single offense involving thirty grams or less of marijuana for the person's own use.

Any drug user or drug addict may be deportable.

G) FIREARMS OFFENSES

Any person may be deportable who has been convicted of any law regarding the purchasing, selling, carrying, using, owning, or attempting or conspiring to purchase, own, use or carry any weapon, part of a weapon or accessory which is a firearm or a destructive device, where a conviction occurred after the person was admitted into the United States.

H) OTHER OFFENSES

Any person may be deportable who has been convicted at any time of espionage, sabotage, or treason for which a term of five years or more may be imposed.

I) DOMESTIC VIOLENCE CRIMES

Any person may be deportable who has been convicted of a crime of domestic violence, stalking, child abuse or child abandonment after being admitted into the United States.

Any person may be deportable who violates an order of protection issued by a state court in connection with domestic violence after being admitted into the United States.

A waiver may be available if the person proves that he or she was acting in self defense, violated the protection order to protect himself or herself, or was arrested or convicted of an offense that did not result in a serious bodily injury and that there was a connection between the crime and the person being subjected to battery or extreme cruelty.

3. Change of address and falsification of documents

Any person who falls under any of the following categories may be deportable.

A) CHANGE OF ADDRESS

Any person may be deportable who fails to report a change of address within ten days of the address change, unless the person can prove that the failure was not willful and was reasonably excusable.

B) FALSIFICATION OF DOCUMENTS

Any person may be deportable who has been convicted of falsification of any immigration documents, visas, permits, etc.

C) DOCUMENT FRAUD

Any person may be deportable who engages in document fraud in order to gain an immigration benefit, unless the offense was done solely to help or assist the person's spouse or child.

D) FALSELY CLAIMING UNITED STATES CITIZENSHIP

Any person may be deportable who falsely claimed that he or she was a U.S. citizen unless each parent of such person was a U.S. citizen, the person permanently resided in the United States before his or her sixteenth birthday, and had reasonably believed that he or she was indeed a U.S. citizen.

4. Security grounds

Any person who falls under any of the following categories may be deportable. The activity must have occurred after the person was admitted into the United States.

A) Sabotage, espionage, danger to national security

Any person may be deportable who engages in sabotage, espionage, or evading any law prohibiting the export of technology or sensitive information from the United States.

Any person may be deportable who engages in an activity which endangers public safety or national security of the United States.

Any person may be deportable who engages in an activity to oppose or overthrow the government of the United States.

B) Terrorist activity

Any person may be deportable who engages in a terrorist activity.

C) Danger to United States foreign policy

Any person may be deportable whose presence in the United States poses serious adverse foreign policy consequences for the United States.

D) Participation in Nazi persecutions, genocide, torture, extrajudicial killings

Any person may be deportable who engaged in Nazi persecution, genocide, torture or extrajudicial killings.

E) Violation of religious freedom

Any person may be deportable who participated in serious violations of religious freedoms.

5. Public charge

Any person may be deportable who has become a public charge within five years after entry into the United States. This may not apply if the causes for being a public charge arose after being admitted into the United States.

6. Unlawful voting in the United States

Any person may be deportable who voted in violation of any federal, state or local law, unless the person's parents were U.S. citizens, he or she permanently lived in the United States before his or her sixteenth birthday, and the person reasonably believed that he or she was a U.S. citizen.

B. Deportation Procedure

The purpose of any deportation proceeding is to remove a person from the United States if the USCIS can prove that the person belongs to one or more categories of deportable persons. A person is deportable if he or she belongs in any of the categories discussed in the previous section. However, the USCIS cannot arbitrarily remove a person without giving him or her a chance to rebut allegations. The USCIS bears the burden of proving its case in an immigration court. Every person in a deportation proceeding will get an opportunity to present his or her case to an immigration judge and possibly assert any defenses he or she may have. The immigration judge will ultimately make a decision whether a person is deportable or not.

1. Deportation of aliens seeking admission into the United States

Before discussing the regular deportation procedure for people who are already in the United States, I will describe the deportation process for people arriving at a U.S. checkpoint (border). This process tends to be much quicker, as you will see.

Each person arriving at a U.S. checkpoint is subject to an inspection. He or she is formally known as an "applicant for admission" into the United States. The purpose of an inspection, similar to one at any international border, is to determine whether the arriving traveler has proper documents to be admitted into the United States. At the time of inspection, the immigration officer has the right to ask questions about the reasons for the person's stay in the United States, length of stay, further intentions, etc. Any person has the right to decide not to apply for admission and to depart immediately, without entering the United States. If the person decides to apply for admission, such person may be removed if the officer determines that the person is inadmissible. The person will be removed immediately unless the person indicates that he or she desires to apply for asylum in the United States or fears persecution if removed from the United States. In that case the immigration officer will refer the person for an interview regarding those issues.

Stowaways (who have traveled aboard a vessel

without permission of the owner of the vessel) are not eligible for admission into the United States. Nevertheless, they are inspected by an immigration officer, as well. A stowaway will be ordered removed unless he or she indicates that he or she desires to apply for asylum in the United States, or fears persecution if removed from the United States. At that time, the officer will refer the person for an interview regarding those issues. A stowaway may be allowed to apply for asylum only if it is proven that the person has a credible fear of persecution.

At the interview, a person must demonstrate to the immigration officer that he or she has a "credible fear of persecution." "Credible fear of persecution" means that there is a significant possibility, taking into account the statements made by the person and other available facts and evidence, that the person could establish eligibility for asylum.

Before the interview, an alien asking for asylum will be allowed to consult a person (attorney) of his or her choosing regarding the interview, and regarding any subsequent review of the interview determination. During this interview, which will occur very quickly after a person shows up at the border and indicates his or her desire to apply for asylum or states that he or she has a credible fear of persecution if removed from the United States, the interviewing officer will make a determination whether the person has a credible fear of persecution. If the officer determines that the credible fear exists, the person will be detained for further consideration. If the officer determines that no credible fear exists, the person will be ordered removed without further hearings. The officer will prepare a written record of the interview, including a summary of facts, analysis of the facts, and the ultimate decision. At this time the alien may request a review by an immigration judge. This hearing will occur no later than seven days after the officer's order to remove. The person will be questioned by an immigration judge either in person or by telephonic or video conference. The immigration judge will make the final decision. Please note that the person will be detained until the final decision is reached regarding the existence of credible fear of persecution.

2. Deportation proceeding

A) NOTICE TO APPEAR

Every deportation proceeding begins with the USCIS giving a "notice to appear" to a person the USCIS believes is deportable. The notice to appear contains certain standard information, such as the charges against the person, time and place where the deportation proceeding will be held, notice of the right to obtain an attorney, and a description of consequences if the person does not appear for the proceeding. This notice may be given in person, or by regular mail at the person's last address as indicated in the USCIS files.

B) ARREST AND BOND FOR RELEASE

A person may be arrested by the USCIS if the USCIS believes that the person is deportable, pursuant to an arrest warrant, Form I-200. If you are arrested, do not sign any documents given to you and do not give out any information regarding your immigration status in the United States. Ask to contact your country's consulate. Ask to speak to your attorney and your family. You have the right to make a phone call. You will be fingerprinted and interviewed and a deportation officer will be assigned to your case. At that time you will receive a notice to appear, from the deportation officer. After being processed you may be moved to another facility. If your family does not have the phone number and address of the detention facility, they may contact the Immigration and Enforcement headquarters via *www.ice.gov* or 202-305-2734.

After a person is arrested, the USCIS will decide on the conditions of custody, including the amount of any bond required for release, and deliver a Notice of Custody Conditions, Form I-286, to the arrested person. Always ask for a bond hearing before an immigration judge. Have your family and attorney present. A person detained may file a request to be heard by an immigration judge asking that the conditions of detention be lessened, including a reduction of the amount of the bond.

If the arrested person is ordered released on a bond, someone must post a bond for his or her release. That person must file Immigration Bond, Form I-352. A bond is essentially a contract between the person posting a bond and the USCIS. If the person for whom the bond is posted does not appear for a hearing at a certain time and place the bond may be forfeited. Bonds can be surety bonds or cash bonds. Surety bonds are issued by companies specializing in this type of bonds, and a number of companies may be found in any yellow pages or via the Internet. Cash bonds must be delivered in the form of cash, money order, cashier's check or U.S. bonds or notes.

If a bond is allowed, the amount of the bond cannot be less than $1,500. If a person is released, he or she will not be authorized to work during the entire deportation procedure, unless the person is a permanent resident alien.

c) Court proceeding

A person who has received a notice to appear must appear in the immigration court specified in the notice, with or without an attorney. If an interpreter is needed, one will be appointed by the court. The immigration judge will advise the person of his or her right to have an attorney present, to examine evidence presented against him or her, and to present evidence in his or her own behalf; read the charges from the notice; and ask the person to answer to the charges from the notice. The answers to the charges could be either admitted, denied or neither admitted or denied. If the charges are admitted, the judge will enter an order of removal. If the charges are denied, the court will proceed with the case and schedule a hearing. The USCIS has the burden of proving their charges, and the person has the burden of proving that the charges are not true, or, even if the charges are found to be true, that he or she is entitled to certain defenses.

d) Failure to appear in court

If a person who has received a notice to appear or if his or her attorney of record who has received a notice to appear on his or her behalf does not appear at a scheduled court hearing, the person will be ordered removed. (This is called removal "in absentia.") Delivery of notice will not be required if the person never gave an address to the USCIS.

This order of removal in absentia may be vacated in two situations. First, if the person files a motion to reopen within 180 days after the original order was entered, demonstrating that the failure to appear occurred because of certain exceptional circumstances. Exceptional circumstances could be battery or extreme cruelty to the person, or any child or parent of the person; the person's serious illness; or the serious illness or death of the person's spouse, parent or child. The person must demonstrate that the existence of any exceptional circumstance was outside that person's control.

The order of removal in absentia may also be vacated by filing a motion to reopen at any time if the person can prove that he or she has never received a notice to appear, and that he or she was not at fault for failure to appear at a hearing (for example, if the person changed address one or more times but has always reported to the USCIS the change of address in a timely manner).

If neither of these two motions may be used or were never filed, the person who was ordered removed pursuant to the order in absentia will not be eligible for any defenses to deportation for ten years after the order was given.

e) Defenses to deportation

Apart from the obvious defense that the USCIS charges are wrong, there are several of other defenses which may be available to a person in a deportation proceeding. They are: cancellation of removal, adjustment of status, asylum and withholding of removal, voluntary departure, suspension of deportation or special rule cancellation of removal under NACARA, suspension of deportation, and of course any available waivers as discussed above to grounds of inadmissibility and deportability. If a defense is available, a person must apply to court to allow him or her to file the appropriate forms with the immigration court.

(I) Cancellation of removal

Cancellation of removal may be available to permanent residents and to nonimmigrants. If proven, the person will be granted permanent-resident status in the United States.

In order for a permanent resident to be eligible for cancellation of removal, such person must prove the following. First, that he or she has been a permanent resident for at least five years. Second, that prior to service of the notice to appear, or prior to committing any offense which gave rise to the charge of deportability, he or she had been residing in the United States for at least seven years. Finally, that he or she has not been convicted of an aggravated felony.

Persons ineligible to use this defense are crewmembers, J1 exchange students, persons inadmissible or deportable based on security grounds, and persons who participated in the persecution of any person based on race, religion, nationality or membership in a political group.

In order for a nonimmigrant to be eligible for cancellation of removal, such person must prove the following. First, that prior to receiving the notice to appear, he or she had been residing in the United States for at least ten years. Second, that the person is of good moral character. Third, that the removal of the person would result in exceptional and extremely unusual hardship to the person's U.S.-citizen or permanent-resident spouse, parent or child.

If a nonimmigrant is a battered spouse or child of a U.S. citizen or permanent resident, or a parent of a battered child, such person must prove the following. First, that prior to receiving the notice to appear, the person had been residing in the United States for at least three years. Second, that the person is of good moral character. Third, that the person is not inadmissible based on criminal and national-security grounds, and has not committed an aggravated felony. Finally, that the removal of such person would result in extreme hardship to that person or that person's child whose parent is a U.S.-citizen or permanent resident.

A permanent resident filing for cancellation of removal must file Form EOIR 42A, Application for Cancellation of Removal for Certain Permanent Residents. A nonimmigrant must file Form I-42B, Application for Cancellation of Removal and Adjustment of Status for Certain Nonpermanent Residents. For cancellation of removal, the person must produce evidence of continuous residence in the United States for the required time period. Necessary documentary evidence may be tax returns, utility bills, bank account records, school records, leases, mortgages, and affidavits of friends and family. To prove that a person is of good moral character, provide testimony of family and friends, clergy, and employers and fellow employees.

Regarding the actual court procedure, note that the form, along with the supporting documentation, must be filed directly with the court, and a copy must be given to the USCIS. The supporting documenta-

tion must also include Form I-325G, Biographic Information, and a biometrics confirmation. In order to get a biometrics confirmation, the person must send a copy of the application, along with the applicable fees and a copy of the Instructions for Submitting Certain Applications in Immigration Court and for providing Biometric and Biographic Information to U.S. Citizenship and Immigration Services to the Texas Service Center. To find these instructions, go to *www.uscis.gov*, click on "Immigration Services and Benefits," then click on "Immigration Benefits in EOIR Removal Proceeding," then click on "Pre-order Instructions." The person will receive a receipt for the fee, and a request to appear for fingerprinting. Once the fingerprinting is done, the person will receive a biometrics confirmation which must be filed with the court.

(II) Adjustment of status

A person eligible for adjustment of status may always raise that defense and file the Adjustment of Status Application (I-485) with the court. Note, however, that unless a family application (Petition for Alien Relative, I-130) or an employment application (Petition for Alien Worker, I-140) is already approved, a person will not be able to file for adjustment of status until the underlying petition is approved. Any family or employment petition is not filed with the immigration court but must be sent to the regular service center processing such applications.

(III) Asylum and withholding of removal

A person who believes that he or she may be eligible for asylum and withholding of removal must raise that defense and file the Asylum and Withholding of Removal Application (I-589) with the court. (See Part I, Chapter 6 for details.) In addition to filing the application with the court, the person must send the following documents to the Nebraska Service Center: a copy of the first three pages of the application and a copy of the Instructions for Submitting Certain Applications in Immigration Court and for providing Biometric and Biographic Information to U.S. Citizenship and Immigration Services (see "Cancellation of removal" above). The person will receive a receipt from the service center, and a request for fingerprints. After the fingerprinting is done, the person will receive a biometrics confirmation.

(IV) Suspension of deportation or special rule cancellation of removal under NACARA

"NACARA" is the Nicaraguan Adjustment and Central American Relief Act. Persons eligible under NACARA may be able to get permanent resident status in the United States. The form may be filed with a USCIS service center or an immigration court.

(1) Eligible persons

• Guatemalan nationals who entered the United States on or before October 1, 1990, registered for benefits under the ABC settlement agreement on or before December 31, 1991, and were not apprehended at the time of entry after December 19, 1990;

• El Salvadoran nationals who entered the United States on or before September 19, 1990, registered for benefits under the ABC settlement agreement on or before October 31, 1991, and were not apprehended at the time of entry after December 19, 1990;

• persons who entered the United States on or before December 31, 1990, filed for asylum on or before December 31, 1991, and at the time of filing were a national of Russia, any republic of the Soviet Union, Albania, Bulgaria, Czechoslovakia, East Germany, Estonia, Hungary, Latvia, Poland, Romania, Yugoslavia, or any state of the former Yugoslavia;

• spouses and unmarried children under twenty-one of the above applicants;

• persons who have been battered or subjected to extreme cruelty by a person described in the first three categories above at the time such person applied for Temporary Protected Status, registered for ABC benefits, applied for asylum, filed an application for suspension of deportation or cancellation of removal, or when such application was granted.

In addition, the applicant from the first four categories above must show that he or she has had at least seven years of continuous presence in the United States, was a good (moral) person during such period, and that his or her U.S.-citizen or permanent-resident spouse, parent or unmarried child under twenty-one would suffer extreme hardship if the person was re-moved from the United States. For applicants under the last category shown above (battery victims), the required time period is three years.

(2) Persons not eligible

A person convicted of an aggravated felony or subject to a final order of deportation is not eligible for suspension of deportation under NACARA.

(V) Suspension of deportation

An application for suspension of deportation, Form EOIR-40, is filed with an immigration court. It applies to persons whose deportation proceedings were commenced before April 1, 1997, and are still pending.

To be eligible, the applicant must show continuous residence in the United States for at least seven years before the application was filed, that he or she is a person of good moral character and that his or her U.S.-citizen or permanent-resident spouse, parent or unmarried child under twenty-one would suffer extreme hardship if the person was deported.

(VI) Voluntary departure

A person may be allowed to depart voluntarily from the United States, at the alien's own expense, instead of being subject to deportation proceedings either before or after the commencement of the proceedings. If a person is allowed to voluntarily depart, the ten-year bar on reentry will not apply.

Before the deportation proceeding, a person may apply at any immigration office. A person may be granted up to 120 days to depart. If an application is made after a deportation proceeding is commenced in immigration court, the USCIS may agree to the voluntary departure. If the person is granted voluntary departure and fails to depart, that person will be barred from asking for voluntary departure and any other defenses for ten years.

Application for voluntary departure may also be granted by the immigration judge, as well, after a deportation proceeding has commenced. Request for voluntary departure must be made at or before the first hearing on the merits of the case. The request may be granted if the applicant agrees that he or she is removable, does not ask for any other relief (adjustment of status, cancellation of removal, etc.), if he or she was not convicted of an aggravated offense, and if he or she waives the right to appeal. Of course, voluntary departure may also be granted, even after the first hearing on the merits, if the USCIS agrees.

Voluntary departure may be granted by the immigration court after the end of the proceedings if the person has been present in the United States for the past twelve months, has not been convicted of an aggravated offense, and the person is of a good moral character.

(VII) Waivers

A person who is in a deportation proceeding and who believes that an I-601 Form waiver is available to him or her, may file a request for a waiver, filing this with the court directly.

(VIII) Alien ordered deported

If a court enters an order that a person shall be deported, the USCIS will deport the person as soon as it is practicable, but usually within ninety days of the court order. During that time, the person will be detained by the USCIS. A person may be released under certain circumstances.

The order of removal may be appealed to the Board of Immigration Appeals (BIA) within thirty days of the court order by filing Form EOIR-26, Notice of Appeal, and the appropriate fee.

If the person being deported is a person who was seeking entry into the United States, then such person will be deported to the country where his or her travel originated. If that country is unwilling to accept the person, he or she may be removed to a country of that person's citizenship, country where he or she was born, or the country where he or she has a residence.

All other persons will be deported to a country which he or she designates if the country is willing to accept him or her and if the person has valid documents for entry into such country. If that country is unwilling to accept the person, the USCIS may deport the person to the country from which he or she was admitted into the United States, country of birth, country of residence, or country of citizenship. Generally, the person will not be deported to a country where the person's life or freedom would be in jeopardy because of the person's race, religion, nationality, or political opinion.

(IX) Stay of deportation

A person who was ordered deported may apply for a stay of deportation by filing Form I-246, Application for Stay of Deportation or Removal. This form may be used if a person ordered deported needs additional time to finish his or her affairs in the United States.

(X) Application to reenter the United States after deportation

A person removed from the United States may apply for admission after removal. Who can apply?

- a person who voluntarily left the United States where no deportation order was entered;
- a person who was denied admission into the United States and was deported more than one year ago;
- a person who has been outside the United States for more than five years after the last deportation.

The grant of admission is at the discretion of the USCIS. The application must be done on Form 212, Application for Permission to Reapply for Admission into the United States after Deportation or Removal.

(XI) Concept of extreme hardship

"Extreme hardship" is a term which I have mentioned a number of times in the context of eligibility for various immigration rights, waivers and defenses. Whether extreme hardship applies in a particular case depends on a number of different circumstances. In the context of a deportation proceeding, specifically defense of cancellation of removal, a person who claims the existence of extreme hardship must produce evidence that his or her deportation would result in an extreme hardship which would be felt more and beyond the hardship ordinarily associated with a deportation. Factors which must be considered are:

- age of the alien;
- age and number of the alien's children and their ability to speak the person's native language (how would they fit in the alien's country or country of deportation);
- alien's health condition and health condition of the children; availability of required medical treatment in the alien's country;
- alien's ability to find a job in the alien's country;
- length of time the alien was in the United States (Are

there any other family members who are staying legally in the United States? Are there any means of the alien getting permanent residence in the United States, through family member for example?);

- psychological, financial, or educational impact of deportation;
- current political and economic conditions in the alien's country;
- whether the alien has any family in his or her country;
- connections the alien made in the United States, and contributions made to the United States. (What is the level of the alien's integration into the United States?)

For a battered or abused spouse or child of a U.S.-citizen or permanent-resident alien, the alien must produce additional evidence about:

- the nature of abuse, and physical and psychological consequences of the abuse;
- the consequences for the alien if the alien were to be deprived of the U.S. court system (child custody and visitation rights, alimony and child support, and any criminal investigations and enforcement of orders of protection);
- the likelihood that the family of the abuser living in the alien's country would continue to abuse the alien once the person was deported there (Would the local authorities help the alien? Are there any domestic violence laws there?);
- the social, medical, mental health and other needs of the alien and his or her children.

Appendix A.
Form Packages for
Various Family Categories

A. *Sponsoring a Spouse*

1. Sponsor is a U.S. citizen, spouse is in the United States
   - Petition for Alien Relative, I-130
   - Biographic Information Form for each person, G-325A
   - Application for Adjustment of Status, I-485
   - Supplement A to Form 485 Adjustment of Status, if applicable
   - Application for Employment, I-765
   - Affidavit of Support, I-864
   - Contract between Sponsor and Household Member, Form I-864A, if applicable
   - Medical Examination I-693
   - Application for Advance Parole, I-131, if applicable

2. Sponsor is a U.S. citizen and spouse is abroad
   - Petition for Alien Relative, I-130
   - Biographic Information Form for each person, G-325A
   - Affidavit of Support, I-864
   - Contract Between Sponsor and Household Member, I-864A, if applicable

3. Sponsor is a permanent resident and spouse is in the United States
   - Petition for Alien Relative, I-130
   - Biographic Information Form, G-325A for each person
   - Affidavit of Support, I-864

   - Contract Between Sponsor and Household Member, I-864A, if applicable

4. Sponsor is a permanent resident and spouse is abroad
   - Petition for Alien Relative, I-130
   - Biographic Information Form, G-325A for each person
   - Affidavit of Support, I-864
   - Contract Between Sponsor and Household Member, I-864A, if applicable

B. *Sponsoring a Child*

1. Sponsor is a U.S. citizen, unmarried child under twenty-one, residing in the United States
   - Petition for Alien Relative, I-130
   - Biographic Information Form for your child, G-325A
   - Application for Adjustment of Status, I-485
   - Supplement A to Form I-485, Adjustment of Status, if applicable
   - Application for Employment, I-765, if applicable
   - Affidavit of Support, I-864;
   - Contract Between Sponsor and Household Member, I-864A, if applicable
   - Medical Examination I-693
   - Application for Advance Parole, I-131, if applicable

2. Sponsor is a U.S. citizen, child is unmarried under twenty-one, residing abroad

- Petition for Alien Relative, I-130
- Affidavit of Support, I-864
- Contract between Sponsor and Household Member, I-864A, if applicable

3. Sponsor is a U.S. citizen; child is unmarried, over twenty-one, residing in the United States, or abroad
   - Petition for Alien Relative, I-130
   - Affidavit of Support, I-864
   - Contract Between Sponsor and Household Member, I-864A, if applicable

4. Sponsor is a U.S. citizen; child is married, over twenty-one, residing in the United States or abroad
   - Petition for Alien Relative, I-130
   - Affidavit of Support, I-864
   - Contract Between Sponsor and Household Member, I-864A, if applicable

5. Sponsor is a permanent resident; child is unmarried, under twenty-one, residing in the United States or abroad
   - Petition for Alien Relative, I-130
   - Affidavit of Support, I-864
   - Contract Between Sponsor and Household Member, I-864A, if applicable

6. Sponsor is a permanent resident; child is unmarried, over twenty-one, residing in the United States or abroad
   - Petition for Alien relative, I-130
   - Affidavit of Support, I-864
   - Contract Between Sponsor and Household Member, I-864A, if applicable

C. Sponsoring a Parent

1. Sponsor is a U.S. citizen, parent is in the United States
   - Petition for Alien Relative, I-130
   - Biographic Information Form for the parent, G-325A
   - Application for Adjustment of Status, I-485
   - Supplement A to Form I-485 Adjustment of Status, if applicable
   - Application for Employment, I-765
   - Affidavit of Support, I-864
   - Contract Between Sponsor and Household Member, I-864A, if applicable
   - Medical Examination I-693
   - Application for Advance parole, Form I-131, if applicable

2. Sponsor is a U.S. citizen, parent is abroad
   - Petition for Alien Relative, I-130
   - Affidavit of Support, I-864
   - Contract Between Sponsor and Household Member, if applicable

D. Sponsor Is a U.S. Citizen, Sponsoring Brother or Sister Living in the United States or Abroad

- Petition for Alien Relative, I-130
- Affidavit of Support, I-864
- Contract Between Sponsor and Household Member, if applicable

E. Orphans

- Application for Advance Processing of Orphan Petition, I-600A
- Petition to Classify Orphan as an Immediate Relative, I-600.

F. Hague Convention Adoptions

- Determination of Suitability to Adopt, I-800A
- Classification of a Child as Immediate Relative, I-800

G. Amerasian

- Petition for Amerasian, Widow(er), or Special Immigrant, I-360
- Affidavit of Financial Support, I-361

H. Widow/Widower of a Deceased U.S. Citizen

- Petition for Amerasian, Widow(er), or Special Immigrant, Form I-360
- Application to Adjust Status, I-485
- Supplement A to Form I-485 Adjustment of Status, if applicable
- Biographic Information G-325A
- Medical Examination I-693
- Application for Employment Authorization I-765
- Intending Immigrant's Affidavit of Support Exemption, Form I-864W
- Application for Advance Parole, I-131, if applicable

I. Battered Spouse or Child of a U.S. Citizen or Permanent Resident

- Petition for Amerasian, Widow(er) or Special Immigrant, Form I-360
- Application for Adjustment of Status I-485, if applicable
- Supplement A to Form — 485 Adjustment of Status, if applicable
- Biographic Information G-325A
- Intending Immigrant's Affidavit of Support Exemption, Form I-864W
- Application for Advance Parole, I-131, if applicable

Appendix B.
Sample Immigration Forms

Note that these forms, current as of April 2008, are for information purposes only. Do not send these to the USCIS. You must obtain new forms from the USCIS.

Department of Homeland Security
U.S. Citizenship and Immigration Services

OMB #1615-0012; Expires 11/30/07

I-130, Petition for Alien Relative

DO NOT WRITE IN THIS BLOCK - FOR USCIS OFFICE ONLY

A#	Action Stamp	Fee Stamp

Section of Law/Visa Category
- [ ] 201(b) Spouse - IR-1/CR-1
- [ ] 201(b) Child - IR-2/CR-2
- [ ] 201(b) Parent - IR-5
- [ ] 203(a)(1) Unm. S or D - F1-1
- [ ] 203(a)(2)(A)Spouse - F2-1
- [ ] 203(a)(2)(A) Child - F2-2
- [ ] 203(a)(2)(B) Unm. S or D - F2-4
- [ ] 203(a)(3) Married S or D - F3-1
- [ ] 203(a)(4) Brother/Sister - F4-1

Petition was filed on: _____ (priority date)
- [ ] Personal Interview
- [ ] Pet. [ ] Ben. " A" File Reviewed
- [ ] Field Investigation
- [ ] 203(a)(2)(A) Resolved
- [ ] Previously Forwarded
- [ ] I-485 Filed Simultaneously
- [ ] 204(g) Resolved
- [ ] 203(g) Resolved

Remarks:

A. Relationship   You are the petitioner. Your relative is the beneficiary.

1. I am filing this petition for my:
[ ] Husband/Wife [ ] Parent [ ] Brother/Sister [ ] Child

2. Are you related by adoption?
[ ] Yes [ ] No

3. Did you gain permanent residence through adoption?
[ ] Yes [ ] No

B. Information about you

1. Name (Family name in CAPS)   (First)   (Middle)

2. Address (Number and Street)   (Apt. No.)

(Town or City)   (State/Country)   (Zip/Postal Code)

3. Place of Birth (Town or City)   (State/Country)

4. Date of Birth

5. Gender
[ ] Male [ ] Female

6. Marital Status
[ ] Married [ ] Widowed [ ] Single [ ] Divorced

7. Other Names Used (including maiden name)

8. Date and Place of Present Marriage (if married)

9. U.S. Social Security (if any)

10. Alien Registration Number

11. Name(s) of Prior Husband(s)/Wive(s)

12. Date(s) Marriage(s) Ended

13. If you are a U.S. citizen, complete the following:

My citizenship was acquired through (check one):
- [ ] Birth in the U.S.
- [ ] Naturalization. Give certificate number and date and place of issuance.
- [ ] Parents. Have you obtained a certificate of citizenship in your own name?
  - [ ] Yes. Give certificate number, date and place of issuance. [ ] No

14. If you are a lawful permanent resident alien, complete the following:

Date and place of admission for or adjustment to lawful permanent residence and class of admission.

14b. Did you gain permanent resident status through marriage to a U.S. citizen or lawful permanent resident?
[ ] Yes [ ] No

C. Information about your relative

1. Name (Family name in CAPS)   (First)   (Middle)

2. Address (Number and Street)   (Apt. No.)

(Town or City)   (State/Country)   (Zip/Postal Code)

3. Place of Birth (Town or City)   (State/Country)

4. Date of Birth

5. Gender
[ ] Male [ ] Female

6. Marital Status
[ ] Married [ ] Widowed [ ] Single [ ] Divorced

7. Other Names Used (including maiden name)

8. Date and Place of Present Marriage (if married)

9. U.S. Social Security (if any)

10. Alien Registration Number

11. Name(s) of Prior Husband(s)/Wive(s)

12. Date(s) Marriage(s) Ended

13. Has your relative ever been in the U.S.? [ ] Yes [ ] No

14. If your relative is currently in the U.S., complete the following:
He or she arrived as a:
(visitor, student, stowaway, without inspection, etc.)

Arrival/Departure Record (I-94)   Date arrived

Date authorized stay expired, or will expire, as shown on Form I-94 or I-95

15. Name and address of present employer (if any)

Date this employment began

16. Has your relative ever been under immigration proceedings?
[ ] No [ ] Yes Where _____ When _____
[ ] Removal [ ] Exclusion/Deportation [ ] Rescission [ ] Judicial Proceedings

INITIAL RECEIPT   RESUBMITTED   RELOCATED: Rec'd ____ Sent ____ COMPLETED: Appv'd ____ Denied ____ Ret'd ____

Form I-130 (Rev. 07/30/07)Y

C. Information about your alien relative (continued)

17. List husband/wife and all children of your relative.

(Name)	(Relationship)	(Date of Birth)	(Country of Birth)

18. Address in the United States where your relative intends to live.

(Street Address)	(Town or City)	(State)

19. Your relative's address abroad. (Include street, city, province and country)   Phone Number (if any)

20. If your relative's native alphabet is other than Roman letters, write his or her name and foreign address in the native alphabet.

(Name)   Address (Include street, city, province and country):

21. If filing for your husband/wife, give last address at which you lived together. (Include street, city, province, if any, and country):

From: To:

22. Complete the information below if your relative is in the United States and will apply for adjustment of status.

Your relative is in the United States and will apply for adjustment of status to that of a lawful permanent resident at the USCIS office in:

If your relative is not eligible for adjustment of status, he or she will apply for a visa abroad at the American consular post in:

(City)	(State)	(City)	(Country)

NOTE: Designation of an American embassy or consulate outside the country of your relative's last residence does not guarantee acceptance for processing by that post. Acceptance is at the discretion of the designated embassy or consulate.

D. Other information

1. If separate petitions are also being submitted for other relatives, give names of each and relationship.

2. Have you ever before filed a petition for this or any other alien? ☐ Yes ☐ No

If "Yes," give name, place and date of filing and result.

WARNING: USCIS investigates claimed relationships and verifies the validity of documents. USCIS seeks criminal prosecutions when family relationships are falsified to obtain visas.

PENALTIES: By law, you may be imprisoned for not more than five years or fined $250,000, or both, for entering into a marriage contract for the purpose of evading any provision of the immigration laws. In addition, you may be fined up to $10,000 and imprisoned for up to five years, or both, for knowlingly and willfully falsifying or concealing a material fact or using any false document in submitting this petition.

YOUR CERTIFICATION: I certify, under penalty of perjury under the laws of the United States of America, that the foregoing is true and correct. Furthermore, I authorize the release of any information from my records that the U.S. Citizenship and Immigration Services needs to determine eligiblity for the benefit that I am seeking.

E. Signature of petitioner.

Date   Phone Number (   )

F. Signature of person preparing this form, if other than the petitioner.

I declare that I prepared this document at the request of the person above and that it is based on all information of which I have any knowledge.

Print Name _____ Signature _____ Date _____

Address _____ **G-28 ID or VOLAG Number, if any.** _____

OMB No. 1615-0015; Exp. 10/31/08

Department of Homeland Security
U.S. Citizenship and Immigration Services

**Form I-140, Immigrant
Petition for Alien Worker**

START HERE - Please type or print in black ink.

	For USCIS Use Only

Part 1. **Information about the person or organization filing this petition.** If an individual is filing, use the top name line. Organizations should use the second line.

Family Name (Last Name)	Given Name (First Name)	Full Middle Name	Returned
			Date
Company or Organization Name			Date
			Resubmitted
Address: (Street Number and Name)		Suite #	Date
Attn:			Date
City	State/Province		Reloc Sent
Country	Zip/Postal Code		Date
IRS Tax #	U.S. Social Security # (if any)	E-Mail Address (if any)	Date
			Reloc Rec'd

Part 2. Petition type.

This petition is being filed for: *(Check one.)*

a. ☐ An alien of extraordinary ability.

b. ☐ An outstanding professor or researcher.

c. ☐ A multinational executive or manager.

d. ☐ A member of the professions holding an advanced degree or an alien of exceptional ability (who is NOT seeking a National Interest Waiver).

e. ☐ A professional (at a minimum, possessing a bachelor's degree or a foreign degree equivalent to a U.S. bachelor's degree) or a skilled worker (requiring at least two years of specialized training or experience).

f. ☐ (Reserved.)

g. ☐ Any other worker (requiring less than two years of training or experience).

h. ☐ Soviet Scientist.

i. ☐ An alien applying for a National Interest Waiver (who IS a member of the professions holding an advanced degree or an alien of exceptional ability).

Date
Date

Classification:
☐ 203(b)(1)(A) Alien of Extraordinary Ability
☐ 203(b)(1)(B) Outstanding Professor or Researcher
☐ 203(b)(1)(C) Multi-National Executive or Manager
☐ 203(b)(2) Member of Professions w/Adv. Degree or Exceptional Ability
☐ 203(b)(3)(A)(i) Skilled Worker
☐ 203(b)(3)(A)(ii) Professional
☐ 203(b)(3)(A)(iii) Other Worker

Certification:
☐ National Interest Waiver (NIW)
☐ Schedule A, Group I
☐ Schedule A, Group II

Part 3. Information about the person you are filing for.

Family Name (Last Name)	Given Name (First Name)	Full Middle Name
Address: (Street Number and Name)		Apt. #
C/O: (In Care Of)		
City	State/Province	
Country	Zip/Postal Code	E-Mail Address (if any)
Daytime Phone # (with area/country codes)	Date of Birth (mm/dd/yyyy)	
City/Town/Village of Birth	State/Province of Birth	Country of Birth
Country of Nationality/Citizenship	A # (if any)	U.S. Social Security # (if any)

Priority Date	**Consulate**

Concurrent Filing:

☐ **I-485 filed concurrently.**

Remarks

Action Block

If in the U.S.

Date of Arrival (mm/dd/yyyy)	I-94 # (Arrival/Departure Document)
Current Nonimmigrant Status	Date Status Expires (mm/dd/yyyy)

To Be Completed by
Attorney or Representative, if any.
☐ Fill in box if G-28 is attached to represent the applicant.

ATTY State License #

Form I-140 (Rev. 10/12/07) Y

Part 4. Processing Information.

1. Please complete the following for the person named in **Part 3**: *(Check one)*

☐ Alien will apply for a visa abroad at the American Embassy or Consulate at:

City   Foreign Country

☐ Alien is in the United States and will apply for adjustment of status to that of lawful permanent resident.

Alien's country of current residence or, if now in the U.S., last permanent residence abroad.

2. If you provided a U.S. address in **Part 3**, print the person's foreign address:

3. If the person's native alphabet is other than Roman letters, write the person's foreign name and address in the native alphabet:

4. Are any other petition(s) or application(s) being filed with this Form I-140?

☐ No   ☐ Yes-(check all that apply)   ☐ Form I-485   ☐ Form I-765

☐ Form I-131   ☐ Other - Attach an explanation.

5. Is the person you are filing for in removal proceedings?   ☐ No   ☐ Yes-Attach an explanation.

6. Has any immigrant visa petition ever been filed by or on behalf of this person?   ☐ No   ☐ Yes-Attach an explanation.

If you answered yes to any of these questions, please provide the case number, office location, date of decision and disposition of the decision on a separate sheet(s) of paper.

Part 5. Additional information about the petitioner.

1. Type of petitioner *(Check one.)*

☐ Employer   ☐ Self   ☐ Other (Explain, e.g., Permanent Resident, U.S. citizen or any other person filing on behalf of the alien.)

2. If a company, give the following:

Type of Business   Date Established *(mm/dd/yyyy)*   Current Number of Employees

Gross Annual Income   Net Annual Income   NAICS Code

DOL/ETA Case Number

3. If an individual, give the following:

Occupation   Annual Income

Part 6. Basic information about the proposed employment.

1. Job Title   **2.** SOC Code

3. Nontechnical Description of Job

4. Address where the person will work if different from address in **Part 1**.

5. Is this a full-time position?   **6.** If the answer to **Number 5** is "No," how many hours per week for the position?

☐ Yes   ☐ No

7. Is this a permanent position?   **8.** Is this a new position?   **9.** Wages per week

☐ Yes   ☐ No   ☐ Yes   ☐ No $

Part 7. Information on spouse and all children of the person for whom you are filing.

List husband/wife and all children related to the individual for whom the petition is being filed. Provide an attachment of additional family members, if needed.

Name *(First/Middle/Last)*	Relationship	Date of Birth *(mm/dd/yyyy)*	Country of Birth

Part 8. Signature.

*Read the information on penalties in the instructions before completing this section. If someone helped you prepare this petition, he or she must complete **Part 9**.*

I certify, under penalty of perjury under the laws of the United States of America, that this petition and the evidence submitted with it are all true and correct. I authorize U.S. Citizenship and Immigration Services to release to other government agencies any information from my USCIS (or former INS) records, if USCIS determines that such action is necessary to determine eligibility for the benefit sought.

Petitioner's Signature   **Daytime Phone Number** *(Area/Country Codes)*   **E-Mail Address**

Print Name   **Date** *(mm/dd/yyyy)*

NOTE: *If you do not fully complete this form or fail to submit the required documents listed in the instructions, a final decision on your petition may be delayed or the petition may be denied.*

Part 9. Signature of person preparing form, if other than above.   *(Sign below.)*

I declare that I prepared this petition at the request of the above person and it is based on all information of which I have knowledge.

Attorney or Representative: In the event of a Request for Evidence (RFE), may the USCIS contact you by Fax or E-mail? ☐ Yes ☐ No

Signature   **Print Name**   **Date** *(mm/dd/yyyy)*

Firm Name and Address

Daytime Phone Number *(Area/Country Codes)*   **Fax Number** *(Area/Country Codes)*   **E-Mail Address**

OMB No. 1615-0009; Expires 05/31/08

Department of Homeland Security
U.S. Citizenship and Immigration Services

I-129, Petition for a
Nonimmigrant Worker

START HERE - Please type or print in black ink.

For USCIS Use Only

Part 1. Information about the employer filing this petition. *If the employer is an individual, complete **Number 1**. Organizations should complete **Number 2**.*

1. Family Name *(Last Name)*   Given Name *(First Name)*

Full Middle Name   Telephone No. w/Area Code
(   )

2. Company or Organization Name   Telephone No. w/Area Code
(   )

Mailing Address: *(Street Number and Name)*   Suite #

C/O: *(In Care Of)*

City   State/Province

Country   Zip/Postal Code   E-Mail Address *(If Any)*

Federal Employer Identification #   U.S. Social Security #   Individual Tax #

Returned	Receipt
Date	
Date	
Resubmitted	
Date	
Date	
Reloc Sent	
Date	
Date	
Reloc Rec'd	
Date	
Date	

☐ Petitioner Interviewed on ____

☐ Beneficiary Interviewed on ____

Part 2. Information about this petition. *(See instructions for fee information.)*

1. Requested Nonimmigrant Classification. *(Write classification symbol):*

2. Basis for Classification *(Check one):*

a. ☐ New employment (including new employer filing H-1B extension).

b. ☐ Continuation of previously approved employment without change with the same employer.

c. ☐ Change in previously approved employment.

d. ☐ New concurrent employment.

e. ☐ Change of employer.

f. ☐ Amended petition.

3. If you checked **Box 2b, 2c, 2d, 2e,** or **2f,** give the petition receipt number.

4. Prior Petition. If the beneficiary is in the U.S. as a nonimmigrant and is applying to change and/or extend his or her status, give the prior petition or application receipt #:

5. Requested Action. *(Check one):*

a. ☐ Notify the office in **Part 4** so the person(s) can obtain a visa or be admitted. (**NOTE:** *a petition is not required for an E-1, E-2 or R visa*).

b. ☐ Change the person(s)' status and extend their stay since the person(s) are all now in the U.S. in another status *(see instructions for limitations).* This is available only where you check "New Employment" in **Item 2**, above.

c. ☐ Extend the stay of the person(s) since they now hold this status.

d. ☐ Amend the stay of the person(s) since they now hold this status.

e. ☐ Extend the status of a nonimmigrant classification based on a Free Trade Agreement. *(See Free Trade Supplement for TN and H1B1 to Form I-129).*

f. ☐ Change status to a nonimmigrant classification based on a Free Trade Agreement. *(See Free Trade Supplement for TN and H1B1 to Form I-129).*

6. Total number of workers in petition *(See instructions relating to when more than one worker can be included):*

Class: _____
# of Workers: _____
Priority Number: _____
Validity Dates: _____
From: _____
To: _____

☐ **Classification Approved**
☐ Consulate/POE/PFI Notified
☐ At _____
☐ Extension Granted
☐ COS/Extension Granted

Partial Approval *(explain)*

Action Block

To Be Completed by
Attorney or Representative, if any.
☐ Fill in box if G-28 is attached to represent the applicant.

ATTY State License #

Part 3. Information about the person(s) you are filing for. *Complete the blocks below. Use the continuation sheet to name each person included in this petition.*

1. If an Entertainment Group, Give the Group Name

Family Name *(Last Name)*	Given Name *(First Name)*	Full Middle Name

All Other Names Used *(include maiden name and names from all previous marriages)*

Date of Birth *(mm/dd/yyyy)*	U.S. Social Security # *(if any)*	A # *(if any)*

Country of Birth	Province of Birth	Country of Citizenship

2. If in the United States, Complete the Following:

Date of Last Arrival *(mm/dd/yyyy)*	I-94 # *(Arrival/Departure Document)*	Current Nonimmigrant Status

Date Status Expires *(mm/dd/yyyy)*	Passport Number	Date Passport Issued *(mm/dd/yyyy)*	Date Passport Expires *(mm/dd/yyyy)*

Current U.S. Address

Part 4. Processing Information.

1. If the person named in **Part 3** is outside the United States or a requested extension of stay or change of status cannot be granted, give the U.S. consulate or inspection facility you want notified if this petition is approved.

   Type of Office *(Check one)*: ☐ Consulate   ☐ Pre-flight inspection   ☐ Port of Entry

Office Address *(City)*	U.S. State or Foreign Country

   Person's Foreign Address

2. Does each person in this petition have a valid passport?

   ☐ Not required to have passport   ☐ No - explain on separate paper   ☐ Yes

3. Are you filing any other petitions with this one?   ☐ No   ☐ Yes - How many?

4. Are applications for replacement/initial I-94s being filed with this petition?   ☐ No   ☐ Yes - How many?

5. Are applications by dependents being filed with this petition?   ☐ No   ☐ Yes - How many?

6. Is any person in this petition in removal proceedings?   ☐ No   ☐ Yes - explain on separate paper

Part 4. Processing Information.   *(Continued)*

7. Have you ever filed an immigrant petition for any person in this petition?   ☐ No   ☐ Yes - explain on separate paper

8. If you indicated you were filing a new petition in **Part 2**, within the past seven years has any person in this petition:

   a. Ever been given the classification you are now requesting?   ☐ No   ☐ Yes - explain on separate paper

   b. Ever been denied the classification you are now requesting?   ☐ No   ☐ Yes - explain on separate paper

9. Have you ever previously filed a petition for this person?   ☐ No   ☐ Yes - explain on separate paper

10. If you are filing for an entertainment group, has any person in this petition not been with the group for at least one year?   ☐ No   ☐ Yes - explain on separate paper

Part 5. Basic information about the proposed employment and employer. *Attach the supplement relating to the classification you are requesting.*

1. Job Title

2. Nontechnical Job Description

3. LCA Case Number

4. NAICS Code

5. Address where the person(s) will work if different from address in **Part 1**. *(Street number and name, city/town, state, zip code)*

6. Is this a full-time position?

   ☐ No - Hours per week: ☐ Yes - Wages per week or per year:

7. Other Compensation *(Explain)*

8. Dates of intended employment *(mm/dd/yyyy)*:

   From: To:

9. Type of Petitioner - *Check one*:

   ☐ U.S. citizen or permanent resident   ☐ Organization   ☐ Other - explain on separate paper

10. Type of Business

11. Year Established

12. Current Number of Employees

13. Gross Annual Income

14. Net Annual Income

Part 6. Signature. *Read the information on penalties in the instructions before completing this section.*

I certify, under penalty of perjury under the laws of the United States of America, that this petition and the evidence submitted with it is all true and correct. If filing this on behalf of an organization, I certify that I am empowered to do so by that organization. If this petition is to extend a prior petition, I certify that the proposed employment is under the same terms and conditions as stated in the prior approved petition. I authorize the release of any information from my records, or from the petitioning organization's records that U.S. Citizenship and Immigration Services needs to determine eligibility for the benefit being sought.

Signature

Daytime Phone Number *(Area/Country Code)*

( )

Print Name

Date *(mm/dd/yyyy)*

NOTE: If you do not completely fill out this form and the required supplement, or fail to submit required documents listed in the instructions, the person(s) filed for may not be found eligible for the requested benefit and this petition may be denied.

Part 7. Signature of person preparing form, if other than above.

I declare that I prepared this petition at the request of the above person and it is based on all information of which I have any knowledge.

Signature

Daytime Phone Number *(Area/Country Code)*

( )

Print Name

Date *(mm/dd/yyyy)*

Firm Name and Address

OMB No. 1615-0009; Expires 05/31/08

Department of Homeland Security
U.S. Citizenship and Immigration Services

E Classification Supplement
to Form I-129

1. Name of person or organization filing petition:

2. Name of person you are filing for:

3. Classification sought *(Check one)*:

☐ E-1 Treaty trader ☐ E-2 Treaty investor

4. Name of country signatory to treaty with U.S.:

Section 1.   Information about the employer outside the United States (if any)

Employer's Name

Total Number of Employees

Employer's Address *(Street number and name, city/town, state/province, zip/postal code)*

Principal Product, Merchandise or Service

Employee's Position - Title, duties and number of years employed

Section 2.   Additional information about the U.S. Employer

1. The U.S. company is to the company outside the United States *(Check one)*:

☐ Parent ☐ Branch ☐ Subsidiary ☐ Affiliate ☐ Joint Venture

2. Date and Place of Incorporation or Establishment in the United States

3. Nationality of Ownership *(Individual or Corporate)*

Name *(First/Middle/Last)*	Nationality	Immigration Status	% Ownership

4. Assets

5. Net Worth

6. Total Annual Income

7. Staff in the United States

   a. How many executive and/or managerial employees does petitioner have who are nationals of the treaty country in either E or L status?

   b. How many specialized qualifications or knowledge persons does the petitioner have who are nationals of the treaty country in either E or L status?

   c. Provide the total number of employees in executive or managerial positions in the United States.

   d. Provide the total number of specialized qualifications or knowledge persons positions in the United States.

8. Total number of employees the alien would supervise; or describe the nature of the specialized skills essential to the U.S. company.

Section 3.   Complete if filing for an E-1 Treaty Trader

1. Total Annual Gross Trade/Business of the U.S. company

2. For Year Ending *(yyyy)*

3. Percent of total gross trade between the United States and the country of which the treaty trader organization is a national.

Section 4.   Complete if filing for an E-2 Treaty Investor

Total Investment: Cash

Equipment

Other

Inventory

Premises

Total

OMB No.1615-0009; Expires 05/31/08

Department of Homeland Security
U.S. Citizenship and Immigration Services

Nonimmigrant Classification Based on Free Trade Agreement-Supplement to Form I-129

---

1. Name of person or organization filing petition:

2. Name of person you are filing for:

3. Employer is a *(Check one)*:

☐ U.S. Employer   ☐ Foreign Employer

4. If Foreign Employer, name the foreign country.

Section 1. Information about requested extension or change *(See instructions attached to this form.)*

1. This is a request for an extension of Free Trade status based on *(Check one)*:   **Or**

  a. ☐ Free Trade, Canada (TN)

  b. ☐ Free Trade, Chile (H1B1)

  c. ☐ Free Trade, Mexico (TN)

  d. ☐ Free Trade, Singapore (H1B1)

  e. ☐ Free Trade, Other

  f. ☐ I am an H-1B1 Free Trade Nonimmigrant from Chile or Singapore and this is my sixth consecutive request for an extension.

2. This is a request for a change of nonimmigrant status to *(Check one)*:

  a. ☐ Free Trade, Canada (TN)

  b. ☐ Free Trade, Chile (H1B1)

  c. ☐ Free Trade, Mexico (TN)

  d. ☐ Free Trade, Singapore (H1B1)

  e. ☐ Free Trade, Other

  f. ☐ I am an H-1B1 Free Trade Nonimmigrant from Chile or Singapore and this is my first request for a change of status to H-1B1 within the past six years.

Part 2. Signature. *Read the information on penalties in the instructions before completing this section.*

I certify, under penalty of perjury under the laws of the United States of America, that this petition and the evidence submitted with it is all true and correct. If filing this on behalf of an organization, I certify that I am empowered to do so by that organization. If this petition is to extend a prior petition, I certify that the proposed employment is under the same terms and conditions as stated in the prior approved petition. I authorize the release of any information from my records, or from the petitioning organization's records, that the U.S. Citizenship and Immigration Services needs to determine eligibility for the benefit being sought.

Signature

Daytime Phone Number *(Area/Country Code)*
( )

Print Name

Date *(mm/dd/yyyy)*

NOTE: If you do not completely fill out this form and the required supplement, or fail to submit required documents listed in the instructions, the person(s) filed for may not be found eligible for the requested benefit and this petition may be denied.

Part 3. Signature of person preparing form, if other than above.

I declare that I prepared this petition at the request of the above person and it is based on all information of which I have any knowledge.

Signature

Daytime Phone Number *(Area/Country Code)*
( )

Print Name

Date *(mm/dd/yyyy)*

Firm Name and Address

OMB No.1615-0009; Expires 05/31/08

H Classification Supplement
to Form I-129

Department of Homeland Security
U.S. Citizenship and Immigration Services

1. Name of person or organization filing petition:

2. Name of person or total number of workers or trainees you are filing for:

3. List the alien's and any dependent family member's prior periods of stay in H classification in the United States for the last six years. Be sure to list only those periods in which the alien and/or family members were actually in the United States in an H classification. **NOTE:** Submit photocopies of Forms I-94, I-797 and/or other USCIS issued documents noting these periods of stay in the H classification. If more space is needed, attach an additional sheet(s). (If applying for H-2A/H-2B classification skip this item.)

Subject's Name	Period of Stay (mm/dd/yyyy)		Subject's Name	Period of Stay (mm/dd/yyyy)	
	From:	To:		From:	To:
	From:	To:		From:	To:

4. Classification sought (*Check one*):

☐ H-1B1 Specialty occupation

☐ H-1B2 Exceptional services relating to a cooperative research and development project administered by the U.S. Department of Defense (DOD)

☐ H-1B3 Fashion model of national or international acclaim

☐ H-2A Agricultural worker

☐ H-2B Non-agricultural worker

☐ H-3 Trainee

☐ H-3 Special education exchange visitor program

Section 1. Complete this section if filing for H-1B classification.

1. Describe the proposed duties

2. Alien's present occupation and summary of prior work experience

Statement for H-1B specialty occupations only:

By filing this petition, I agree to the terms of the labor condition application for the duration of the alien's authorized period of stay for H-1B employment.

Petitioner's Signature	Print or Type Name	Date (mm/dd/yyyy)

Statement for H-1B specialty occupations and U.S. Department of Defense projects:

As an authorized official of the employer, I certify that the employer will be liable for the reasonable costs of return transportation of the alien abroad if the alien is dismissed from employment by the employer before the end of the period of authorized stay.

Signature of Authorized Official of Employer	Print or Type Name	Date (mm/dd/yyyy)

Statement for H-1B U.S. Department of Defense projects only:

I certify that the alien will be working on a cooperative research and development project or a co-production project under a reciprocal government-to-government agreement administered by the U.S. Department of Defense.

DOD Project Manager's Signature	Print or Type Name	Date (mm/dd/yyyy)

Section 2. Complete this section if filing for H-2A or H-2B classification.

1. Employment is: *(Check one)*

    a. ☐ Seasonal   **c.** ☐ Intermittent

    b. ☐ Peakload   **d.** ☐ One-time occurence

2. Temporary need is: *(Check one)*

    a. ☐ Unpredictable   **c.** ☐ Recurrent annually

    b. ☐ Periodic

3. Explain your temporary need for the alien's services *(attach a separate sheet(s) paper if additional space is needed).*

Section 3. Complete this section if filing for H-2A classification.

The petitioner and each employer consent to allow government access to the site where the labor is being performed for the purpose of determining compliance with H-2A requirements. The petitioner further agrees to notify USCIS in the manner and within the time frame specified if an H-2A worker absconds, or if the authorized employment ends more than five days before the relating certification document expires, and pay liquidated damages of ten dollars ($10.00) for each instance where it cannot demonstrate compliance with this notification requirement. The petitioner agrees also to pay liquidated damages of two hundred dollars ($200.00) for each instance where it cannot be demonstrated that the H-2A worker either departed the United States or obtained authorized status during the period of admission or within five days of early termination, whichever comes first.

The petitioner must execute **Part A.** If the petitioner is the employer's agent, the employer must execute **Part B**. If there are joint employers, they must each execute **Part C.**

Part A. Petitioner:

By filing this petition, I agree to the conditions of H-2A employment and agree to the notice requirements and limited liabilities defined in 8 CFR 214.2(h)(3)(vi).

Petitioner's Signature	Print or Type Name	Date *(mm/dd/yyyy)*

Part B. Employer who is not the petitioner:

I certify that I have authorized the party filing this petition to act as my agent in this regard. I assume full responsibility for all representations made by this agent on my behalf and agree to the conditions of H-2A eligibility

Employer's Signature	Print or Type Name	Date *(mm/dd/yyyy)*

Part C. Joint Employers:

I agree to the conditions of H-2A eligibility.

Joint Employer's Signature(s)	Print or Type Name	Date *(mm/dd/yyyy)*

Joint Employer's Signature(s)	Print or Type Name	Date *(mm/dd/yyyy)*

Joint Employer's Signature(s)	Print or Type Name	Date *(mm/dd/yyyy)*

Joint Employer's Signature(s)	Print or Type Name	Date *(mm/dd/yyyy)*

Section 4. Complete this section if filing for H-3 classification.

1. If you answer "yes" to any of the following questions, attach a full explanation.

    a. Is the training you intend to provide, or similar training, available in the alien's country? ☐ No ☐ Yes

    b. Will the training benefit the alien in pursuing a career abroad? ☐ No ☐ Yes

    c. Does the training involve productive employment incidental to training? ☐ No ☐ Yes

    d. Does the alien already have skills related to the training? ☐ No ☐ Yes

    e. Is this training an effort to overcome a labor shortage? ☐ No ☐ Yes

    f. Do you intend to employ the alien abroad at the end of this training? ☐ No ☐ Yes

2. If you do not intend to employ this person abroad at the end of this training, explain why you wish to incur the cost of providing this training and your expected return from this training.

OMB No.1615-0009; Expires 05/31/08

Department of Homeland Security
U.S. Citizenship and Immigration Services

H-1B Data Collection and
Filing Fee Exemption Supplement

Petitioner's Name [   ]

Part A. General Information.

1. **Employer Information** - *(check all items that apply)*

   a. Is the petitioner a dependent employer?   ☐ No   ☐ Yes

   b. Has the petitioner ever been found to be a willful violator?   ☐ No   ☐ Yes

   c. Is the beneficiary an exempt H-1B nonimmigrant?   ☐ No   ☐ Yes

   　　1. If yes, is it because the beneficiary's annual rate of pay is equal to at least $60,000?   ☐ No   ☐ Yes

   　　2. Or is it because the beneficiary has a master's or higher degree in a speciality related to the employment?   ☐ No   ☐ Yes

2. Beneficiary's Last Name　　　　　　First Name　　　　　　　　Middle Name

   [   ]   [   ]   [   ]

   Attention To or In Care Of　　　　Current Residential Address - Street Number and Name　　　Apt. #

   [   ]   [   ]   [   ]

   City　　　　　　　　　　　　　State　　　　　　　　　　　　Zip/Postal Code

   [   ]   [   ]   [   ]

   U.S. Social Security # *(If Any)*　　I-94 # *(Arrival/Departure Document)*　　Previous Receipt # *(If Any)*

   [   ]   [   ]   [   ]

3. **Beneficiary's Highest Level of Education.** Please check one box below.

   ☐ NO DIPLOMA

   ☐ HIGH SCHOOL GRADUATE - high school
   　 DIPLOMA or the equivalent (example: GED)

   ☐ Some college credit, but less than one year

   ☐ One or more years of college, no degree

   ☐ Associate's degree *(for example: AA, AS)*

   ☐ Bachelor's degree *(for example: BA, AB, BS)*

   ☐ Master's degree *(for example: MA, MS, MEng, MEd, MSW, MBA)*

   ☐ Professional degree *(for example: MD, DDS, DVM, LLB, JD)*

   ☐ Doctorate degree *(for example: PhD, EdD)*

4. Major/Primary Field of Study.

   [ ]

5. Has the beneficiary of this petition earned a master's or higher degree from a U.S. institution of higher education as defined in 20 U.S.C. section 1001(a)?

   ☐ No   ☐ Yes (If "Yes" provide the following information):

   Name of the U.S. institution of higher education　　Date Degree Awarded　　Type of U.S. Degree

   [   ]   [   ]   [   ]

   Address of the U.S. institution of higher education

   [   ]

6. Rate of Pay Per Year.　　　　7. LCA Code.　　　　8. NAICS Code.

   [   ]   [ ][ ][ ]   [ ][ ][ ][ ][ ][ ]

Part B. Fee Exemption and/or Determination

In order for USCIS to determine if you must pay the additional $1,500 or $750 fee, please answer all of the following questions:

1.　☐ Yes   ☐ No   Are you an institution of higher education as defined in the Higher Education Act of 1965, section 101 (a), 20 U.S.C. section 1001(a)?

2.　☐ Yes   ☐ No   Are you a nonprofit organization or entity related to or affiliated with an institution of higher education, as such institutions of higher education are defined in the Higher Education Act of 1965, section 101 (a), 20 U.S.C. section 1001(a)?

3. ☐ Yes ☐ No Are you a nonprofit research organization or a governmental research organization, as defined in 8 CFR 214.2(h)(19)(iii)(C)?

4. ☐ Yes ☐ No Is this the second or subsequent request for an extension of stay that you have filed for this alien?

5. ☐ Yes ☐ No Is this an amended petition that does not contain any request for extensions of stay?

6. ☐ Yes ☐ No Are you filing this petition in order to correct a USCIS error?

7. ☐ Yes ☐ No Is the petitioner a primary or secondary education institution?

8. ☐ Yes ☐ No Is the petitioner a non-profit entity that engages in an established curriculum-related clinical training of students registered at such an institution?

If you answered "Yes" to any of the questions above, then you are required to submit the fee for your H-1B Form I-129 petition, which is $320. If you answered "No" to all questions, please answer Question 9.

9. ☐ Yes ☐ No Do you currently employ a total of no more than 25 full-time equivalent employees in the United States, including any affiliate or subsidiary of your company?

If you answered "Yes" to Question 9 above, then you are required to pay an additional fee of $750. If you answered "No", then you are required to pay an additional fee of $1,500.

NOTE: On or after March 8, 2005, a U.S. employer seeking initial approval of H-1B or L nonimmigrant status for a beneficiary, or seeking approval to employ an H-1B or L nonimmigrant currently working for another U.S. employer, must submit an additional $500 fee. This additional $500 Fraud Prevention and Detection fee was mandated by the provisions of the H-1B Visa Reform Act of 2004. **There is no exemption from this fee.**

Part C. Numerical Limitation Exemption Information.

1. ☐ Yes ☐ No Are you an institution of higher education as defined in the Higher Education Act of 1965, section 101 (a), 20 U.S.C. section 1001(a)?

2. ☐ Yes ☐ No Are you a nonprofit organization or entity related to or affiliated with an institution of higher education, as such institutions of higher education as defined in the Higher Education Act of 1965, section 101(a), 20 U.S.C. section 1001(a)?

3. ☐ Yes ☐ No Are you a nonprofit research organization or a governmental research organization, as defined in 8 CFR 214.2(h)(19)(iii)(C)?

4. ☐ Yes ☐ No Is the beneficiary of this petition a J-1 nonimmigrant alien who received a waiver of the two-year foreign residency requirement described in section 214 (l)(1)(B) or (C) of the Act?

5. ☐ Yes ☐ No Has the beneficiary of this petition been previously granted status as an H-1B nonimmigrant in the past 6 years and not left the United States for more than one year after attaining such status?

6. ☐ Yes ☐ No If the petition is to request a change of employer, did the beneficiary previously work as an H-1B for an institution of higher education, an entity related to or affiliated with an institution of higher education, or a nonprofit research organization or governmental research institution defined in questions 1, 2 and 3 of Part C of this form?

7. ☐ Yes ☐ No Has the beneficiary of this petition earned a master's or higher degree from a U.S. institution of higher education, as defined in the Higher Education Act of 1965, section 101(a), 20 U.S.C. section 1001(a)?

I certify under penalty of perjury, under the laws of the United States of America, that this attachment and the evidence submitted with it is true and correct. If filing this on behalf of an organization or entity, I certify that I am empowered to do so by that organization or entity. I authorize the release of any information from my records, or from the petitioning organization or entity's records, that U.S. Citizenship and Immigration Services may need to determine eligibility for the exemption being sought.

Certification.

Signature	Print Name

Title	Date *(mm/dd/yyyy)*

OMB No.1615-0009; Expires 05/31/08

Department of Homeland Security
U.S. Citizenship and Immigration Services

L Classification Supplement
to Form I-129

---

1. Name of person or organization filing petition:

2. Name of person you are filing for:

3. This petition is *(Check one)*:

    a. ☐ An individual petition   **b.** ☐ A blanket petition

---

Section 1. Complete this section if filing for an individual petition.

1. Classification sought *(Check one)*:

    a. ☐ L-1A manager or executive   **b.** ☐ L-1B specialized knowledge

2. List the alien's and any dependent family member's prior periods of stay in an H or L classification in the United States for the last seven years. Be sure to list only those periods in which the alien and/or family members were actually in the U.S. in an H or L classification. **NOTE:** Submit photocopies of Forms I-94, I-797 and/or other USCIS issued documents noting these periods of stay in the H or L classification. If more space is needed, attach an additional sheet(s).

Subject's Name	Period of Stay *(mm/dd/yyyy)*	
	From:	To:
	From:	To:
	From:	To:
	From:	To:
	From:	To:

3. Name of employer abroad

4. Address of employer abroad *(Street number and name, city/town, state/province, zip/postal code)*

5. Dates of alien's employment with this employer. Explain any interruptions in employment.

Dates of Employment *(mm/dd/yyyy)*	Explanation of Interruptions
From: To:	
From: To:	
From: To:	

6. Description of the alien's duties for the past three years.

7. Description of the alien's proposed duties in the United States.

8. Summary of the alien's education and work experience.

1. Name of person or organization filing petition:

2. Name of person you are filing for:

Section 1. Complete this section if filing for an individual petition. *(Continued)*

9. The U.S. company is to the company abroad: *(Check one)*

   a. ☐ Parent   b. ☐ Branch   c. ☐ Subsidiary   d. ☐ Affiliate   e. ☐ Joint Venture

10. Describe the stock ownership and managerial control of each company. Provide the U.S. Tax Code Number for each company.

Company stock ownership and managerial control of each company	U.S. Tax Code Number

11. Do the companies currently have the same qualifying relationship as they did during the one-year period of the alien's employment with the company abroad?   ☐ Yes   ☐ No *(Attach explanation)*

12. Is the alien coming to the United States to open a new office?   ☐ Yes *(Attach explanation)*   ☐ No

13. If you are seeking L-1B specialized knowledge status for an individual, answer the following question:

   Will the beneficiary be stationed primarily offsite (at the worksite of an employer other than the petitioner or its affiliate, subsidiary, or parent)?   ☐ Yes   ☐ No

   If you answered "Yes" to the preceding question, describe how and by whom the beneficiary's work will be controlled and supervised. Include a description of the amount of time each supervisor is expected to control and supervise the work. Use an attachment if needed.

   If you answered "Yes" to the preceding question, also describe the reasons why placement at another worksite outside the petitioner, subsidiary or parent is needed. Include a description of how the beneficiary's duties at another worksite relate to the need for the specialized knowledge he or she possesses. Use an attachment if needed.

Section 2. Complete this section if filing a blanket petition.

List all U.S. and foreign parent, branches, subsidiaries and affiliates included in this petition. *(Attach a separate sheet(s) of paper if additional space is needed.)*

Name and Address	Relationship

Section 3. Fraud Prevention and Detection Fee.

As of **March 8, 2005**, a U.S. employer seeking initial approval of L nonimmigrant status for a beneficiary, or seeking approval to employ an L nonimmigrant currently working for another U.S. employer, must submit an additional **$500.00** fee. This additional **$500.00** Fraud Prevention and Detection fee was mandated by the provisions of the H-1B Visa Reform Act of 2004. **There is no exemption from this fee.** You must include payment of this **$500.00** fee with your submission of this form. Failure to submit the fee when required will result in rejection or denial of your submission.

OMB No.1615-0009; Expires 05/31/08

Department of Homeland Security
U.S. Citizenship and Immigration Services

O and P Classifications
Supplement to Form I-129

1. **Name of person or organization filing petition:**

2. **Name of person or group or total number of workers you are filing for:**

3. **Classification sought** *(Check one)*:

   a. ☐ O-1A Alien of extraordinary ability in sciences, education, business or athletics (not including the arts, motion picture or television industry.)

   b. ☐ O-1B Alien of extraordinary ability in the arts or extraordinary achievement in the motion picture or television industry.

   c. ☐ O-2 Accompanying alien who is coming to the U.S. to assist in the performance of the O-1.

   d. ☐ P-1 Athletic/Entertainment group.

   e. ☐ P-1S Essential Support Personnel for P-1.

   f. ☐ P-2 Artist or entertainer for reciprocal exchange program.

   g. ☐ P-2S Essential Support Personnel for P-2.

   h. ☐ P-3 Artist/Entertainer coming to the United States to perform, teach or coach under a program that is culturally unique.

   i. ☐ P-3S Essential Support Personnel for P-3.

4. Explain the nature of the event

5. Describe the duties to be performed

6. If filing for an O-2 or P support alien, list dates of the alien's prior experience with the O-1 or P alien

7. Have you obtained the required written consultation(s)?   ☐ Yes - Attached   ☐ No - Copy of request attached

   If not, give the following information about the organization(s) to which you have sent a duplicate of this petition.

O-1 Extraordinary Ability

Name of Recognized Peer Group	Daytime Telephone # *(Area/Country Code)* ( )
Complete Address	Date Sent *(mm/dd/yyyy)*

O-1 Extraordinary achievement in motion pictures or television

Name of Labor Organization	Daytime Telephone # *(Area/Country Code)* ( )
Complete Address	Date Sent *(mm/dd/yyyy)*
Name of Management Organization	Daytime Telephone # *(Area/Country Code)* ( )
Complete Address	Date sent *(mm/dd/yyyy)*

O-2 or P alien

Name of Labor Organization	Daytime Telephone # *(Area/Country Code)* ( )
Complete Address	Date Sent *(mm/dd/yyyy)*

OMB No.1615-0009; Expires 05/31/08

Q-1 and R-1 Classifications
Supplement to Form I-129

Department of Homeland Security
U.S. Citizenship and Immigration Services

1. Name of person or organization filing petition:	2. Name of person you are filing for:

Section 1. Complete this section if you are filing for a Q-1 international cultural exchange alien.

I hereby certify that the participant(s) in the international cultural exchange program:

- Is at least 18 years of age,
- Is qualified to perform the service or labor or receive the type of training stated in the petition,
- Has the ability to communicate effectively about the cultural attributes of his or her country of nationality to the American public, and
- Has resided and been physically present outside the United States for the immediate prior year, if he or she was previously admitted as a Q-1.

I also certify that I will offer the alien(s) the same wages and working conditions comparable to those accorded local domestic workers similarly employed.

Petitioner's signature   **Date** *(mm/dd/yyyy)*

Section 2. Complete this section if you are filing for an R-1 religious worker.

1. List the alien's and any dependent family member's prior periods of stay in R classification in the United States for the last six years. Be sure to list only those periods in which the alien and/or family members were actually in the United States in an R classification. **NOTE:** Submit photocopies of Forms I-94, I-797 and/or other USCIS issued documents noting these periods of stay in the R classification. If more space is needed, attach an additional sheet(s).

Subject's Name	Period of Stay *(mm/dd/yyyy)*		Subject's Name	Period of Stay *(mm/dd/yyyy)*	
	From:	To:		From:	To:
	From:	To:		From:	To:
	From:	To:		From:	To:

2. Describe the alien's proposed duties in the United States.

3. Describe the alien's qualifications for the vocation or occupation.

4. Description of the relationship between the religious organization in the United States and the organization abroad of which the alien was a member.

Attachment - 1

Attach to Form I-129 when more than one person is included in the petition. *(List each person separately. Do not include the person you named on the Form I-129.)*

Family Name *(Last Name)*   Given Name *(First Name)*   Full Middle Name   Date of Birth *mm/dd/yyyy*

Country of Birth   Country of Citizenship   U.S. Social Security # *(if any)*   A # *(if any)*

IF IN THE U.S.

Date of Arrival *(mm/dd/yyyy)*   I-94 # (Arrival/Departure Document)   Current Nonimmigrant Status   Date Status Expires *(mm/dd/yyyy)*

Country Where Passport Issued   Date Passport Expires *(mm/dd/yyyy)*   Date Started With Group *(mm/dd/yyyy)*

Family Name *(Last Name)*   Given Name *(First Name)*   Full Middle Name   Date of Birth *mm/dd/yyyy*

Country of Birth   Country of Citizenship   U.S. Social Security # *(if any)*   A # *(if any)*

IF IN THE U.S.

Date of Arrival *(mm/dd/yyyy)*   I-94 # (Arrival/Departure Document)   Current Nonimmigrant Status   Date Status Expires *(mm/dd/yyyy)*

Country Where Passport Issued   Date Passport Expires *(mm/dd/yyyy)*   Date Started With Group *(mm/dd/yyyy)*

Family Name *(Last Name)*   Given Name *(First Name)*   Full Middle Name   Date of Birth *mm/dd/yyyy*

Country of Birth   Country of Citizenship   U.S. Social Security # *(if any)*   A # *(if any)*

IF IN THE U.S.

Date of Arrival *(mm/dd/yyyy)*   I-94 # (Arrival/Departure Document)   Current Nonimmigrant Status   Date Status Expires *(mm/dd/yyyy)*

Country Where Passport Issued   Date Passport Expires *(mm/dd/yyyy)*   Date Started With Group *(mm/dd/yyyy)*

Family Name *(Last Name)*   Given Name *(First Name)*   Full Middle Name   Date of Birth *mm/dd/yyyy*

Country of Birth   Country of Citizenship   U.S. Social Security # *(if any)*   A # *(if any)*

IF IN THE U.S.

Date of Arrival *(mm/dd/yyyy)*   I-94 # (Arrival/Departure Document)   Current Nonimmigrant Status   Date Status Expires *(mm/dd/yyyy)*

Country Where Passport Issued   Date Passport Expires *(mm/dd/yyyy)*   Date Started With Group *(mm/dd/yyyy)*

OMB No. 1615-0023; Expires 09/30/08

Department of Homeland Security
U.S. Citizenship and Immigration Services

I-485, Application to Register
Permanent Residence or Adjust Status

START HERE - Please type or print in black ink.	For USCIS Use Only

Part 1. Information about you.

Family Name	Given Name	Middle Name

Address- C/O

Street Number and Name		Apt. #

City

State	Zip Code

Date of Birth (*mm/dd/yyyy*)	Country of Birth:
	Country of Citizenship/Nationality:

U.S. Social Security #	A # (*if any*)

Date of Last Arrival (*mm/dd/yyyy*)	I-94 #

Current USCIS Status	Expires on (*mm/dd/yyyy*)

For USCIS Use Only

Returned	Receipt

Resubmitted

Reloc Sent

Reloc Rec'd

Applicant Interviewed

Part 2. Application type. (*Check one.*)

I am applying for an adjustment to permanent resident status because:

a. ☐ an immigrant petition giving me an immediately available immigrant visa number has been approved. (Attach a copy of the approval notice, or a relative, special immigrant juvenile or special immigrant military visa petition filed with this application that will give you an immediately available visa number, if approved.)

b. ☐ my spouse or parent applied for adjustment of status or was granted lawful permanent residence in an immigrant visa category that allows derivative status for spouses and children.

c. ☐ I entered as a K-1 fiancé(e) of a United States citizen whom I married within 90 days of entry, or I am the K-2 child of such a fiancé(e). (Attach a copy of the fiancé(e) petition approval notice and the marriage certificate).

d. ☐ I was granted asylum or derivative asylum status as the spouse or child of a person granted asylum and am eligible for adjustment.

e. ☐ I am a native or citizen of Cuba admitted or paroled into the United States after January 1, 1959, and thereafter have been physically present in the United States for at least one year.

f. ☐ I am the husband, wife or minor unmarried child of a Cuban described above in (e) and I am residing with that person, and was admitted or paroled into the United States after January 1, 1959, and thereafter have been physically present in the United States for at least one year.

g. ☐ I have continuously resided in the United States since before January 1, 1972.

h. ☐ Other basis of eligibility. Explain (for example, I was admitted as a refugee, my status has not been terminated, and I have been physically present in the U.S. for one year after admission). If additional space is needed, use a separate piece of paper.

I am already a permanent resident and am applying to have the date I was granted permanent residence adjusted to the date I originally arrived in the United States as a nonimmigrant or parolee, or as of May 2, 1964, whichever date is later, and: (*Check one.*)

i. ☐ I am a native or citizen of Cuba and meet the description in (e) above.

j. ☐ I am the husband, wife or minor unmarried child of a Cuban, and meet the description in (f) above.

Section of Law
☐ Sec. 209(b), INA
☐ Sec. 13, Act of 9/11/57
☐ Sec. 245, INA
☐ Sec. 249, INA
☐ Sec. 1 Act of 11/2/66
☐ Sec. 2 Act of 11/2/66
☐ Other

Country Chargeable

Eligibility Under Sec. 245
☐ Approved Visa Petition
☐ Dependent of Principal Alien
☐ Special Immigrant
☐ Other

Preference

Action Block

To be Completed by
Attorney or Representative, if any
☐ Fill in box if G-28 is attached to represent the applicant.

VOLAG #

ATTY State License #

Form I-485 (Rev. 07/30/07) Y

Part 3. Processing information.

A. City/Town/Village of Birth | Current Occupation

Your Mother's First Name | Your Father's First Name

Give your name exactly as it appears on your Arrival/Departure Record (Form I-94)

Place of Last Entry Into the United States (*City/State*)	In what status did you last enter? (*Visitor, student, exchange alien, crewman, temporary worker, without inspection, etc.*)
Were you inspected by a U.S. Immigration Officer? ☐ Yes ☐ No	
Nonimmigrant Visa Number	Consulate Where Visa Was Issued

Date Visa Was Issued (mm/dd/yyyy)	Gender: ☐ Male ☐ Female	Marital Status: ☐ Married ☐ Single ☐ Divorced ☐ Widowed

Have you ever before applied for permanent resident status in the U.S.?   ☐ No   ☐ Yes. If you checked "Yes," give date and place of filing and final disposition.

B. List your present husband/wife, all of your sons and daughters (If you have none, write "none." If additional space is needed, use separate paper).

Family Name	Given Name	Middle Initial	Date of Birth (*mm/dd/yyyy*)
Country of Birth	Relationship	A #	Applying with you? ☐ Yes ☐ No
Family Name	Given Name	Middle Initial	Date of Birth (*mm/dd/yyyy*)
Country of Birth	Relationship	A #	Applying with you? ☐ Yes ☐ No
Family Name	Given Name	Middle Initial	Date of Birth (*mm/dd/yyyy*)
Country of Birth	Relationship	A #	Applying with you? ☐ Yes ☐ No
Family Name	Given Name	Middle Initial	Date of Birth (*mm/dd/yyyy*)
Country of Birth	Relationship	A #	Applying with you? ☐ Yes ☐ No
Family Name	Given Name	Middle Initial	Date of Birth (*mm/dd/yyyy*)
Country of Birth	Relationship	A #	Applying with you? ☐ Yes ☐ No

C. List your present and past membership in or affiliation with every organization, association, fund, foundation, party, club, society or similar group in the United States or in other places since your 16th birthday. Include any foreign military service in this part. If none, write "none." Include the name(s) of organization(s), location(s), dates of membership, from and to, and the nature of the organization(s). If additional space is needed, use a separate piece of paper.

_____

_____

_____

_____

_____

_____

Part 3. Processing information. *(Continued)*

Please answer the following questions. (If your answer is **"Yes"** on any one of these questions, explain on a separate piece of paper and refer to "What Are the General Filing Instructions? Initial Evidence" to determine what documentation to include with your application. Answering **"Yes"** does not necessarily mean that you are not entitled to adjust status or register for permanent residence.)

1. Have you ever, in or outside the United States:

   a. knowingly committed any crime of moral turpitude or a drug-related offense for which you have not been arrested? ☐ Yes ☐ No

   b. been arrested, cited, charged, indicted, fined or imprisoned for breaking or violating any law or ordinance, excluding traffic violations? ☐ Yes ☐ No

   c. been the beneficiary of a pardon, amnesty, rehabilitation decree, other act of clemency or similar action? ☐ Yes ☐ No

   d. exercised diplomatic immunity to avoid prosecution for a criminal offense in the United States? ☐ Yes ☐ No

2. Have you received public assistance in the United States from any source, including the United States government or any state, county, city or municipality (other than emergency medical treatment), or are you likely to receive public assistance in the future? ☐ Yes ☐ No

3. Have you ever:

   a. within the past ten years been a prostitute or procured anyone for prostitution, or intend to engage in such activities in the future? ☐ Yes ☐ No

   b. engaged in any unlawful commercialized vice, including, but not limited to, illegal gambling? ☐ Yes ☐ No

   c. knowingly encouraged, induced, assisted, abetted or aided any alien to try to enter the United States illegally? ☐ Yes ☐ No

   d. illicitly trafficked in any controlled substance, or knowingly assisted, abetted or colluded in the illicit trafficking of any controlled substance? ☐ Yes ☐ No

4. Have you ever engaged in, conspired to engage in, or do you intend to engage in, or have you ever solicited membership or funds for, or have you through any means ever assisted or provided any type of material support to any person or organization that has ever engaged or conspired to engage in sabotage, kidnapping, political assassination, hijacking or any other form of terrorist activity? ☐ Yes ☐ No

5. Do you intend to engage in the United States in:

   a. espionage? ☐ Yes ☐ No

   b. any activity a purpose of which is opposition to, or the control or overthrow of, the government of the United States, by force, violence or other unlawful means? ☐ Yes ☐ No

   c. any activity to violate or evade any law prohibiting the export from the United States of goods, technology or sensitive information? ☐ Yes ☐ No

6. Have you ever been a member of, or in any way affiliated with, the Communist Party or any other totalitarian party? ☐ Yes ☐ No

7. Did you, during the period from March 23, 1933 to May 8, 1945, in association with either the Nazi Government of Germany or any organization or government associated or allied with the Nazi Government of Germany, ever order, incite, assist or otherwise participate in the persecution of any person because of race, religion, national origin or political opinion? ☐ Yes ☐ No

8. Have you ever engaged in genocide, or otherwise ordered, incited, assisted or otherwise participated in the killing of any person because of race, religion, nationality, ethnic origin or political opinion? ☐ Yes ☐ No

9. Have you ever been deported from the United States, or removed from the United States at government expense, excluded within the past year, or are you now in exclusion, deportation, removal or recission proceedings? ☐ Yes ☐ No

10. Are you under a final order of civil penalty for violating section 274C of the Immigration and Nationality Act for use of fraudulent documents or have you, by fraud or willful misrepresentation of a material fact, ever sought to procure, or procured, a visa, other documentation, entry into the United States or any immigration benefit? ☐ Yes ☐ No

11. Have you ever left the United States to avoid being drafted into the U.S. Armed Forces? ☐ Yes ☐ No

12. Have you ever been a J nonimmigrant exchange visitor who was subject to the two-year foreign residence requirement and have not yet complied with that requirement or obtained a waiver? ☐ Yes ☐ No

13. Are you now withholding custody of a U.S. citizen child outside the United States from a person granted custody of the child? ☐ Yes ☐ No

14. Do you plan to practice polygamy in the United States? ☐ Yes ☐ No

Part 4. Signature.   *(Read the information on penalties in the instructions before completing this section. You must file this application while in the United States.)*

Your registration with U.S. Citizenship and Immigration Services.

"I understand and acknowledge that, under section 262 of the Immigration and Nationality Act (Act), as an alien who has been or will be in the United States for more than 30 days, I am required to register with U.S. Citizenship and Immigration Services. I understand and acknowledge that, under section 265 of the Act, I am required to provide USCIS with my current address and written notice of any change of address within **ten** days of the change. I understand and acknowledge that USCIS will use the most recent address that I provide to USCIS, on any form containing these acknowledgements, for all purposes, including the service of a Notice to Appear should it be necessary for USCIS to initiate removal proceedings against me. I understand and acknowledge that if I change my address without providing written notice to USCIS, I will be held responsible for any communications sent to me at the most recent address that I provided to USCIS. I further understand and acknowledge that, if removal proceedings are initiated against me and I fail to attend any hearing, including an initial hearing based on service of the Notice to Appear at the most recent address that I provided to USCIS or as otherwise provided by law, I may be ordered removed in my absence, arrested and removed from the United States."

Selective Service Registration.

The following applies to you if you are a male at least 18 years old, but not yet 26 years old, who is required to register with the Selective Service System: "I understand that my filing this adjustment of status application with U.S. Citizenship and Immigration Services authorizes USCIS to provide certain registration information to the Selective Service System in accordance with the Military Selective Service Act. Upon USCIS acceptance of my application, I authorize USCIS to transmit to the Selective Service System my name, current address, Social Security Number, date of birth and the date I filed the application for the purpose of recording my Selective Service registration as of the filing date. If, however, USCIS does not accept my application, I further understand that, if so required, I am responsible for registering with the Selective Service by other means, provided I have not yet reached age 26."

Applicant's Certification

I certify, under penalty of perjury under the laws of the United States of America, that this application and the evidence submitted with it is all true and correct. I authorize the release of any information from my records that U.S. Citizenship and Immigration Services (USCIS) needs to determine eligibility for the benefit I am seeking.

Signature	*Print Your Name*	*Date*	*Daytime Phone Number*
			( )

NOTE: *If you do not completely fill out this form or fail to submit required documents listed in the instructions, you may not be found eligible for the requested document and this application may be denied.*

Part 5. Signature of person preparing form, if other than above. (sign below)

I declare that I prepared this application at the request of the above person and it is based on all information of which I have knowledge.

Signature	*Print Your Full Name*	*Date*	**Phone Number** *(Include Area Code)*
			( )

Firm Name and Address	*E-Mail Address (if any)*

OMB No. 1615-0023; Expires 09/30/08

Department of Homeland Security
U.S. Citizenship Immigration and Service

Supplement A to Form I-485,
Adjustment of Status Under Section 245(i)

NOTE: Use this form only if you are applying to adjust status to that of a lawful permanent resident under section 245(i) of the Immigration and Nationality Act.

Part A. Information about you.	**For USCIS Use Only**

Last Name	First Name	Middle Name

Action Block

Address: In Care Of

Street Number and Name   Apt. #

City   State   Zip Code

Alien Registration Number (A #) if any   Date of Birth *(mm/dd/yyyy)*

Country of Birth   Country of Citizenship/Nationality

Telephone Number   E-Mail Address, if any

(   )

Part B. Eligibility. *(Check the correct response.)*

1. I am filing Supplement A to Form I-485 because:

  a. ☐ I am the beneficiary of a visa petition filed on or before January 14, 1998.

  b. ☐ I am the beneficiary of a visa petition filed on or after January 15, 1998, and on or before April 30, 2001.

  c. ☐ I am the beneficiary of an application for a labor certification filed on or before January 14, 1998.

  d. ☐ I am the beneficiary of an application for a labor certification filed on or after January 15, 1998, and on or before April 30, 2001.

If you checked box b or d in Question 1, you must submit evidence demonstrating that you were physically present in the United States on December 21, 2000.

2. And I fall into one or more of these categories: *(Check all that apply to you.)*

  a. ☐ I entered the United States as an alien crewman;

  b. ☐ I have accepted employment without authorization;

  c. ☐ I am in unlawful immigration status because I entered the United States without inspection or I remained in the United States past the expiration of the period of my lawful admission;

  d. ☐ I have failed (except through no fault of my own or for technical reasons) to maintain, continuously, lawful status;

  e. ☐ I was admitted to the United States in transit without a visa;

  f. ☐ I was admitted as a nonimmigrant visitor without a visa;

  g. ☐ I was admitted to the United States as a nonimmigrant in the S classification; or

  h. ☐ I am seeking employment-based adjustment of status and am not in lawful nonimmigrant status.

Part C. Additional eligibility information.

1. Are you applying to adjust status based on any of the below reasons?

  a. You were granted asylum in the United States;

  b. You have continuously resided in the United States since January 1, 1972;

  c. You entered as a K-1 fiancé(e) of a U.S. citizen;

  d. You have an approved Form I-360, Petition for Amerasian, Widow(er), Battered or Abused Spouse or Child, or Special Immigrant, and are applying for adjustment as a special immigrant juvenile court dependent or a special immigrant who has served in the U.S. armed forces, or a battered or abused spouse or child;

  e. You are a native or citizen of Cuba, or the spouse or child of such alien, who was not lawfully inspected or admitted to the United States;

  f. You are a special immigrant retired international organization employee or family member;

  g. You are a special immigrant physician;

Part C. Additional eligibility information. *(Continued.)*

h. You are a public interest parolee, who was denied refugee status, and are from the former Soviet Union, Vietnam, Laos or Cambodia (a "Lautenberg Parolee" under Public Law 101-167); or

i. You are eligible under the Immigration Nursing Relief Act.

☐ **No.** I am not applying for adjustment of status for any of these reasons. *(Go to next question.)*

☐ **Yes.** I am applying for adjustment of status for any one of these reasons. **(If you answered "Yes," do not file this form.)**

2. Do any of the following conditions describe you?

    a. You are already a lawful permanent resident of the United States.

    b. You have continuously maintained lawful immigration status in the United States since November 5, 1986.

    c. You are applying to adjust status as the spouse or unmarried minor child of a U.S. citizen or the parent of a U.S. citizen child at least 21 years of age, and you were inspected and lawfully admitted to the United States.

    ☐ **No.** None of these conditions describe me. *(Go to **Part D.** Signature.)*

    ☐ **Yes. If you answered "Yes," do not file this form.**

Part D. Signature. *Read the information on penalties in the instructions before completing this section.*

I certify, under penalty of perjury under the laws of the United States of America, that this application and the evidence submitted with it is all true and correct. I authorize the release of any information from my records that the U.S. Citizenship and Immigration Services needs to determine eligibility for the benefit being sought.

Signature	Print Name	Date

Part E. Signature of person preparing form, if other than above. *Read the information on penalties in the instructions before completing this section.*

I certify, under penalty of perjury under the laws of the United States of America, that I prepared this form at the request of the above person and that to the best of my knowledge the contents of this application are all true and correct.

Signature	Print Name	Date

Firm Name and Address	Daytime Phone Number *(Area Code and Number)*
	( )
	E-Mail Address, if any

Department of Homeland Security
U.S. Citizenship and Immigration Services

OMB No. 1615-0008; Exp. 05/31/09

G-325A, Biographic Information

(Family Name)	(First Name)	(Middle Name)	☐ Male ☐ Female	Birth Date (mm/dd/yyyy)	Citizenship/Nationality	File Number A

All Other Names Used (Including names by previous marriages)	City and Country of Birth	U.S. Social Security # *(If any)*

	Family Name	First Name	Date, City and Country of Birth (If known)	City and Country of Residence
Father				
Mother (Maiden Name)				

Husband or Wife (If none, so state.) Family Name (For wife, give maiden name)	First Name	Birth Date (mm/dd/yyyy)	City and Country of Birth	Date of Marriage	Place of Marriage

Former Husbands or Wives (If none, so state) Family Name (For wife, give maiden name)	First Name	Birth Date (mm/dd/yyyy)	Date and Place of Marriage	Date and Place of Termination of Marriage

Applicant's residence last five years. List present address first.

Street and Number	City	Province or State	Country	From Month	From Year	To Month	To Year
						Present Time	

Applicant's last address outside the United States of more than one year.

Street and Number	City	Province or State	Country	From Month	From Year	To Month	To Year

Applicant's employment last five years. (If none, so state.) List present employment first.

Full Name and Address of Employer	Occupation (Specify)	From Month	From Year	To Month	To Year
				Present Time	

Show below last occupation abroad if not shown above. (Include all information requested above.)

This form is submitted in connection with an application for: ☐ Naturalization ☐ Other (Specify): _____ ☐ Status as Permanent Resident	Signature of Applicant	Date

Submit all copies of this form.	If your native alphabet is in other than Roman letters, write your name in your native alphabet below:

Penalties: Severe penalties are provided by law for knowingly and willfully falsifying or concealing a material fact.

Applicant: Be sure to put your name and Alien Registration Number in the box outlined by heavy border below.

Complete This Box (Family Name)	(Given Name)	(Middle Name)	(Alien Registration Number)

OMB No. 1615-0075; Expires 10/31/10

Department of Homeland Security
U.S. Citizenship and Immigration Services

I-864, Affidavit of Support
Under Section 213A of the Act

Part 1. Basis for filing Affidavit of Support.

1. I, _____ ,

am the sponsor submitting this affidavit of support because (Check only one box):

a. ☐ **I am the petitioner. I filed or am filing for the immigration of my relative.**

b. ☐ **I filed an alien worker petition on behalf of the intending immigrant, who is related to me as my** _____

c. ☐ **I have an ownership interest of at least 5 percent in** _____ , **which filed an alien worker petition on behalf of the intending immigrant, who is related to me as my** _____

d. ☐ **I am the only joint sponsor.**

e. ☐ **I am the** ☐ **first** ☐ **second of two joint sponsors.** *(Check appropriate box.)*

f. ☐ **The original petitioner is deceased. I am the substitute sponsor. I am the intending immigrant's** _____

For Government Use Only

This I-864 is from:

☐ the Petitioner

☐ a Joint Sponsor #

☐ the Substitute Sponsor

☐ 5% Owner

This I-864:

☐ does not meet the requirements of section 213A.

☐ meets the requirements of section 213A.

Reviewer

Location

Date *(mm/dd/yyyy)*

Number of Affidavits of Support in file:

☐ 1   ☐ 2

Part 2. Information on the principal immigrant.

2. Last Name

First Name | Middle Name

3. Mailing Address Street Number and Name *(Include Apartment Number)*

City | State/Province | Zip/Postal Code | Country

4. Country of Citizenship | 5. Date of Birth *(mm/dd/yyyy)*

6. Alien Registration Number *(if any)*
   A-
   | 7. U.S. Social Security Number *(if any)*

Part 3. Information on the immigrant(s) you are sponsoring.

8. ☐ I am sponsoring the principal immigrant named in Part 2 above.

   ☐ Yes   ☐ No (Applicable only in cases with two joint sponsors)

9. ☐ I am sponsoring the following family members immigrating at the same time or within six months of the principal immigrant named in **Part 2** above. Do not include any relative listed on a separate visa petition.

Name	Relationship to Sponsored Immigrant	Date of Birth *(mm/dd/yyyy)*	A-Number *(if any)*	U.S.Social Security Number *(if any)*
a.				
b.				
c.				
d.				
e.				

10. Enter the total number of immigrants you are sponsoring on this form from **Part 3**, Items **8** and **9**.   ☐☐

Part 4. Information on the Sponsor.

			For Government Use Only
11. Name	Last Name		
	First Name	Middle Name	
12. Mailing Address	Street Number and Name *(Include Apartment Number)*		
	City	State or Province	
	Country	Zip/Postal Code	
13. Place of Residence *(if different from mailing address)*	Street Number and Name *(Include Apartment Number)*		
	City	State or Province	
	Country	Zip/Postal Code	

14. Telephone Number *(Include Area Code or Country and City Codes)*

15. Country of Domicile

16. Date of Birth *(mm/dd/yyyy)*

17. Place of Birth *(City)*	State or Province	Country

18. U.S. Social Security Number *(Required)*

19. Citizenship/Residency

   ☐ I am a U.S. citizen.

   ☐ I am a U.S. national (for joint sponsors only).

   ☐ I am a lawful permanent resident. My alien registration number is A-_____

If you checked box (b), (c), (d), (e) or (f) in line 1 on Page 1, you must include proof of your citizen, national, or permanent resident status.

20. Military Service (To be completed by petitioner sponsors only.)

I am currently on active duty in the U.S. armed services.   ☐ Yes   ☐ No

Part 5. Sponsor's household size.

		For Government Use Only

21. Your Household Size - <u>DO NOT COUNT ANYONE TWICE</u>

Persons you are sponsoring in this affidavit:

    a. Enter the number you entered on line 10.   ☐☐

Persons NOT sponsored in this affidavit:

    b. Yourself.   **1**

    c. If you are currently married, enter "1" for your spouse.   ☐

    d. If you have dependent children, enter the number here.   ☐☐

    e. If you have any other dependents, enter the number here.   ☐☐

    f. If you have sponsored any other persons on an I-864 or I-864 EZ who are now lawful permanent residents, enter the number here.   ☐☐

    g. **OPTIONAL**: If you have <u>siblings, parents, or adult children</u> with the same principal residence who are combining their income with yours by submitting Form I-864A, enter the number here.   ☐☐

    h. Add together lines and enter the number here. **Household Size:**   ☐☐

Part 6. Sponsor's income and employment.

22. I am currently:

    a. ☐ Employed as a/an _____ .

         Name of Employer #1 *(if applicable)* _____ .

         Name of Employer #2 *(if applicable)* _____ .

    b. ☐ Self-employed as a/an _____ .

    c. ☐ Retired from _____ since _____ .
                           (Company Name)   *(Date)*

    d. ☐ Unemployed since _____ .
                                     (Date)

23. My current individual annual income is: $ _____
                                                           (See Step-by-Step Instructions)

24. My current annual household income:

    a. List your income from line 23 of this form. $ _____

    b. Income you are using from any other person who was counted in your household size, including, in certain conditions, the intending immigrant. (See step-by-step instructions.) Please indicate name, relationship and income.

Name	Relationship	Current Income
_____	_____	$ _____
_____	_____	$ _____
_____	_____	$ _____
_____	_____	$ _____

    c. Total Household Income: $ _____

    (Total all lines from 24a and 24b. Will be Compared to Poverty Guidelines -- See Form I-864P.)

    d. ☐ The persons listed above have completed Form I-864A. I am filing along with this form all necessary Forms I-864A completed by these persons.

    e. ☐ The person listed above, _____ does not need to
                                      (Name)
       complete Form I-864A because he/she is the intending immigrant and has no accompanying dependents.

25. Federal income tax return information.

    ☐ I have filed a Federal tax return for each of the three most recent tax years. I have attached the required photocopy or transcript of my Federal tax return for only the most recent tax year.

    My total income (adjusted gross income on IRS Form 1040EZ) as reported on my Federal tax returns for the most recent three years was:

Tax Year		Total Income
_____	*(most recent)*	$ _____
_____	*(2nd most recent)*	$ _____
_____	*(3rd most recent)*	$ _____

    ☐ *(Optional)* I have attached photocopies or transcripts of my Federal tax returns for my second and third most recent tax years.

For Government Use Only

Household Size =

_____

Poverty line for year

_____ is:

$ _____

Part 7. Use of assets to supplement income. *(Optional)*	**For Government Use Only**

If your income, or the total income for you and your household, from line 24c exceeds the Federal Poverty Guidelines for your household size, YOU ARE NOT REQUIRED to complete this Part. Skip to Part 8.

26. Your assets *(Optional)*

   a. Enter the balance of all savings and checking accounts. $ _____

   b. Enter the net cash value of real-estate holdings. (Net means current assessed value minus mortgage debt.) $ _____

   c. Enter the net cash value of all stocks, bonds, certificates of deposit, and any other assets not already included in lines 26 (a) or (b). $ _____

   d. Add together lines 26 a, b and c and enter the number here.   **TOTAL:** $ _____

27. Your household member's assets from Form I-864A. *(Optional)*

   Assets from Form I-864A, line 12d for $ _____

_____
(Name of Relative)

28. Assets of the principal sponsored immigrant. *(Optional)*

   The principal sponsored immigrant is the person listed in line 2.

   a. Enter the balance of the sponsored immigrant's savings and checking accounts. $ _____

   b. Enter the net cash value of all the sponsored immigrant's real estate holdings. (Net means investment value minus mortgage debt.) $ _____

   c. Enter the current cash value of the sponsored immigrant's stocks, bonds, certificates of deposit, and other assets not included on line a or b. $ _____

   d. Add together lines 28a, b, and c, and enter the number here. $ _____

29. Total value of assets.

   Add together lines 26d, 27 and 28d and enter the number here.   **TOTAL:** $ _____

For Government Use Only

Household Size =

_____

Poverty line for year

_____ is:

$ _____

The total value of all assests, line 29, must equal 5 times (3 times for spouses and children of USCs, or 1 time for orphans to be formally adopted in the U.S.) the difference between the poverty guidelines and the sponsor's household income, line 24c.

Part 8. Sponsor's Contract.

Please note that, by signing this Form I-864, you agree to assume certain specific obligations under the Immigration and Nationality Act and other Federal laws. The following paragraphs describe those obligations. Please read the following information carefully before you sign the Form I-864. If you do not understand the obligations, you may wish to consult an attorney or accredited representative.

What is the Legal Effect of My Signing a Form I-864?

If you sign a Form I-864 on behalf of any person (called the "intending immigrant") who is applying for an immigrant visa or for adjustment of status to a permanent resident, and that intending immigrant submits the Form I-864 to the U.S. Government with his or her application for an immigrant visa or adjustment of status, under section 213A of the Immigration and Nationality Act these actions create a contract between you and the U. S. Government. The intending immigrant's becoming a permanent resident is the "consideration" for the contract.

Under this contract, you agree that, in deciding whether the intending immigrant can establish that he or she is not inadmissible to the United States as an alien likely to become a public charge, the U.S. Government can consider your income and assets to be available for the support of the intending immigrant.

What If I choose Not to Sign a Form I-864?

You cannot be made to sign a Form I-864 if you do not want to do so. But if you do not sign the Form I-864, the intending immigrant may not be able to become a permanent resident in the United States.

What Does Signing the Form I-864 Require Me to do?

If an intending immigrant becomes a permanent resident in the United States based on a Form I-864 that you have signed, then, until your obligations under the Form I-864 terminate, you must:

-- Provide the intending immigrant any support necessary to maintain him or her at an income that is at least 125 percent of the Federal Poverty Guidelines for his or her household size (100 percent if you are the petitioning sponsor and are on active duty in the U.S. Armed Forces and the person is your husband, wife, unmarried child under 21 years old.)

-- Notify USCIS of any change in your address, within 30 days of the change, by filing Form I-865.

What Other Consequences Are There?

If an intending immigrant becomes a permanent resident in the United States based on a Form I-864 that you have signed, then until your obligations under the Form I-864 terminate, your income and assets may be considered ("deemed") to be available to that person, in determining whether he or she is eligible for certain Federal means-tested public benefits and also for State or local means-tested public benefits, if the State or local government's rules provide for consideration ("deeming") of your income and assets as available to the person.

This provision does **not** apply to public benefits specified in section 403(c) of the Welfare Reform Act such as, but not limited to, emergency Medicaid, short-term, non-cash emergency relief; services provided under the National School Lunch and Child Nutrition Acts; immunizations and testing and treatment for communicable diseases; and means-tested programs under the Elementary and Secondary Education Act.

Contract continued on following page.

What If I Do Not Fulfill My Obligations?

If you do not provide sufficient support to the person who becomes a permanent resident based on the Form I-864 that you signed, that person may sue you for this support.

If a Federal, State or local agency, or a private agency provides any covered means-tested public benefit to the person who becomes a permanent resident based on the Form I-864 that you signed, the agency may ask you to reimburse them for the amount of the benefits they provided. If you do not make the reimbursement, the agency may sue you for the amount that the agency believes you owe.

If you are sued, and the court enters a judgment against you, the person or agency that sued you may use any legally permitted procedures for enforcing or collecting the judgment. You may also be required to pay the costs of collection, including attorney fees.

If you do not file a properly completed Form I-865 within 30 days of any change of address, USCIS may impose a civil fine for your failing to do so.

When Will These Obligations End?

Your obligations under a Form I-864 will end if the person who becomes a permanent resident based on a Form I-864 that you signed:

- Becomes a U.S. citizen;
- Has worked, or can be credited with, 40 quarters of coverage under the Social Security Act;
- No longer has lawful permanent resident status, and has departed the United States;
- Becomes subject to removal, but applies for and obtains in removal proceedings a new grant of adjustment of status, based on a new affidavit of support, if one is required; or
- Dies.

Note that divorce **does not** terminate your obligations under this Form I-864.

Your obligations under a Form I-864 also end if you die. Therefore, if you die, your Estate will not be required to take responsibility for the person's support after your death. Your Estate may, however, be responsible for any support that you owed before you died.

30. I, _____ ,

(Print Sponsor's Name)

certify under penalty of perjury under the laws of the United States that:

- **a.** I know the contents of this affidavit of support that I signed.

- **b.** All the factual statements in this affidavit of support are true and correct.

- **c.** I have read and I understand each of the obligations described in Part 8, and I agree, freely and without any mental reservation or purpose of evasion, to accept each of those obligations in order to make it possible for the immigrants indicated in Part 3 to become permanent residents of the United States;

- **d.** I agree to submit to the personal jurisdiction of any Federal or State court that has subject matter jurisdiction of a lawsuit against me to enforce my obligations under this Form I-864;

- **e.** Each of the Federal income tax returns submitted in support of this affidavit are true copies, or are unaltered tax transcripts, of the tax returns I filed with the U.S. Internal Revenue Service; and

Sign on following page.

f. I authorize the Social Security Administration to release information about me in its records to the Department of State and U.S. Citizenship and Immigration Services.

g. Any and all other evidence submitted is true and correct.

31. _____   _____
    (Sponsor's Signature)   *(Date-- mm/dd/yyyy)*

Part 9. Information on Preparer, if prepared by someone other than the sponsor.

I certify under penalty of perjury under the laws of the United States that I prepared this affidavit of support at the sponsor's request and that this affidavit of support is based on all information of which I have knowledge.

Signature: _____   **Date:** _____
                                                                  (mm/dd/yyyy)

Printed Name: _____

Firm Name: _____

Address: _____

Telephone Number: _____

E-Mail Address : _____

Business State ID # *(if any)* _____

OMB No. 1615-0075; Expires 10/31/10

Department of Homeland Security
U.S. Citizenship and Immigration Services

I-864A, Contract Between
Sponsor and Household Member

Part 1. Information on the Household Member. (You.)	For Government Use Only
1. Name Last Name First Name Middle Name	**This I-864A relates to a household member who:** ☐ is the intending immigrant. ☐ is not the intending immigrant.
2. Mailing Address Street Number and Name *(include apartment number)* City State or Province Country Zip/Postal Code	
3. Place of Residence *(if different from mailing address)* Street Number and Name *(include apartment number)* City State or Province Country Zip/Postal Code	_____ Reviewer _____ Location
4. Telephone Number *(Include area code or country and city codes)*	
5. Date of Birth *(mm/dd/yyyy)*	Date *(mm/dd/yyyy)*
6. Place of Birth City State/Province Country	
7. U.S. Social Security Number *(if any)*	

8. Relationship to Sponsor (Check either a, b or c)

   a. ☐ I am the intending immigrant and also the sponsor's spouse.

   b. ☐ I am the intending immigrant and also a member of the sponsor's household.

   c. ☐ I am not the intending immigrant. I am the sponsor's household member. I am related to the sponsor as his/her.

     ☐ Spouse

     ☐ Son or daughter *(at least 18 years old)*

     ☐ Parent

     ☐ Brother or sister

     ☐ Other dependent (specify)

Form I-864A (Rev.10/18/07)Y

9. I am currently:

<table>
<tr><td></td><td></td><td>For Government
Use Only</td></tr>
</table>

a. ☐ Employed as a/an _____ .

      Name of Employer # 1 *(if applicable)* _____ .

      Name of Employer #2 *(if applicable)* _____ .

b. ☐ Self-employed as a/an _____ .

c. ☐ Retired from_____ since _____ .
                   (Company Name)   *(mm/dd/yyyy)*

d. ☐ Unemployed since _____
                           (mm/dd/yyyy)

---

10. My current individual annual income is: $_____

---

11. Federal income tax information.

☐ I have filed a Federal tax return for each of the three most recent tax years. I have attached the required photocopy or transcript of my Federal tax return for only the most recent tax year.

My total income (adjusted gross income on IRS Form 1040EZ) as reported on my Federal tax returns for the most recent three years was:

Tax Year		Total Income
_____ *(most recent)*	$	_____
_____ *(2nd most recent)*	$	_____
_____ *(3rd most recent)*	$	_____

☐ *(Optional)* I have attached photocopies or transcripts of my Federal tax returns for my second and third most recent tax years.

---

12. My assets (complete only if necessary)

a. Enter the balance of all cash, savings, and checking accounts. $_____ .

b. Enter the net cash value of real-estate holdings. (Net means assessed value minus mortgage debt.) $_____ .

c. Enter the cash value of all stocks, bonds, certificates of deposit, and other assets not listed on line a or b. $_____ .

d. **Add together Lines a, b, and c and enter the number here.** $_____ .

Part 2. Sponsor's Promise.

	For Government Use Only

13. I, THE SPONSOR, _____
(Print Name)

in consideration of the household member's promise to support the following intending immigrant(s)

and to be jointly and severally liable for any obligations I incur under the affidavit of support, promise

to complete and file an affidavit of support on behalf of the following _____ named intending
(Indicate Number)

immigrant(s) (see Step-by-Step instructions).

	Name	Date of Birth *(mm/dd/yyyy)*	A-number *(if any)*	U.S. Social Security Number *(if any)*
a.				
b.				
c.				
d.				
e.				

14. _____   _____
(Sponsor's Signature)   *(Date--mm/dd/yyyy)*

Part 3. Household Member's Promise.

15. I, THE HOUSEHOLD MEMBER, _____
(Print Name)

in consideration of the sponsor's promise to complete and file an affidavit of support on behalf of the

above _____named intending immigrant(s):
(Number from line 13)

a. Promise to provide any and all financial support necessary to assist the sponsor in maintaining the sponsored immigrant(s) at or above the minimum income provided for in section 213A(a)(1)(A) of the Act (not less than 125 percent of the Federal Poverty Guidelines) during the period in which the affidavit of support is enforceable;

b. Agree to be jointly and severally liable for payment of any and all obligations owed by the sponsor under the affidavit of support to the sponsored immigrant(s), to any agency of the Federal Government, to any agency of a State or local government, or to any other private entity that provides means-tested public benefit;

c. Certify under penalty under the laws of the United States that all the information provided on this form is true and correct to the best of my knowledge and belief and that the Federal income tax returns submitted in support of the contract are true copies or unaltered tax transcripts filed with the Internal Revenue Service.

d. **Consideration where the household member is also the sponsored immigrant:** I understand that if I am the sponsored immigrant and a member of the sponsor's household that this promise relates only to my promise to be jointly and severally liable for any obligation owed by the sponsor under the affidavit of support to any of my dependents, to any agency of the Federal Government, to any agency of a State or local government, and to provide any and all financial support necessary to assist the sponsor in maintaining any of my dependents at or above the minimum income provided for in section 213A(s)(1)(A) of the Act (not less than 125 percent of the Federal poverty line) during the period which the affidavit of support is enforceable.

e. I authorize the Social Security Administration to release information about me in its records to the Department of State and U.S. Citizenship and Immigration Services.

16. _____   _____
(Household Member's Signature)   *(Date--mm/dd/yyyy)*

Department of Homeland Security
U. S. Citizenship and Immigration Services

OMB No. 1615-0013; Expires 11/30/07

I-131, Application for Travel Document

DO NOT WRITE IN THIS BLOCK	FOR USCIS USE ONLY (except G-28 block below)	
Document Issued ☐ Reentry Permit ☐ Refugee Travel Document ☐ Single Advance Parole ☐ Multiple Advance Parole Valid to: _____ **If Reentry Permit or Refugee Travel Document, mail to:** ☐ Address in Part 1 ☐ American embassy/consulate at: _____ ☐ Overseas DHS office at: _____	**Action Block**	**Receipt** ☐ Document Hand Delivered On _____ By _____ *To be completed by Attorney/Representative, if any.* Attorney State License # _____ ☐ Check box if G-28 is attached.

Part 1.   Information about you. *(Please type or print in black ink.)*

1. A #

2. Date of Birth *(mm/dd/yyyy)*

3. Class of Admission

4. Gender   Male ☐   Female ☐

5. Name *(Family name in capital letters)*   *(First)*   *(Middle)*

6. Address *(Number and Street)*   Apt. #

City   State or Province   Zip/Postal Code   Country

7. Country of Birth

8. Country of Citizenship

9. Social Security # *(if any.)*

Part 2.   Application type *(check one).*

a. ☐ I am a permanent resident or conditional resident of the United States and I am applying for a reentry permit.

b. ☐ I now hold U.S. refugee or asylee status and I am applying for a refugee travel document.

c. ☐ I am a permanent resident as a direct result of refugee or asylee status and I am applying for a refugee travel document.

d. ☐ I am applying for an advance parole document to allow me to return to the United States after temporary foreign travel.

e. ☐ I am outside the United States and I am applying for an advance parole document.

f. ☐ I am applying for an advance parole document for a person who is outside the United States. *If you checked box "f", provide the following information about that person:*

1. Name *(Family name in capital letters)*   *(First)*   *(Middle)*

2. Date of Birth *(mm/dd/yyyy)*

3. Country of Birth

4. Country of Citizenship

5. Address *(Number and Street)*   Apt. #   Daytime Telephone # *(area/country code)*

City   State or Province   Zip/Postal Code   Country

Form I-131 (Rev. 11/16/07)Y

Part 3. Processing information.

1. Date of Intended Departure *(mm/dd/yyyy)*

2. Expected Length of Trip

3. Are you, or any person included in this application, now in exclusion, deportation, removal or recission proceedings? ☐ No ☐ Yes *(Name of DHS office):*

If you are applying for an Advance Parole Document, skip to Part 7.

4. Have you ever before been issued a reentry permit or refugee travel? *for the last document issued to you):* ☐ No ☐ Yes *(Give the following information*

Date Issued *(mm/dd/yyyy):*   Disposition *(attached, lost, etc.):*

5. Where do you want this travel document sent? *(Check one)*

a. ☐ To the U.S. address shown in **Part 1** on the first page of this form.

b. ☐ To an American embassy or consulate at: City: Country:

c. ☐ To a DHS office overseas at: City: Country:

d. If you checked "b" or "c", where should the notice to pick up the travel document be sent?

    ☐ To the address shown in **Part 2** on the first page of this form.

    ☐ To the address shown below:

Address *(Number and Street)*   Apt. #   Daytime Telephone # *(area/country code)*

City   State or Province   Zip/Postal Code   Country

Part 4. Information about your proposed travel.

Purpose of trip. *If you need more room, continue on a seperate sheet(s) of paper.*	List the countries you intend to visit.

Part 5. Complete only if applying for a reentry permit.

Since becoming a permanent resident of the United States (or during the past five years, whichever is less) how much total time have you spent outside the United States?

☐ less than six months   ☐ two to three years
☐ six months to one year   ☐ three to four years
☐ one to two years   ☐ more than four years

Since you became a permanent resident of the United States, have you ever filed a federal income tax return as a nonresident, or failed to file a federal income tax return because you considered yourself to be a nonresident? *(If "Yes," give details on a separate sheet(s) of paper.)*   ☐ Yes ☐ No

Part 6. Complete only if applying for a refugee travel document.

1. Country from which you are a refugee or asylee:

If you answer "Yes" to any of the following questions, you must explain on a separate sheet(s) of paper.

2. Do you plan to travel to the above named country?   ☐ Yes ☐ No

3. Since you were accorded refugee/asylee status, have you ever:
   a. returned to the above named country?   ☐ Yes ☐ No
   b. applied for and/or obtained a national passport, passport renewal or entry permit of that country?   ☐ Yes ☐ No
   c. applied for and/or received any benefit from such country (for example, health insurance benefits).   ☐ Yes ☐ No

4. Since you were accorded refugee/asylee status, have you, by any legal procedure or voluntary act:
   a. reacquired the nationality of the above named country?   ☐ Yes ☐ No
   b. acquired a new nationality?   ☐ Yes ☐ No
   c. been granted refugee or asylee status in any other country?   ☐ Yes ☐ No

Part 7. Complete only if applying for advance parole.

On a separate sheet(s) of paper, please explain how you qualify for an advance parole document and what circumstances warrant issuance of advance parole. Include copies of any documents you wish considered. *(See instructions.)*

1. For how many trips do you intend to use this document?　　□ One trip　　□ More than one trip

2. If the person intended to receive an advance parole document is outside the United States, provide the location (city and country) of the American embassy or consulate or the DHS overseas office that you want us to notify.

City

Country

3. If the travel document will be delivered to an overseas office, where should the notice to pick up the document be sent:

□ To the address shown in **Part 2** on the first page of this form.

□ To the address shown below:

Address *(Number and Street)*　　　Apt. #　　Daytime Telephone # *(area/country code)*

City　　　State or Province　　　Zip/Postal Code　　Country

Part 8. Signature. *Read the information on penalties in the instructions before completing this section. If you are filing for a reentry permit or refugee travel document, you must be in the United States to file this application.*

I certify, under penalty of perjury under the laws of the United States of America, that this application and the evidence submitted with it are all true and correct. I authorize the release of any information from my records that the U.S. Citizenship and Immigration Services needs to determine eligibility for the benefit I am seeking.

Signature　　　Date *(mm/dd/yyyy)*　　　**Daytime Telephone Number** *(with area code)*

Please Note: If you do not completely fill out this form or fail to submit required documents listed in the instructions, you may not be found eligible for the requested document and this application may be denied.

Part 9. Signature of person preparing form, if other than the applicant. *(Sign below.)*

I declare that I prepared this application at the request of the applicant and it is based on all information of which I have knowledge.

Signature　　　Print or Type Your Name

Firm Name and Address　　　Daytime Telephone Number *(with area code)*

Fax Number *(if any.)*　　　Date *(mm/dd/yyyy)*

OMB No. 1615-0040; Expires 08/31/08

Department of Homeland Security
U.S. Citizenship and Immigration Services

I-765, Application For
Employment Authorization

Do not write in this block.

Remarks	Action Block	Fee Stamp
A#		
Applicant is filing under §274a.12 _____		

☐ Application Approved. Employment Authorized / Extended *(Circle One)*   until _____ (Date).
_____ (Date).

☐ Subject to the following conditions: _____
☐ Application Denied.
☐ Failed to establish eligibility under 8 CFR 274a.12 (a) or (c).
☐ Failed to establish economic necessity as required in 8 CFR 274a.12(c)(14), (18) and 8 CFR 214.2(f)

I am applying for:
☐ Permission to accept employment.
☐ Replacement *(of lost employment authorization document)*
☐ Renewal of my permission to accept employment *(attach previous employment authorization document)*.

1. Name (Family Name in CAPS) (First)   (Middle)

2. Other Names Used (Include Maiden Name)

3. Address in the United States (Number and Street)   (Apt. Number)

   (Town or City)   (State/Country)   (ZIP Code)

4. Country of Citizenship/Nationality

5. Place of Birth (Town or City)   (State/Province)   (Country)

6. Date of Birth (mm/dd/yyyy)   7. Gender
                                   ☐ Male ☐ Female

8. Marital Status   ☐ Married   ☐ Single
                    ☐ Widowed   ☐ Divorced

9. Social Security Number (Include all numbers you have ever used) (if any)

10. Alien Registration Number (A-Number) or I-94 Number (if any)

11. Have you ever before applied for employment authorization from USCIS?

   ☐ Yes (If yes, complete below)   ☐ No

   Which USCIS Office?   Date(s)

   Results (Granted or Denied - attach all documentation)

12. Date of Last Entry into the U.S.   (mm/dd/yyyy)

13. Place of Last Entry into the U.S.

14. Manner of Last Entry (Visitor, Student, etc.)

15. Current Immigration Status (Visitor, Student, etc.)

16. Go to **Part 2** of the Instructions, Eligibility Categories. In the space below, place the letter and number of the category you selected from the instructions (For example, (a)(8), (c)(17)(iii), etc.).

   Eligibility under 8 CFR 274a.12

   (   ) (   ) (   )

Certification.

Your Certification: I certify, under penalty of perjury under the laws of the United States of America, that the foregoing is true and correct. Furthermore, I authorize the release of any information that the U.S. Citizenship and Immigration Services needs to determine eligibility for the benefit I am seeking. I have read the Instructions in **Part 2** and have identified the appropriate eligibility category in **Block 16.**

Signature   Telephone Number   Date

Signature of person preparing form, if other than above: I declare that this document was prepared by me at the request of the applicant and is based on all information of which I have any knowledge.

Print Name   Address   *Signature*   Date

Remarks	Initial Receipt	Resubmitted	Relocated		Completed		
			Rec'd	Sent	Approved	Denied	Returned

Form I-765 (Rev.07/30/07) Y

DEPARTMENT OF HOMELAND SECURITY
U.S. Customs and Border Protection   OMB No. 1651-0111

Admission Number

Welcome to the United States

I-94 Arrival/Departure Record - Instructions

This form must be completed by all persons except U.S. Citizens, returning resident aliens, aliens with immigrant visas, and Canadian Citizens visiting or in transit.

Type or print legibly with pen in ALL CAPITAL LETTERS. Use English. Do not write on the back of this form.

This form is in two parts. Please complete both the Arrival Record (Items 1 through 13) and the Departure Record (Items 14 through 17).

When all items are completed, present this form to the CBP Officer.

Item 7 - If you are entering the United States by land, enter **LAND** in this space. If you are entering the United States by ship, enter **SEA** in this space.

CBP Form I-94 (10/04)

Admission Number   OMB No. 1651-0111

Arrival Record

1. Family Name

2. First (Given) Name

3. Birth Date (Day/Mo/Yr)

4. Country of Citizenship

5. Sex (Male or Female)

6. Passport Number

7. Airline and Flight Number

8. Country Where You Live

9. City Where You Boarded

10. City Where Visa was Issued

11. Date Issued (Day/Mo/Yr)

12. Address While in the United States (Number and Street)

13. City and State

CBP Form I-94 (10/04)

Departure Number   OMB No. 1651-0111

I-94
Departure Record

14. Family Name

15. First (Given) Name

16. Birth Date (Day/Mo/Yr)

17. Country of Citizenship

CBP Form I-94 (10/04)

See Other Side   **STAPLE HERE**

U.S. Department of State
NONIMMIGRANT VISA APPLICATION

Approved OMB 1405-0018
Expires 11/30/2010
Estimated Burden 1 hour
See Page 2

PLEASE TYPE OR PRINT YOUR ANSWERS IN THE SPACE PROVIDED BELOW EACH ITEM

1. Passport Number

2. Place of Issuance:
City   Country   State/Province

DO NOT WRITE IN THIS SPACE

B-1/B-2 MAX   B-1 MAX   B-2 MAX

Other _____ MAX
Visa Classification

3. Issuing Country

4. Issuance Date (dd-mmm-yyyy)

5. Expiration Date (dd-mmm-yyyy)

Mult or _____
Number of Applications

6. Surnames (As in Passport)

Months _____
Validity

Issued/Refused

On _____ By _____

7. First and Middle Names (As in Passport)

Under SEC.   214(b)   221(g)

8. Other Surnames Used (Maiden, Religious, Professional, Aliases)

Other _____ INA

Reviewed By _____

9. Other First and Middle Names Used

10. Date of Birth (dd-mmm-yyyy)

11. Place of Birth:
City   Country   State/Province

12. Nationality

13. Sex
☐ Male
☐ Female

14. National Identification Number (If applicable)

15. Home Address (Include apartment number, street, city, state or province, postal zone and country)

16. Home Telephone Number

Business Phone Number

Mobile/Cell Number

Fax Number

Business Fax Number

Pager Number

17. Marital Status
☐ Married ☐ Single (Never Married)
☐ Widowed ☐ Divorced ☐ Separated

18. Spouse's Full Name (Even if divorced or separated. Include maiden name.)

19. Spouse's DOB (dd-mmm-yyyy)

20. Name and Address of Present Employer or School
Name: Address:

21. Present Occupation (If retired, write "retired". If student, write "student".)

22. When Do You Intend To Arrive In The U.S.? (Provide specific date if known)

23. E-Mail Address

24. At What Address Will You Stay in The U.S.?

‖‖‖‖‖‖‖‖‖‖‖‖‖‖‖

O1G72DLFCL

DO NOT WRITE IN THIS SPACE

25. Name and Telephone Numbers of Person in U.S. Who You Will Be Staying With or Visiting for Tourism or Business

Name   Home Phone

Business Phone   Cell Phone

50 mm x 50 mm

PHOTO

staple or glue photo here

26. How Long Do You Intend To Stay in The U.S.?

27. What is The Purpose of Your Trip?

28. Who Will Pay For Your Trip?

29. Have You Ever Been in The U.S.?   ☐ Yes   ☐ No

WHEN? _____

FOR HOW LONG? _____

30. Have You Ever Been Issued a U.S. Visa? ☐ Yes ☐ No
WHEN? _____
WHERE? _____
WHAT TYPE OF VISA? _____

31. Have You Ever Been Refused a U.S. Visa? ☐ Yes ☐ No
WHEN? _____
WHERE? _____
WHAT TYPE OF VISA? _____

32. Do You Intend To Work in The U.S.? ☐ Yes ☐ No
(If YES, give the name and complete address of U.S. employer.)

33. Do You Intend To Study in The U.S.? ☐ Yes ☐ No
(If YES, give the name and complete address of the school.)

34. Names and Relationships of Persons Traveling With You

35. Has Your U.S. Visa Ever Been Cancelled or Revoked? ☐ Yes ☐ No

36. Has Anyone Ever Filed an immigrant Visa Petition on Your Behalf? ☐ Yes ☐ No If Yes, Who?

37. Are Any of The Following Persons in The U.S., or Do They Have U.S. Legal Permanent Residence or U.S. Citizenship?
Mark YES or NO and indicate that person's status in the U.S. (i.e., U.S. legal permanent resident, U.S. citizen, visiting, studying, working, etc.).

☐ YES ☐ NO Husband/Wife _____
☐ YES ☐ NO Fiance/Fiancee _____
☐ YES ☐ NO

☐ YES ☐ NO Father/Mother _____
☐ YES ☐ NO Son/Daughter _____
Brother/Sister _____

38. IMPORTANT: ALL APPLICANTS MUST READ AND CHECK THE APPROPRIATE BOX FOR EACH ITEM.
A visa may not be issued to persons who are within specific categories defined by law as inadmissible to the United States (except when a waiver is obtained in advance). Is any of the following applicable to you?

● Have you ever been arrested or convicted for any offense or crime, even though subject of a pardon, amnesty or other similar legal action? Have you ever unlawfully distributed or sold a controlled substance (drug), or been a prostitute or procurer for prostitutes? ☐ YES ☐ NO

● Have you ever been refused admission to the U.S., or been the subject of a deportation hearing, or sought to obtain or assist others to obtain a visa, entry into the U.S., or any other U.S. immigration benefit by fraud or willful misrepresentation or other unlawful means? Have you attended a U.S. public elementary school on student (F) status or a public secondary school after November 30, 1996 without reimbursing the school? ☐ YES ☐ NO

● Do you seek to enter the United States to engage in export control violations, subversive or terrorist activities, or any other unlawful purpose? Are you a member or representative of a terrorist organization as currently designated by the U.S. Secretary of State? Have you ever participated in persecutions directed by the Nazi government of Germany; or have you ever participated in genocide? ☐ YES ☐ NO

● Have you ever violated the terms of a U.S. visa, or been unlawfully present in, or deported from, the United States? ☐ YES ☐ NO

● Have you ever withheld custody of a U.S. citizen child outside the United States from a person granted legal custody by a U.S. court, voted in the United States in violation of any law or regulation, or renounced U.S. citizenship for the purpose of avoiding taxation? ☐ YES ☐ NO

● Have you ever been afflicted with a communicable disease of public health significance or a dangerous physical or mental disorder, or ever been a drug abuser or addict? ☐ YES ☐ NO

While a YES answer does not automatically signify ineligibility for a visa, if you answered YES you may be required to personally appear before a consular officer.

39. Was this Application Prepared by Another Person on Your Behalf?
(If answer is YES, then have that person complete item 40.) ☐ Yes ☐ No

40. Application Prepared By:
NAME: _____ Relationship to Applicant: _____
ADDRESS: _____
Signature of Person Preparing Form: _____ DATE *(dd-mmm-yyyy)* _____

41. I certify that I have read and understood all the questions set forth in this application and the answers I have furnished on this form are true and correct to the best of my knowledge and belief. I understand that any false or misleading statement may result in the permanent refusal of a visa or denial of entry into the United States. I understand that possession of a visa does not automatically entitle the bearer to enter the United States of America upon arrival at a port of entry if he or she is found inadmissible.

APPLICANT'S SIGNATURE _____ DATE *(dd-mmm-yyyy)* _____

Privacy Act and Paperwork Reduction Act Statements

INA Section 222(f) provides that visa issuance and refusal records shall be considered confidential and shall be used only for the formulation, amendment, administration, or enforcement of the immigration, nationality, and other laws of the United States. Certified copies of visa records may be made available to a court which certifies that the information contained in such records is needed in a case pending before the court.

Public reporting burden for this collection of information is estimated to average 1 hour per response, including time required for searching existing data sources, gathering the necessary data, providing the information required, and reviewing the final collection. You do not have to provide the information unless this collection displays a currently valid OMB number. Send comments on the accuracy of this estimate of the burden and recommendations for reducing it to: U.S. Department of State, A/RPS/DIR, Washington, DC 20520.

DS-156

U.S. DEPARTMENT OF LABOR
Employment and Training Administration

APPLICATION
FOR
ALIEN EMPLOYMENT CERTIFICATION

OMB Approval No. 1205-0015   Expires: 01/31/2011

IMPORTANT: READ CAREFULLY BEFORE COMPLETING THIS FORM

PRINT legibly in ink or use a typewriter. If you need more space to answer questions in this form, use a separate sheet. Identify each answer with the number of the corresponding question. SIGN AND DATE each sheet in original signature.

To knowingly furnish any false information in the preparation of this form and any supplemental thereto or to aid, abet, or counsel another to do so is a felony punishable by $10,000 fine or 5 years in the penitentiary, or both (18 U.S.C. 1001)

PART A. OFFER OF EMPLOYMENT

1. Name of Alien   (Family name in capital letter, First, Middle, Maiden)

2. Present Address of Alien   (Number, Street, City and Town, State ZIP code or Province, Country)

3. Type of Visa (if in U.S.)

The following information is submitted as an offer of employment

4. Name of Employer   (Full name of Organization)

5. Federal Taxpayer ID – EIN

6. Address   (Number, Street, City and Town, State ZIP code)

7. Address Where Alien Will Work   (if different than Item 6)

8. Nature of Employer's Business Activity	9. Name of Job Title	10. Total Hours Per Week		11. Work Schedule (Hourly)	12. Rate of Pay	
		a. Basic	b. Overtime	a.m. p.m.	a. Basic $ per	b. Overtime $ per

13. Describe Fully the job to be Performed   (Duties)

14. State in detail the MINIMUM education, training, and experience for a worker to perform satisfactorily the job duties described in item 13 above.

15. Other Special Requirements

EDU-CATION (Enter number of years)	Grade School	High School	College	College Degree Required (specify)
				Major Field of Study

TRAIN-ING	No. Yrs.		No. Mos.	Type of Training

EXPERI-ENCE	Job Offered		Related Occupation	Related Occupation (specify)
	Number			
	Yrs.	Mos.	Yrs.	Mos.

16. Occupational Title of Person Who Will Be Alien's Immediate Supervisor

17. Number of Employees Alien Will Supervise

ENDORSEMENTS
(Make no entry in section – for Government use only)

Date Forms Received

L.O.	S.O.
R.O.	N.O.
Ind. Code	Occ. Code
Occ. Title	

ETA 750 (Nov. 2007)

OMB Control No. 1205-0015   Expires: 01/31/2011

18. COMPLETE ITEMS ONLY IF JOB IS TEMPORARY			19. IF JOB IS UNIONIZED (Complete)	
a. No. of Openings To Be Filled by Aliens Under Job Offer	b. Exact Dates You Expect To Employ Alien		a. Number of Local	b. Name of Local
	From	To		
				c. City and State

20. STATEMENT FOR LIVE-AT-WORK JOB OFFERS   (Complete for Private Household ONLY)

a. Description of Residence		b. No. Persons residing at Place of Employment				c. Will free board and private room not shared with anyone be provided?	("X" one)
("X" one)	Number of Rooms	Adults		Children	Ages		❑ YES ❑ NO
❑ House			BOYS				
❑ Apartment			GIRLS				

21. DESCRIBE EFFORTS TO RECRUIT U.S. WORKERS AND THE RESULTS. (Specify Sources of Recruitment by Name)

22. Applications require various types of documentation. Please read Part II of the instructions to assure that appropriate supporting documentation is included with your application.

23. EMPLOYER CERTIFICATIONS

By virtue of my signature below, I HEREBY CERTIFY the following conditions of employment.

a. I have enough funds available to pay the wage or salary offered the alien.

b. The wage offered equal or exceeds the prevailing wage and I guarantee that, if a labor certification is granted, the wage paid to the alien when the alien begins work will equal or exceed the prevailing wage which is applicable at the time the alien begins work.

c. The wage offered is not based on commissions, bonuses, or other incentives, unless I guarantee a wage paid on a weekly, bi-weekly, or monthly basis.

d. I will be able to place the alien on the payroll on or before the date of the alien's proposed entrance into the United States.

e. The job opportunity does not involve unlawful discrimination by race, creed, color, national origin, age, sex, religion, handicap, or citizenship.

f. The job opportunity is not:

   (1) Vacant because the former occupant is on strike or is being locked out in the course of a labor dispute involving a work stoppage.

   (2) At issue in a labor dispute involving a work stoppage.

g. The job opportunity's terms, conditions and occupational environment are not contrary to Federal, State or local law.

h. The job opportunity has been and is clearly open to any qualified U.S. worker.

24. DECLARATIONS

DECLARATION OF EMPLOYER	Pursuant to 28 U.S.C. 1746, I declare under penalty of perjury the foregoing is true and correct.	
SIGNATURE		DATE
NAME (Type or Print)	TITLE	
EMAIL ADDRESS	CONTACT TELEPHONE	FAX TELEPHONE
AUTHORIZATION OF AGENT OF EMPLOYER	I HEREBY DESIGNATE the agent below to represent me for the purposes of labor certification and I TAKE FULL RESPONSIBILITY for accuracy of any representations made by my agent.	
SIGNATURE OF EMPLOYER		DATE
NAME OF AGENT (Type or Print)	ADDRESS OF AGENT (Number, Street, City, State, ZIP code)	
EMAIL ADDRESS	CONTACT TELEPHONE	FAX TELEPHONE

OMB No.: 1205-0015 OMB Expiration Date: 01/31/2011 OMB Burden Hours averages 1.5 hours. OMB Burden Statement: These reporting instructions have been approved under the Paperwork Reduction Act of 1995. Persons are not required to respond to this collection of information unless it displays a currently valid OMB control number. Obligations to reply are mandatory. (Title 8 U.S.C. §§ 1882, 1884, and 1188) Public reporting burden for this collection of information, which is to assist with planning and program management, includes the time to review instructions, search existing data sources, gather and maintain the data needed, and complete and review the collection of information. Send comments regarding this burden estimate or any other aspect of this collection of information, including suggestions for reducing this burden, to the U.S. Department of Labor, Room C-4312, 200 Constitution Ave. NW, Washington, DC 20210. (Paperwork Reduction Project OMB 1205-0015.)

| Labor Condition Application for Nonimmigrant Workers | **U.S. Department of Labor** Employment and Training Administration | **Form ETA 9035** OMB Approval: 1205-0310 Expiration Date: 11/30/2008 |

A. Program Designation   ○ H-1B   ○ H-1B1 Chile   ○ H-1B1 Singapore
You must choose one: ○ E-3 Australian

B. Employer's Information

1. Return Fax Number

If you want the application returned by mail, leave the Return Fax Number blank.   (___) ____ - ____

2. Employer's Name

3. Employer's Address (Number and Street)

4. Employer's City   State   Zip/Postal Code

5. Employer's EIN Number   6. Employer's Phone Number   Extension
___ - _____   (___) ____ - ____

C. Rate of Pay

1. Wage Rate (or Rate From) (Required):   3. Rate is Per: 4. Is this position part-time?
$ _____ . __
                                            ○ Year   ○ Week
2. Rate Up To (Optional):   ○ Month   ○ Hour   ○ Yes
$ _____ . __   ○ 2 Weeks   ○ No

Please Note: Part-time hours worked by nonimmigrant(s) will be in the range of hours stated on the USCIS Form(s) I-129.

D. Period of Employment and Occupation Information   *Please Note: The Date Information MUST be in MM/DD/YYYY format*

1. Begin Date
__ / __ / ____

3. Occupational Code
①②③④⑤⑥⑦⑧⑨⓪
①②③④⑤⑥⑦⑧⑨⓪
①②③④⑤⑥⑦⑧⑨⓪

4. Number of Nonimmigrant Workers
①②③④⑤⑥⑦⑧⑨⓪
①②③④⑤⑥⑦⑧⑨⓪
①②③④⑤⑥⑦⑧⑨⓪

2. End Date
__ / __ / ____

5. Job Title

E. Information Relating to Work Location for the Nonimmigrant Worker(s)   This section is REQUIRED

1. City   *Do NOT write "Same As Above". This section MUST be filled out.*   State

2. Prevailing Wage   3. Wage is Per: 4. Wage Source
$ _____ . __
                     ○ Year   ○ Week   ○ OES
5. Year Source Published   ○ Month   ○ Hour   ○ Collective Bargaining Agreement
____   ○ 2 Weeks   ○ Other

If OTHER is chosen as the Wage Source, Numbers 5 and 6 in this section MUST be filled out.

6. Other Wage Source

Page Link
| 4 | 4 | 5 | 8 | 1 | 3 |

If filing the form electronically, the Page Link field will be automatically created for you upon printing. If filing the form manually, please ensure that the Page Link field contains a 6 digit number that is repeated on all 3 pages.

3417

| Labor Condition Application for Nonimmigrant Workers | **U.S. Department of Labor** Employment and Training Administration | **Form ETA 9035** OMB Approval: 1205-0310 Expiration Date: 11/30/2008 |

E. Subsection A Information for Additional or Subsequent Work Location
  This Section should be completed only if filing for more than 1 work location.

1. City

☐☐☐☐☐☐☐☐☐☐☐☐☐☐☐☐☐☐☐☐☐☐   State ☐☐

2. Prevailing Wage

$ ☐☐☐☐☐☐ . ☐☐

  5. Year Source Published

☐☐☐☐

3. Wage is Per:
  ○ Year   ○ Week
  ○ Month ○ Hour
  ○ 2 Weeks

4. Wage Source
  ○ OES
  ○ Collective Bargaining Agreement
  ○ Other

If OTHER is chosen as the Wage Source, Numbers 5 and 6 in this section MUST be filled out.

6. Other Wage Source

☐☐☐☐☐☐☐☐☐☐☐☐☐☐☐☐☐☐☐☐☐☐☐☐

F. Employer Labor Condition Statements

  ! **Please Note: In order for your application to be processed, you MUST read section E of the Labor Condition Application cover pages under the heading "Employer Labor Condition Statements" and agree to all 4 labor condition statements summarized below:**

(1) Wages: Pay nonimmigrants at least the local prevailing wage or the employer's actual wage, whichever is higher, and pay for non-productive time. Offer nonimmigrants benefits on the same basis as U.S. workers.

(2) Working Conditions: Provide working conditions for nonimmigrants which will not adversely affect the working conditions of workers similarly employed.

(3) Strike, Lockout, or Work Stoppage: No strike or lockout in the occupational classification at the place of employment.

(4) Notice: Notice to union or to workers at the place of employment. A copy of this form to the nonimmigrant worker(s).

  I have read and agree to Employer Labor Condition Statements 1, 2, 3, and 4 as set forth in Section E of the Labor Condition Application Cover Pages.   ○ Yes   ○ No

F-1. Additional Employer Labor Condition Statements - H-1B Employers Only
  Please Note: In order for an application regarding H-1B nonimmigrants to be processed, you MUST read Section F-1 - Subsections 1 and 2 of the Labor Condition Application cover pages under the heading "Additional Employer Labor Condition Statements" and choose one of the 3 alternatives (A, B, or C) listed below in Subsection 1. If you mark Alternative B, you MUST read Section F-1 - Subsection 2 of the cover pages under the heading "Additional Employer Labor Condition Statements" and indicate your agreement to all 3 additional statements summarized below in Subsection 2.

1. Subsection 1
  Choose ONE of the following 3 alternatives:

A ○ **Employer is not H-1B dependent and is not a willful violator.**

B ○ **Employer is H-1B dependent and/or a willful violator.**

C ○ **Employer is H-1B dependent and/or a willful violator BUT will use this application ONLY to support H-1B petitions for exempt nonimmigrants.**

2. Subsection 2
  If Alternative B in Subsection 1 is marked, the following Additional Labor Condition Statements are applicable:

A. **Displacement:** Non-displacement of the U.S. workers in employer s work force;

B. **Secondary Displacement:** Non-displacement of U.S. workers in another employer's work force; and

C. **Recruitment and Hiring:** Recruitment of U.S. workers and hiring of U.S. worker applicant(s) who are equally or better qualified than the H-1B nonimmigrant(s).

  I have read and agree to Additional Labor Condition Statements 2 A, B, and C.   ○ Yes   ○ No

Page Link					
4	4	5	8	1	3

If filing the form electronically, the Page Link field will be automatically created for you upon printing. If filing the form manually, please ensure that the Page Link field contains a 6 digit number that is repeated on all 3 pages.

3417

| Labor Condition Application for Nonimmigrant Workers | **U.S. Department of Labor** Employment and Training Administration | **Form ETA 9035** OMB Approval: 1205-0310 Expiration Date: 11/30/2008 |

G. Public Disclosure Information

You must choose one of the two options listed in this Section.

1. Public disclosure information will be kept at:

   ○ Employer's principal place of business

   ○ Place of employment

H. Declaration of Employer

By signing this form, I, on behalf of the employer, attest that the information and labor condition statements provided are true and accurate; that I have read the sections E, F, and F-1 of the cover pages (Form ETA 9035CP), and that I agree to comply with the Labor Condition Statements as set forth in the cover pages and with the Department of Labor regulations (20 CFR part 655, Subparts H and I). I agree to make this application, supporting documentation, and other records available to officials of the Department of Labor upon request during any investigation under the Immigration and Nationality Act.

1. First Name of Hiring or Other Designated Official   MI

2. Last Name of Hiring or Other Designated Official

3. Hiring or Other Designated Official Title

5. Date Signed [ ] / [ ] / [   ]

4. Signature - Do NOT let signature extend beyond the box

Making fraudulent representations on this Form can lead to civil or criminal action under 18 U.S.C. 1001, 18 U.S.C. 1546, or other provisions of law.

I. Contact Information

1. Contact First Name   MI

2. Contact Last Name

3. Contact Phone Number   Extension

([   ]) [   ] - [   ]   [   ]

J. U.S. Government Agency Use Only

By virtue of my signature below, I hereby acknowledge this application certified for

Date Starting _____   and Date Ending _____

_____   _____   _____
Signature and Title of Authorized DOL Official   ETA Case Number   Date
The Department of Labor is not the guarantor of the accuracy, truthfulness, or adequacy of a certified labor condition application.

K. Complaints

Complaints alleging misrepresentation of material facts in the labor condition application and/or failure to comply with the terms of the labor condition application may be filed with any office of the Wage and Hour Division, U.S. Department of Labor. Complaints alleging failure to offer employment to an equally or better qualified U.S. worker, or an employer's misrepresentation regarding such offer(s) of employment, may be filed with: U.S Department of Justice * Office of the Special Counsel for Immigration-Related Unfair Employment Practices* 950 Pennsylvania Ave. NW * Washington. DC * 20530.

| Page Link | | | | | | **If filing the form electronically, the Page Link field will be automatically created for you upon printing. If filing the form manually, please ensure that the Page Link field contains a 6 digit number that is repeated on all 3 pages.** |
| 4 | 4 | 5 | 8 | 1 | 3 | |

3417

OMB Approval: 1205-0451
Expiration Date: 03/31/2008

Application for Permanent Employment Certification
ETA Form 9089
U.S. Department of Labor

Please read and review the filing instructions before completing this form. A copy of the instructions can be found at http://www.foreignlaborcert.doleta.gov/pdf/9089inst.pdf

Employing or continuing to employ an alien unauthorized to work in the United States is illegal and may subject the employer to criminal prosecution, civil money penalties, or both.

A. Refiling Instructions

1. Are you seeking to utilize the filing date from a previously submitted Application for Alien Employment Certification (ETA 750)?	❏ Yes ❏ No

1-A. If Yes, enter the previous filing date

1-B. Indicate the previous SWA or local office case number OR if not available, specify state where case was originally filed:

B. Schedule A or Sheepherder Information

1. Is this application in support of a Schedule A or Sheepherder Occupation?	❏ Yes ❏ No

If Yes, do NOT send this application to the Department of Labor. All applications in support of Schedule A or Sheepherder Occupations must be sent directly to the appropriate Department of Homeland Security office.

C. Employer Information (Headquarters or Main Office)

1. Employer's name

2. Address 1

   Address 2

3. City	State/Province	Country	Postal code

4. Phone number	Extension

5. Number of employees	6. Year commenced business

7. FEIN (Federal Employer Identification Number)	8. NAICS code

9. Is the employer a closely held corporation, partnership, or sole proprietorship in which the alien has an ownership interest, or is there a familial relationship between the owners, stockholders, partners, corporate officers, incorporators, and the alien?	❏ Yes ❏ No

D. Employer Contact Information (This section must be filled out. This information must be different from the agent or attorney information listed in Section E).

1. Contact's last name	First name	Middle initial

2. Address 1

   Address 2

3. City	State/Province	Country	Postal code

4. Phone number	Extension

5. E-mail address

OMB Approval: 1205-0451   Application for Permanent Employment Certification
Expiration Date: 03/31/2008   ETA Form 9089
                                            U.S. Department of Labor

E. Agent or Attorney Information (If applicable)

1. Agent or attorney's last name	First name	Middle initial
2. Firm name		
3. Firm EIN	4. Phone number	Extension
5. Address 1		
Address 2		

6. City	State/Province	Country	Postal code

7. E-mail address

F. Prevailing Wage Information (as provided by the State Workforce Agency)

1. Prevailing wage tracking number (if applicable)	2. SOC/O*NET(OES) code
3. Occupation Title	4. Skill Level

5. Prevailing wage   Per: (Choose only one)
   $ ❑ Hour   ❑ Week   ❑ Bi-Weekly   ❑ Month   ❑ Year

6. Prevailing wage source (Choose only one)
   ❑ OES   ❑ CBA   ❑ Employer Conducted Survey   ❑ DBA   ❑ SCA   ❑ Other

6-A. If Other is indicated in question 6, specify:

7. Determination date	8. Expiration date

G. Wage Offer Information

1. Offered wage
   From: To: (Optional)   Per: (Choose only one)
   $ $ ❑ Hour   ❑ Week   ❑ Bi-Weekly   ❑ Month   ❑ Year

H. Job Opportunity Information (Where work will be performed)

1. Primary worksite (where work is to be performed) address 1

   Address 2

2. City	State	Postal code

3. Job title

4. Education: minimum level required:

❑ None   ❑ High School   ❑ Associate's   ❑ Bachelor's   ❑ Master's   ❑ Doctorate   ❑ Other

4-A. If Other is indicated in question 4, specify the education required:

4-B. Major field of study

5. Is training required in the job opportunity?   5-A. If Yes, number of months of training required:
   ❑ Yes   ❑ No

OMB Approval: 1205-0451   Application for Permanent Employment Certification
Expiration Date: 03/31/2008   ETA Form 9089
U.S. Department of Labor

H. Job Opportunity Information Continued

5-B. Indicate the field of training:

6. Is experience in the job offered required for the job?   6-A. If Yes, number of months experience required: ❑ Yes   ❑ No

7. Is there an alternate field of study that is acceptable?	❑ Yes ❑ No

7-A. If Yes, specify the major field of study:

8. Is there an alternate combination of education and experience that is acceptable?	❑ Yes ❑ No

8-A. If Yes, specify the alternate level of education required: ❑ None   ❑ High School   ❑ Associate's   ❑ Bachelor's   ❑ Master's   ❑ Doctorate   ❑ Other

8-B. If Other is indicated in question 8-A, indicate the alternate level of education required:

8-C. If applicable, indicate the number of years experience acceptable in question 8:

9. Is a foreign educational equivalent acceptable?   ❑ Yes   ❑ No

10. Is experience in an alternate occupation acceptable?   10-A. If Yes, number of months experience in alternate occupation required: ❑ Yes   ❑ No

10-B. Identify the job title of the acceptable alternate occupation:

11. Job duties – If submitting by mail, add attachment if necessary. Job duties description must begin in this space.

12. Are the job opportunity's requirements normal for the occupation? *If the answer to this question is No, the employer must be prepared to provide documentation demonstrating that the job requirements are supported by business necessity.*	❑ Yes ❑ No
13. Is knowledge of a foreign language required to perform the job duties? *If the answer to this question is Yes, the employer must be prepared to provide documentation demonstrating that the language requirements are supported by business necessity.*	❑ Yes ❑ No

14. Specific skills or other requirements – If submitting by mail, add attachment if necessary. Skills description must begin in this space.

OMB Approval: 1205-0451   Application for Permanent Employment Certification
Expiration Date: 03/31/2008   ETA Form 9089
                                          U.S. Department of Labor

H. Job Opportunity Information Continued

15. Does this application involve a job opportunity that includes a combination of occupations?	❑ Yes ❑ No
16. Is the position identified in this application being offered to the alien identified in Section J?	❑ Yes ❑ No
17. Does the job require the alien to live on the employer's premises?	❑ Yes ❑ No
18. Is the application for a live-in household domestic service worker?	❑ Yes ❑ No
8-A. If Yes, have the employer and the alien executed the required employment contract and has the employer provided a copy of the contract to the alien?	❑ Yes ❑ No ❑ NA

I. Recruitment Information

a. *Occupation Type – All must complete this section.*

1. Is this application for a **professional occupation**, other than a college or university teacher? Professional occupations are those for which a bachelor's degree (or equivalent) is normally required.	❑ Yes ❑ No
2. Is this application for a college or university teacher? **If Yes, complete questions 2-A and 2-B below.**	❑ Yes ❑ No
2-A. Did you select the candidate using a competitive recruitment and selection process?	❑ Yes ❑ No
2-B. Did you use the basic recruitment process for professional occupations?	❑ Yes ❑ No

b. *Special Recruitment and Documentation Procedures for College and University Teachers – Complete only if the answer to question I.a.2-A is Yes.*

3. Date alien selected:
4. Name and date of national professional journal in which advertisement was placed:
5. Specify additional recruitment information in this space. Add an attachment if necessary.

c. *Professional/Non-Professional Information – Complete this section unless your answer to question B.1 or I.a.2-A is YES.*

6. Start date for the SWA job order	7. End date for the SWA job order
8. Is there a Sunday edition of the newspaper in the area of intended employment?	❑ Yes ❑ No
9. Name of newspaper (of general circulation) in which the first advertisement was placed:	
10. Date of first advertisement identified in question 9:	
11. Name of newspaper or professional journal (if applicable) in which second advertisement was placed: ❑ Newspaper ❑ Journal	

OMB Approval: 1205-0451
Expiration Date: 03/31/2008

Application for Permanent Employment Certification
ETA Form 9089
U.S. Department of Labor

I. Recruitment Information Continued

12. Date of second newspaper advertisement or date of publication of journal identified in question 11:

d. Professional Recruitment Information – Complete if the answer to question I.a.1 is YES or if the answer to I.a.2-B is YES. Complete at least 3 of the items.

13. Dates advertised at job fair From: To:	14. Dates of on-campus recruiting From: To:
15. Dates posted on employer web site From: To:	16. Dates advertised with trade or professional organization From: To:
17. Dates listed with job search web site From: To:	18. Dates listed with private employment firm From: To:
19. Dates advertised with employee referral program From: To:	20. Dates advertised with campus placement office From: To:
21. Dates advertised with local or ethnic newspaper From: To:	22. Dates advertised with radio or TV ads From: To:

e. General Information – All must complete this section.

23. Has the employer received payment of any kind for the submission of this application?	❑ Yes ❑ No	
23-A. If Yes, describe details of the payment including the amount, date and purpose of the payment :		
24. Has the bargaining representative for workers in the occupation in which the alien will be employed been provided with notice of this filing at least 30 days but not more than 180 days before the date the application is filed?	❑ Yes ❑ No ❑ NA	
25. If there is no bargaining representative, has a notice of this filing been posted for 10 business days in a conspicuous location at the place of employment, ending at least 30 days before but not more than 180 days before the date the application is filed?	❑ Yes ❑ No ❑ NA	
26. Has the employer had a layoff in the area of intended employment in the occupation involved in this application or in a related occupation within the six months immediately preceding the filing of this application?	❑ Yes ❑ No	
26-A. If Yes, were the laid off U.S. workers notified and considered for the job opportunity for which certification is sought?	❑ Yes ❑ No ❑ NA	

J. Alien Information (This section must be filled out. This information must be different from the agent or attorney information listed in Section E).

1. Alien's last name	First name	Full middle name
2. Current address 1		
Address 2		
3. City State/Province	Country	Postal code
4. Phone number of current residence		
5. Country of citizenship	6. Country of birth	
7. Alien's date of birth	8. Class of admission	
9. Alien registration number (A#)	10. Alien admission number (I-94)	
11. Education: highest level achieved relevant to the requested occupation: ❑ None ❑ High School ❑ Associate's ❑ Bachelor's ❑ Master's ❑ Doctorate ❑ Other		

OMB Approval: 1205-0451   Application for Permanent Employment Certification
Expiration Date: 03/31/2008   ETA Form 9089
                                            U.S. Department of Labor

J. Alien Information Continued

11-A. If Other indicated in question 11, specify	
12. Specify major field(s) of study	
13. Year relevant education completed	
14. Institution where relevant education specified in question 11 was received	
15. Address 1 of conferring institution	
Address 2	

16. City	State/Province	Country	Postal code

17. Did the alien complete the training required for the requested job opportunity, as indicated in question H.5?	❏ Yes ❏ No ❏ NA
18. Does the alien have the experience as required for the requested job opportunity indicated in question H.6?	❏ Yes ❏ No ❏ NA
19. Does the alien possess the alternate combination of education and experience as indicated in question H.8?	❏ Yes ❏ No ❏ NA
20. Does the alien have the experience in an alternate occupation specified in question H.10?	❏ Yes ❏ No ❏ NA
21. Did the alien gain any of the qualifying experience with the employer in a position substantially comparable to the job opportunity requested?	❏ Yes ❏ No ❏ NA
22. Did the employer pay for any of the alien's education or training necessary to satisfy any of the employer's job requirements for this position?	❏ Yes ❏ No
23. Is the alien currently employed by the petitioning employer?	❏ Yes ❏ No

K. Alien Work Experience

List all jobs the alien has held during the past 3 years. Also list any other experience that qualifies the alien for the job opportunity for which the employer is seeking certification.

a. Job 1

1. Employer name			
2. Address 1			
Address 2			
3. City	State/Province	Country	Postal code
4. Type of business		5. Job title	
6. Start date	7. End date	8. Number of hours worked per week	

OMB Approval: 1205-0451
Expiration Date: 03/31/2008

Application for Permanent Employment Certification
ETA Form 9089
U.S. Department of Labor

K. Alien Work Experience Continued

9. Job details (duties performed, use of tools, machines, equipment, skills, qualifications, certifications, licenses, etc. Include the phone number of the employer and the name of the alien's supervisor.)

b. Job 2

1. Employer name	
2. Address 1	
Address 2	

3. City	State/Province	Country	Postal code

4. Type of business	5. Job title

6. Start date	7. End date	8. Number of hours worked per week

9. Job details (duties performed, use of tools, machines, equipment, skills, qualifications, certifications, licenses, etc. Include the phone number of the employer and the name of the alien's supervisor.)

c. Job 3

1. Employer name	
2. Address 1	
Address 2	

3. City	State/Province	Country	Postal code

4. Type of business	5. Job title

6. Start date	7. End date	8. Number of hours worked per week

OMB Approval: 1205-0451   Application for Permanent Employment Certification
Expiration Date: 03/31/2008   ETA Form 9089
                                           U.S. Department of Labor

K. Alien Work Experience Continued

> 9. Job details (duties performed, use of tools, machines, equipment, skills, qualifications, certifications, licenses, etc.
> Include the phone number of the employer and the name of the alien's supervisor.)

L. Alien Declaration

*I declare under penalty of perjury that Sections J and K are true and correct. I understand that to knowingly furnish
false information in the preparation of this form and any supplement thereto or to aid, abet, or counsel another to do so is
a federal offense punishable by a fine or imprisonment up to five years or both under 18 U.S.C. §§ 2 and 1001. Other
penalties apply as well to fraud or misuse of ETA immigration documents and to perjury with respect to such documents
under 18 U.S.C. §§ 1546 and 1621.*

*In addition, I **further declare** under penalty of perjury that I intend to accept the position offered in Section H of this
application if a labor certification is approved and I am granted a visa or an adjustment of status based on this
application.*

1. Alien's last name	First name	Full middle name
2. Signature	Date signed	

Note – The signature and date signed do not have to be filled out when electronically submitting to the Department of Labor for
processing, but must be complete when submitting by mail. If the application is submitted electronically, any resulting certification
MUST be signed *immediately upon receipt* from DOL before it can be submitted to USCIS for final processing.

M. Declaration of Preparer

1. **Was the application completed by the employer?** If No, you must complete this section.	☐ Yes	☐ No

*I hereby certify that I have prepared this application at the direct request of the employer listed in Section C and
that to the best of my knowledge the information contained herein is true and correct. I understand that to
knowingly furnish false information in the preparation of this form and any supplement thereto or to aid, abet, or counsel
another to do so is a federal offense punishable by a fine, imprisonment up to five years or both under 18 U.S.C. §§ 2 and
1001. Other penalties apply as well to fraud or misuse of ETA immigration documents and to perjury with respect to such
documents under 18 U.S.C. §§ 1546 and 1621.*

2. Preparer's last name	First name	Middle initial
3. Title		
4. E-mail address		
5. Signature	Date signed	

Note – The signature and date signed do not have to be filled out when electronically submitting to the Department of Labor for
processing, but must be complete when submitting by mail. If the application is submitted electronically, any resulting certification MUST
be signed *immediately upon receipt* from DOL before it can be submitted to USCIS for final processing.

OMB Approval: 1205-0451
Expiration Date: 03/31/2008

Application for Permanent Employment Certification
ETA Form 9089
U.S. Department of Labor

N. Employer Declaration

*By virtue of my signature below, **I HEREBY CERTIFY** the following conditions of employment:*

1. The offered wage equals or exceeds the prevailing wage and I will pay at least the prevailing wage.
2. The wage is not based on commissions, bonuses or other incentives, unless I guarantees a wage paid on a weekly, bi-weekly, or monthly basis that equals or exceeds the prevailing wage.
3. I have enough funds available to pay the wage or salary offered the alien.
4. I will be able to place the alien on the payroll on or before the date of the alien's proposed entrance into the United States.
5. The job opportunity does not involve unlawful discrimination by race, creed, color, national origin, age, sex, religion, handicap, or citizenship.
6. The job opportunity is not:
   a. Vacant because the former occupant is on strike or is being locked out in the course of a labor dispute involving a work stoppage; or
   b. At issue in a labor dispute involving a work stoppage.
7. The job opportunity's terms, conditions, and occupational environment are not contrary to Federal, state or local law.
8. The job opportunity has been and is clearly open to any U.S. worker.
9. The U.S. workers who applied for the job opportunity were rejected for lawful job-related reasons.
10. The job opportunity is for full-time, permanent employment for an employer other than the alien.

I hereby designate the agent or attorney identified in section E (if any) to represent me for the purpose of labor certification and, by virtue of my signature in Block 3 below, **I take full responsibility** for the accuracy of any representations made by my agent or attorney.

I declare under penalty of perjury that I have read and reviewed this application and that to the best of my knowledge the information contained herein is true and accurate. *I understand that to knowingly furnish false information in the preparation of this form and any supplement thereto or to aid, abet, or counsel another to do so is a federal offense punishable by a fine or imprisonment up to five years or both under 18 U.S.C. §§ 2 and 1001. Other penalties apply as well to fraud or misuse of ETA immigration documents and to perjury with respect to such documents under 18 U.S.C. §§ 1546 and 1621.*

1. Last name	First name	Middle initial
2. Title		
3. Signature	Date signed	

Note – The signature and date signed do not have to be filled out when electronically submitting to the Department of Labor for processing, but must be complete when submitting by mail. If the application is submitted electronically, any resulting certification MUST be signed *immediately upon receipt* from DOL before it can be submitted to USCIS for final processing.

O. U.S. Government Agency Use Only

Pursuant to the provisions of Section 212 (a)(5)(A) of the Immigration and Nationality Act, as amended, I hereby certify that there are not sufficient U.S. workers available and the employment of the above will not adversely affect the wages and working conditions of workers in the U.S. similarly employed.

Signature of Certifying Officer

Date Signed

Case Number

Filing Date

OMB Approval: 1205-0451
Expiration Date: 03/31/2008

Application for Permanent Employment Certification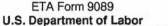
ETA Form 9089
U.S. Department of Labor

P. OMB Information   *Paperwork Reduction Act Information Control Number 1205-0451*

Persons are not required to respond to this collection of information unless it displays a currently valid OMB control number.

Respondent's reply to these reporting requirements is required to obtain the benefits of permanent employment certification (Immigration and Nationality Act, Section 212(a)(5)). Public reporting burden for this collection of information is estimated to average 1¼ hours per response, including the time for reviewing instructions, searching existing data sources, gathering and maintaining the data needed, and completing and reviewing the collection of information. Send comments regarding this burden estimate to the Division of Foreign Labor Certification * U.S. Department of Labor * Room C4312 * 200 Constitution Ave., NW * Washington, DC * 20210.
Do NOT send the completed application to this address.

Q. Privacy Statement Information

In accordance with the Privacy Act of 1974, as amended (5 U.S.C. 552a), you are hereby notified that the information provided herein is protected under the Privacy Act. The Department of Labor (Department or DOL) maintains a System of Records titled Employer Application and Attestation File for Permanent and Temporary Alien Workers (DOL/ETA-7) that includes this record.

Under routine uses for this system of records, case files developed in processing labor certification applications, labor condition applications, or labor attestations may be released as follows: in connection with appeals of denials before the DOL Office of Administrative Law Judges and Federal courts, records may be released to the employers that filed such applications, their representatives, to named alien beneficiaries or their representatives, and to the DOL Office of Administrative Law Judges and Federal courts; and in connection with administering and enforcing immigration laws and regulations, records may be released to such agencies as the DOL Office of Inspector General, Employment Standards Administration, the Department of Homeland Security, and the Department of State.

Further relevant disclosures may be made in accordance with the Privacy Act and under the following circumstances: in connection with federal litigation; for law enforcement purposes; to authorized parent locator persons under Pub. L. 93-647; to an information source or public authority in connection with personnel, security clearance, procurement, or benefit-related matters; to a contractor or their employees, grantees or their employees, consultants, or volunteers who have been engaged to assist the agency in the performance of Federal activities; for Federal debt collection purposes; to the Office of Management and Budget in connection with its legislative review, coordination, and clearance activities; to a Member of Congress or their staff in response to an inquiry of the Congressional office made at the written request of the subject of the record; in connection with records management; and to the news media and the public when a matter under investigation becomes public knowledge, the Solicitor of Labor determines the disclosure is necessary to preserve confidence in the integrity of the Department, or the Solicitor of Labor determines that a legitimate public interest exists in the disclosure of information, unless the Solicitor of Labor determines that disclosure would constitute an unwarranted invasion of personal privacy.

Illinois Department of Employment Security

33 South State Street, Chicago, Illinois 60603

www.ides.state.il.us

PLEASE TYPE OR PRINT

NAME AND ADDRESS OF PERSON REQUESTING WAGE:

_____

_____

_____

FAX NO: _____

PHONE NO: _____

REPLY REQUESTED BY: FAX ☐ MAIL ☐

Employer Name _____

REQUEST FOR PREVAILING WAGE STATEMENT

YOUR REQUEST MAY BE MAILED OR FAXED TO US.

OUR FAX NUMBER:

(312) 793-5151

PLEASE DO NOT SUBMIT DUPLICATE REQUESTS. ALLOW 14 WORKING DAYS FOR PROCESSING

Job Location: CITY, **COUNTY**, STATE (all required)				PLEASE PROVIDE ALL INFORMATION REQUESTED				
NATURE OF EMPLOYER'S BUSINESS	Job Title			Total Hours Per Week		Work Schedule (Hourly)	Rate of Pay	
				a. Basic	b. Overtime		a. Basic $	b. Overtime $
	Job Title of Worker's Immediate Supervisor:					a.m. p.m.	per	per hour

DESCRIBE FULLY THE JOB TO BE PERFORMED:

SUGGESTED DOT _____   SUGGESTED OES/SOC _____

STATE IN DETAIL THE MINIMUM EDUCATION, TRAINING & EXPERIENCE REQUIRED					OTHER SPECIAL REQUIREMENTS:
EDU-CATION *(Enter number of years)*	Grade	High	College	College Degree Required	
				Major Field of Study	
TRAIN-ING	No. Yrs.		No. Mos.	Type of Training	
EXPERI-ENCE	Job Offered		Related Occupation	Related Occupation *(specify)*	
	Yrs.	Mos.	Yrs.	Mos.	NUMBER OF OTHER EMPLOYEES TO BE SUPERVISED *(if any)*:
		O	**R**		

This rate is valid for: ☐ date issued thru 6/30/2009   ☐ **90 days from the date of this determination.**

The prevailing wage for the above occupation in the area indicated

IS: $ _____ PER _____ DATE _____

S.O.C. Title _____

OES/SOC Code _____
(Rev. 07/08)

Wage Source:

☐ OES

☐ Other _____

Level _____

IDES Prevailing Wage Specialist
(312) 793-3216

Appendix C.
Web Sites

Centers for Disease Control and Prevention: *www.cdc.gov*.
Executive Office for Immigration Review: *www.usdoj.gov/eoir*.
Foreign Labor Certification, U.S. Department of Labor: *www.foreignlaborcert.doleta.gov*.
Internal Revenue Service: *www.irs.gov*.
Selective Service System: *www.sss.gov*.
U.S. Citizenship and Immigration Services (Immigration Forms, Fees and Mailing Addresses): *www.uscis.gov*.
U.S. Customs and Border Protection: *www.cbp.gov*.
U.S. Department of Homeland Security: *www.dhs.gov*.
U.S. Department of Justice: *www.usdoj.gov*.
U.S. Department of Labor: *www.dol.gov*.
U.S. Department of State: *www.state.gov*.
U.S. Department of State, Bureau of Consular Affairs: *www.travel.state.gov*.
U.S. Immigration and Customs Enforcement: *www.ice.gov*.

Sources

Federal Register Publications, Citizenship and Immigration Service — CIS, Immigration and Customs Enforcement — ICE, Customs and Border Protection — CBP, 2008 edition.

Federal Register Publications, Department of Homeland Security — DHS, 2007 edition.

USCIS Adjudicator's Field Manual, Public Version, February 2008 edition, Chapter 1, et seq.

USCIS Affirmative Asylum Procedure Manual, November 2007 edition.

USCIS Interpretations, Sec 301.1, et seq.

USCIS Operations Instructions, Section OI 3, et seq.

United States Code of Federal Regulations, 8 C.F.R., Part 1, *et seq.*; 20 C.F.R., Parts 655 and 656; 22 C.F.R., Parts 22, 40, 41, 42, 45, 51, 52, 53, 62, 97, 99 and 104; 28 C.F.R., Parts 0, 16, 17, 65, 200 and 1100; 32 C.F.R., Parts 94, 1602 and 1630; 42 C.F.R., Parts 34 and 435; 45 C.F.R., Parts 50 and 233.

United States Immigration and Nationality Act, United States Code, 8 U.S.C., Section 1101, et seq.

Index